The State
OF
Black America

PROGRESS, PITFALLS, AND THE PROMISE OF THE REPUBLIC

CENTER FOR URBAN RENEWAL AND EDUCATION

Edited by William B. Allen

With the Assistance of the Claremont Institute
for the Study of Statesmanship and Political Philosophy

Encounter
BOOKS

New York • London

First American edition published in 2022 by Encounter Books,
an activity of Encounter for Culture and Education, Inc.,
a nonprofit, tax-exempt corporation.
Encounter Books website address: www.encounterbooks.com
Center for Urban Renewal and Education website address: www.curepolicy.org

Manufactured in the United States and printed on
acid-free paper. The paper used in this publication meets
the minimum requirements of ANSI/NISO Z39.48–1992
(R 1997) (*Permanence of Paper*).

FIRST AMERICAN EDITION

LIBRARY OF CONGRESS CATALOGING-IN-PUBLICATION DATA

Names: Center for Urban Renewal and Education (Washington, D.C.), author.
Allen, W. B. (William Barclay), 1944– editor.
Title: The State of Black America: Progress, Pitfalls, and the Promise of
the Republic / by the Center for Urban Renewal and Education; edited by
W. B. Allen; with the assistance of the Claremont Institute for the
Study of Statesmanship and Political Philosophy.
Description: First American edition. | New York: Encounter Books, 2022.
Includes bibliographical references and index. | Identifiers: LCCN 2021048435 (print)
LCCN 2021048436 (ebook) | ISBN 9781641772662 (hardcover) | ISBN 9781641772679 (ebook)
Subjects: LCSH: African Americans—Social conditions—History. | African
Americans—Cultural assimilation—History. | African Americans—Economic
conditions—History. | United States—Race relations—Political aspects.
Race awareness—United States.
Classification: LCC E185.86 .C394 2022 (print) | LCC E185.86 (ebook) |
DDC 305.896/073—dc23/eng/20211007
LC record available at https://lccn.loc.gov/2021048435
LC ebook record available at https://lccn.loc.gov/2021048436

1 2 3 4 5 6 7 8 9 20 22

This book is dedicated to Star Parker, president and founder of the Center for Urban Renewal and Education (CURE). Her ceaseless efforts, personal sacrifice, and uncompromising ideals are the heart of CURE and this groundbreaking new publication. The State of Black America *is a testament to Star's unswerving belief in our nation's ideals.*

"Who can find a woman of valor? For her value is far above rubies...Grace is deceitful, and beauty is vain, but a woman who fears the Lord, *she shall be praised. Give her the fruit of her hands, and let her deeds praise her in the gates." —Proverbs 31:10, 30-31*

CONTENTS

FOREWORD

Thomas Klingenstein

We find ourselves in a cold civil war. The enemy—what I call "Woke Communists," "Woke Comms" for short—want to destroy the American way of life. To this end, the Woke Comm must convince Americans that their country is "systemically racist," in particular, that black Americans are oppressed by white Americans. If we are to preserve America, we must defeat this lie. The fact is, black Americans are not oppressed. Opportunities for black Americans have never been better. Our leaders must say these things—loudly and often.

Rebutting the lie requires describing the current state of black America. This is the purpose of the volume you hold in your hands.

The war is between those who believe that America is built on freedom and those who believe that America is built on oppression and exploitation; those who are convinced that America is good and those who are convinced that America is bad. These differences are too large to bridge. One side or the other must prevail. This is what makes it a war, if still a cold civil war.

The Woke Comms seek to impose a totalitarian regime. In a traditional totalitarian regime, the government uses repression to control every aspect of public and private life, all the way down to Little League.

In America, the government does *not* control everything, but it *influences* a lot. And where the government leaves off, the cultural/business complex takes over. Education, corporate media, entertainment, big business (especially Big Tech), and the military to varying degrees align with the Democratic

Party, which has become, effectively, a subsidiary of the Woke Comms. These institutions—together with the government—function as a totalitarian regime, crafting narratives to advance their agenda and suppressing narratives that do not. Canceling replaces violence.

At the center of the Woke Comm strategy for overturning the American way of life is the sweeping claim that America is systemically racist. This claim, in turn, is a justification for overturning not just specific policies but the entire American way of life. After all, if, as the Woke Comms contend, racism is systemic, if it has insinuated itself into all the values and institutions that make up the American way of life, then obviously we must throw out that way of life. That America is systemically racist is the foundational claim of the Woke Comm narrative that America was conceived in oppression. This narrative includes many other claims that support the big claim. These claims are false and American patriots must expose them as such.

In addition to promoting a false narrative, the Woke Communists try to silence those who challenge it. Today, anyone who dares to challenge the dominant story about race is called a "racist," shamed, canceled, or denied access to social media. As a result, many have been intimidated into silence. But the cost of silence is very high. When we fail to rebut lies, we perpetuate them.

Thus, we owe a great debt to the essayists in this volume who refute the lies without flinching or pulling punches. Unlike the Woke Comms, they provide evidence for their claims. They understand that we must sustain our traditional narrative, that of a country striving, however imperfectly, toward its noble ideals. If instead we succumb to the Woke Communist narrative, we will lose America.

We Must Change the Narrative

Preserving our traditional narrative requires that we teach it to our citizens, future and current. We must choose between our narrative and theirs.

Is the narrative going to be, as the Woke Communists have it, that racism runs in America's DNA? Or is it going to be truth: that freedom and the principles of the American founding run in our DNA, and that these principles have been the greatest force for human liberty on the planet? We must follow Edward J. Erler, who shows why America's founding principles provide the best opportunity for blacks and everyone else.

Are we going to teach our citizens that our founders were hypocrites who preached equality yet practiced slavery? Or are we going to teach them the truth: that the founding was remarkable not for its hypocrisy but for the fact that a country saturated with slavery included in its founding charter, the Declaration of Independence, a principle that would ultimately lead to the abolition of slavery as well as the abolition of other discriminatory practices? By proclaiming "all men are equal," the founders, said Lincoln,

> did not mean to assert the obvious untruth, that all were then actually enjoying that equality, nor yet, that they were about to confer it immediately upon them. In fact they had no power to confer such a boon. They meant simply to declare the *right*, so that the *enforcement* of it might follow as fast as circumstances should permit. They meant to set up a standard maxim for free society, which should be familiar to all, and revered by all; constantly looked to, constantly labored for, and even though never perfectly attained, constantly approximated, and thereby constantly spreading and

deepening its influence, and augmenting the happiness and value of life to all people of all colors everywhere.[1]

Are we going to insist that American blacks are helpless in the face of so-called "structural racism" or, rather, proclaim the truth: They can go as far as their talents and resolve take them? As Frederick Douglass said 150 years ago when asked what to do with the black man, "Do nothing with us!" he said. "Your doing with us has already played the mischief with us." Douglass understood that what black people needed—self-respect and respect from others—they could acquire only through agency.

Are we going to teach our children that hard work and self-reliance are racist inventions designed to suppress blacks (as the Woke Communists contend) or the truth: Hard work and self-reliance are essential? Both Douglass and Booker T. Washington believed that for children to improve, they must avail themselves of American culture.

Do we believe that America consists of many separate cultures? Or is it not true that America is a single culture that fuses with numerous subcultures? W. B. Allen argues that Martin Luther King Jr., toward the end of his career, began to lose faith in assimilation, proposing instead to distinguish American blacks from American culture. We must dedicate ourselves instead to the vision of a common American political life. Dividing ourselves by race and ethnicity will not end well.

Are we going to teach our children that blacks have never succeeded in America or the truth: Blacks have been remarkably successful if one considers the formidable barriers that have been placed in their way? The fact is, many blacks in the twentieth century—both African Americans and blacks from elsewhere—have been very successful. Moreover, as Robert D. Bland shows, contrary to the conventional understanding, in the second half of the nineteenth century, African Americans made astonishing strides in acquiring literacy and bourgeois values and integrating themselves into American society. Indeed, it was only starting in the 1960s that regressive patterns emerged. This historical evidence is necessary to guide and inspire American blacks today.

Are we going tell our citizens that there is a white supremacist behind every tree or the truth: There are very few actual white supremacists in America and most of those have gone underground? I, for one, do not know a single white supremacist in a position of authority. Of course, if one defines a white supremacist as someone who does not kneel before Black Lives Matter, then there are millions. All Americans should see this as the sleight of hand it is. Americans should also see Black Lives Matter as a racist organization trying to destroy the American way of life.

Are we going to tell our children that they should fear the police or tell them the truth: The police are there to help? Former President Obama says he worries every time his children leave the house that they will be killed or brutalized by the police. This, as Glenn C. Loury points out, is ridiculous. The fact is, blacks have a greater chance of being killed by lightning.

Are we are going to teach our citizens, black as well as white, that they should despise their country? Or will we teach our citizens the truth that, despite her sins, America is worthy of their love? There are many blacks today who have grown up proud to be American. They have never doubted they live in the greatest country in the world.

Likely, these children had intact families. We need more such families. As Star Parker and Robert Borens argue, it is not racism so much as the breakdown of the black family, itself hastened by the decline of Christianity, that accounts for many of the pathologies suffered by those in distressed communities, black or otherwise. Ian V. Rowe agrees. He, too, supports strengthening the family as well as school choice and reducing dependency on the government.

These choices all lie within our power to make. How we choose will determine whether we survive.

INTRODUCTION

Mikael Rose Good

In the twenty-first century it is increasingly perilous to try to tell the truth about the state of black America. Those who embark toward this destination find the path littered with dangers and diversions on all sides. The lone traveler first confronts the obstacle of plain bewilderment; he is caught among various distortions of reality and unequipped to make informed judgments on them. He then all too easily succumbs to the temptations of hysteria, expediency, or sentimentalism. What is needed is to furnish the seeker of truth with resources to fortify him for his journey and, even better, to send him traveling companions. This is what we hope to accomplish in the present volume. We have assembled a company of scholars who through diverse tools of analysis bring clarity to the murky darkness of our country's long troubled racial issues. These authors have begun to clear the path; now it is up to us to heed the call and forge ahead.

The following essays provide a sketch of the "state of black America" that illuminates its many dimensions, employing the tools of history, economics, legal analysis, social science, and political philosophy to move beyond surface views and rhetorically powerful narratives in pursuit of real understanding. Such a broad topic, considered from so many vantage points, cannot be explored exhaustively in just one volume. We do not claim to offer a comprehensive and infallible account of the character, shape, and tendencies of life for black Americans; but we do claim to make a significant contribution toward that end. Most importantly, in compiling these essays we offer to the world a "toolbox" of intellectual resources, encompassing a variety of disciplines, to aid careful and sound thinking on one of the most fraught issues of our time.

In the introductory essay, "Yesterday, Today, and Tomorrow: The State of Black America," William B. Allen and I provide the general architecture in light of which the individual contributions should be evaluated, assessing the most recent and most imminently significant scholarship on the "state of black America." In the process, however, we lay out a positive case to dismiss fears of absorbing minorities into the American mainstream and, also, to liberate thinking from the false premises of a "permanent underclass" that had come to color social science thinking in the 1960s and 1970s. In the same vein, we illustrate both the extraordinary fertility of exertions by American blacks and the nagging shortcomings of a political culture that has never fully embraced the story of those exertions as exemplary of the promise of America. Nevertheless, we insist, a march of social transformation occurs unperceived beneath our very eyes, but one that is locked in a race toward destruction predicated on the notion that there has been no real progress in America. Our sanguine expectations of a transformed society nevertheless acknowledge that the open question remains, whether the transformed society will also be truly "American." We suggest little confidence in such eventuality, apart from the emergence of a robust black patriotism that self-consciously embraces the mission to save America from itself.

Edward J. Erler's essay, "The Fourteenth Amendment and the Completion of the Constitution: Abraham Lincoln and Reconstruction," lays a foundation for our thinking by describing the process by which blacks living in America became "American blacks" rightly understood—i.e., full participants in the rights and privileges conferred on all citizens in America's founding documents. Erler demonstrates that the elevation of blacks to full legal equality with non-blacks was not an aberration but, rather, the logical conclusion of the principles articulated by the founders, realized (belatedly) in the political realm through the brilliant wartime statesmanship of Abraham Lincoln. The principles of the Declaration of Independence, as Lincoln understood, "when implemented to their fullest extent would embrace the whole panoply of rights and privileges for black men and women." Only then could the nation purge "race consciousness" from its laws and mores and embrace the truth that "individuals possess rights—not classes and especially not racial classes." Erler argues that despite our significant progress toward equal rights under the law, the contemporary development of racial class entitlements now threatens the full realization of Lincoln's vision.

Erler's essay provides us with three starting-points: First, vital historical perspective on the question of American blacks' situation vis-à-vis their country; second, constitutional analysis that elucidates the meaning and significance of "equality before the law" and the promise it contains for American blacks; and third, an account of America as it was understood by the emancipator of the slaves himself, as a nation whose proper founding contains an imperative to extend the goods of justice and equality to blacks and non-blacks alike.

Robert D. Bland, in "The Last Generation of Radical Republicans: Race and the Legacy of Reconstruction in the American South, 1877–1915," presents a forgotten history of black political participation in the twilight years of Reconstruction, highlighting the tenacity and creativity of American blacks who refused to abandon the dream of Reconstruction when their former allies in the Republican Party had largely given up the fight. Bland writes the next chapter of the story Erler began, showing how American blacks themselves seized the promise of equal rights granted in the Thirteenth, Fourteenth, and Fifteenth Amendments and at the same time granted the entire nation "its first glimpse of multiracial democracy." Even at the end of the nineteenth century, a period which historians usually describe as "a low tide moment of formal political activity in black America" defined by increasing disfranchisement, Bland argues that "black Republican leaders and voters continued to organize within the GOP," armed with the belief that "they stood on a powerful moral argument related to voting rights and the meaning of the Civil War and Reconstruction that could ultimately win the day in the public sphere." Far from being rendered powerless by their political opposition, American blacks "built a rival political world" and "established a coherent political vision" that continued to reverberate through the Jim Crow era.

In addition, Bland complicates simplistic narratives about American blacks' relationship to the U.S. party system. He shows how American blacks embraced the Republican Party as their best hope for equal rights in the face of intimidation and suppression by Southern Democrats. At the same time, blacks met with increasing ambivalence from many in their party who no longer believed in Reconstruction, and even among black Republicans, there was considerable dissension as various individuals and factions promoted competing visions of black political participation. Importantly, blacks did not take a passive role as beneficiaries of either political party following their emancipation, nor did they act as a homogenous racial "group" or "class." Rather, individual blacks actively shaped American party politics as they engaged in a dynamic debate over the best means to realize their shared goal of social and political equality. This historical tour opens our imagination to possibilities of political life that lie beyond the horizon of the present discourse.

In "Competing Visions," William B. Allen completes our brief historical overview, tracing the developments by which the vision of black self-reliance fell out of fashion in the mid-twentieth century. This was the vision of such leaders as Frederick Douglass and Booker T. Washington, who in the late nineteenth and early twentieth centuries maintained confidence in "the nexus between self-sufficiency and eventual assimilation, resting on the efficacy of the free market" and who preached "mutual respect and independence of parties rather than dependence of one party on another." Allen argues that Martin Luther King Jr. ultimately steered the country away from this vision when he began to lose faith in assimilation, purposing instead "to extract American blacks from the warp and woof of an American culture regarded as fatally flawed." Contrary to Lincoln's ideal of an America united by equality under the law, and contrary also to the valiant efforts of Reconstruction-era blacks to seize that equality and integrate themselves fully into the broader society, "black America" came to be seen as a community defined by oppression and fundamentally at odds with America as a whole.

Allen makes the case that this shift in American attitudes regarding the situation of American blacks contradicts the actual evidence of post–Civil War history revealing "demonstrable progress . . . in the accomplishments and advances to date of the black middle class." That historical evidence ought to have greater influence on our thinking about the *future* of black America. The best hope for American blacks, Allen says, still lies in the reality of "plural communities fused (and continuing to fuse) into a single American culture." But the full realization of this hope requires something of us: "Both black and white Americans must commit themselves to the project of *American* identity before they can experience the results of that project." Going forward, we must reject King's error and dedicate ourselves instead to the vision of common American political life espoused by Douglass and Washington.

Glenn C. Loury brings us face-to-face with the present challenges confronting black America in his essay "Whose Fourth of July? Black Patriotism and Racial Inequality in America." While acknowledging the persistence of racial inequality, Loury critiques the racialized narrative which attributes every disparity to "structural racism" and thus totally absolves struggling black communities of responsibility for their members. On this view, the only solution to racial inequality is a rejection of America itself, an error stemming from the failure "to understand the foundations of [our] own security and prosperity." This dubious narrative is safeguarded by a "cancel culture" that prevents honest inquiry into the "complex historical and contemporary causes" that impact black communities. Hence the truth about black America is obscured and real solutions to racial inequality elude us.

As an alternative, Loury argues that the best strategy for American blacks is to seize social and economic equality by their own agency (as they did in the decades following the Civil War, although the suppression of their legal and political rights in the Jim Crow era did much to set them back). Furthermore, they ought to wholeheartedly embrace the American project as "the most effective way to advance their best interests in the twenty-first century." After all, Loury says, the history of blacks in America is that of "the greatest transformation in the status of an enserfed people...that is to be found anywhere in world history." This was not an arbitrary outcome, but the outworking of the principles of freedom and equality upon which the republic was founded—the same ones that animated Lincoln. To be sure, the outcome was never *inevitable*; in 1852, Frederick Douglass did not know whether he as a black man had any share in the American civic inheritance. But in 2022, though American blacks still "face profound, existential challenges," they now face an immense opportunity to partake of the blessings of freedom and even, indeed, "to save the prospect of freedom in the United States." The question is whether they will take hold of that destiny.

In "Creating an Opportunity Society and Upward Mobility for the Black Community and People of All Races," Ian V. Rowe provides a practical turn to the vision painted by the previous authors, presenting detailed research on the social and economic conditions of flourishing for American blacks in the twenty-first century. Like Loury, Rowe is worried that the dominant narrative disregards the complex array of factors *besides* race that impact the flourishing of individuals and communities. Likewise, fixation on the elusive goal of racial equity "sets a ceiling on black achievement" and has the unintended consequence of instilling "learned helplessness" in young American blacks. Rowe's research indicates that far more effective than top-down attempts to eliminate racial inequity are "developmental strategies that invest in strengthening stable families, expanding educational opportunities and school choice, and incentivizing work over government dependency," which increase upward mobility for *both* blacks and non-blacks. One need not deny the ongoing presence of racial discrimination to affirm that there are concrete steps individual blacks can take to raise their chances of prosperity.

The contemporary tendency, Rowe says, is "to treat individual black people as just stand-ins for a larger group identity—i.e., 'black America'"—that is indelibly marked by oppression and victimhood. But this is to ignore the fact that "the state of individual black Americans is strong because increasingly individual black Americans have greater control over their destiny." Despite the legacy of slavery and racial discrimination, American principles have made possible a situation where "a formerly enslaved people can now regularly produce some of the country's most influential leaders in virtually every facet of American life." In this light, it is manifestly counterproductive to impress upon American blacks that there is nothing they can do to determine the course of their life.

In their essay "Poverty in the African American Community: A Twenty-First-Century Approach to Measuring Economic Progress," Precious D. Hall and Daphne Cooper offer a contrasting perspective, making the case that past and present racial discrimination have disadvantaged American blacks to the extent that it is difficult or impossible for them to flourish without substantial outside intervention. Hall and Cooper concur with previous authors that black Americans have seen significant progress in education and economic prosperity in recent decades. But they attribute more weight to the inequalities that still remain, taking "success stories" as the exception rather than the rule. Central to their argument is the contention that "systematic racial oppression" is still sufficient to "keep African Americans as a permanent underclass, thus withholding from them any measure of true equality." Contrary to Rowe, they posit that *more* emphasis on the structural factors contributing to racial inequality, not less, is essential to black America's progress.

Pointing out the failures of New Deal and Great Society policies to meaningfully alleviate poverty, Cooper and Hall posit that at the root of these failures was an attempt "to blame or fix the individual on a micro level" without adequately addressing larger structural problems. While acknowledging that there are social and cultural problems within black communities that perpetuate the cycle of poverty, Cooper and Hall maintain that the "culture of poverty" theory "ultimately places the blame for poverty on the victim, thus removing the social duty of the government to alleviate poverty." They make a similar critique of the "bootstrap mentality," quoting Martin Luther King Jr.'s argument late in his life that emancipation was insufficient to truly free American blacks from oppression. Ultimately, Cooper and Hall propose a model that integrates various theories of poverty in an effort to illuminate "the political, economic, and social structures of government" that perpetuate racial disparities. This essay, posing as it does a clear challenge to the overarching argument of this volume, sharpens the contrast between two fundamental approaches to thinking about the "state of black America" even as it encourages nuanced dialogue across ideological lines.

Star Parker and Robert Borens conclude the volume with a sweeping overview of the social and economic factors contributing to persistent poverty in some black communities. In "Marriage, Family, Abortion, and Poverty in Black America," they inquire to what extent we can attribute the difficulties facing black America to racial discrimination. They conclude, based on their survey of available data, that it is plausible that in the twenty-first century, family structure, abortion rates, and marriage rates have at least as much influence on black poverty rates as does ongoing racial discrimination (if not more). While the traditional family structure has taken hits across racial lines since the 1960s, it has suffered a steeper decline among American blacks than across the population as a whole, a social reality that poses unique challenges to black communities.

Attempting to offer some account for this social breakdown, Parker and Borens explore the rising unpopularity of Christian moral teaching concerning marriage and family, as well as the parallel shift in attitudes concerning the role of government in society and the outworking of this shift in several key Supreme Court cases. They hypothesize that the breakdown of traditional Christianity imperils the social, political, and economic goods that are vital to black America's flourishing, since in American history it is deep religious faith that has prompted the people to set limits on the role of civil government in human life and to "act worthily of their freedom." They reaffirm the conviction that the prospects for *black* America are inseparable from the prospects for the nation overall: The same requirements of faith, patriotism, and social capital apply equally to the part and the whole.

At this crucial moment in the American story, we need at our disposal a constructive account of black America's past, present, and future that equips us to cut through appearances and bear witness to the reality. Building such an account will help us to address the current state of affairs with greater clarity and wisdom. We have not completed the task; but we have begun the conversation. We hope to be joined by many others who care deeply about the fate of black America, but who think it neither necessary nor prudent to attempt to save American blacks by sacrificing the nation.

I

YESTERDAY, TODAY, AND TOMORROW
The State of Black America

W. B. Allen with Mikael Rose Good

> Thy righteousness *is* like the great mountains;
> thy judgments *are* a great deep:
> O LORD, thou preservest man and beast.
> —*Psalm 36:6*

Understanding the "state of black America" requires first gauging the perspective from which to observe it. From the mountaintops, the valleys below appear static, changeless, and dormant (while, in fact, they broil in ferment). From the valleys, the mountaintops appear remote and impenetrable (while, in fact, they sit in peril of volcanic eruptions). The appearances, however, disfigure the reality. Two recent works well illustrate the effect of these distortions, while nevertheless opening windows looking onto the reality with powerful effect. These works are Robert Putnam's *The Upswing* and Richard Alba's *The Great Demographic Illusion*. The present essay reviews the findings of these works in order to disclose the present state of black America *in relation to its absorption into mainstream American life.*

It is appropriate to frame this appraisal in light of a metaphor deriving from the fifteenth century. The metaphor was applied in the "Epistle Dedicatory" of Niccolò Machiavelli's *The Prince*. That fifteenth-century treatise, in turn, informs the development of modern political alternatives in a decisive manner, elevating politics (power) above culture (influence) in shaping the functions of human society in a manner that eventually came to be universal. At the same time, the contemporary movement to define the state of black America in light of what has come to be called "critical race theory" shapes its understanding completely in light of the Machiavellian revolution (albeit likely unknowingly). In doing that, it does not depart from numerous characterizations ranging from Peter Drucker's counsels in business/corporate management to social science analyses in general. Critical race theory has identified the fifteenth century as the point of departure for its political and cultural analyses not accidentally but rather subject to the determining influence of processes of analysis set forth by Machiavelli. For that reason, in addition to the analysis of the works by Putnam and Alba, this essay must also place in relationship to those works that by Ibram X. Kendi, *How to Be an Antiracist*. For ultimately, most of the distortions that appear in the works of Putnam and Alba derive from the intimidating influence of critical race theory.

Before unfolding the appraisal, it would be helpful to clarify terminology that must be fully understood in order to follow this presentation. For example, the reader will observe that we offer the term "absorption" as preferable to the terms "integration," "assimilation," "domination," etc., when referring to the social dynamics that measure the relations of blacks and non-blacks in the United States. Similarly, it will be observed that we contextualize on the basis of "blacks and non-blacks" in place of the familiar "whites and non-whites." As for the term "white" (and its substantive "whiteness"), we will explain why the term "European" is preferable, since it indicates a mode of functioning in the world. Moreover, we will unpack the term "minority," not avoiding the usage but clearly distinguishing its use in reference to political leverage (electoral weight) and its use in reference to ethno-racial hierarchy (which we shall argue has no analytical force). We will, in conclusion, address the terms "racism" and "systemic racism" based on a working definition of "racism" as the substitution of social codifications for human sympathies or sentiments of humanity. Finally, we shall parse the term "inequality" in a manner that separates political inequalities from inequalities in wealth and income (indicating that mobility analysis must vary in each case albeit intersecting). We shall abjure reference to the terms "diversity" and "inclusion." Those terms have been rendered useless through abuse.[1]

Back to mountains and valleys. To understand the metaphorical power of the mountains and valleys trope, it suffices to contrast the approaches of W. E. B. Du Bois and Booker T. Washington to the state of black America in their time. The one, Du Bois, focused his labor on distinguishing the "talented tenth" and storming the citadels of power. The other, Washington, focused on fostering growth from the bottom up. The former approach suggests that reformation is dependent upon provision from above, while the latter approach suggests that reformation results from organic growth from below. Du Bois took the view from the mountaintop; Washington took the view from the valley. Du Bois helped form the NAACP and launched a sixty-year civil rights movement that eventually produced legal changes. Washington enlarged enormously the indigenous resources of communities on the ground, enlisting the aid of Julius Rosenwald to inseminate distressed communities with some *5,000 schools* before the mid-twentieth century. The one focused on political capital; the other focused on human capital.

It may be said that both approaches were necessary. It is

nonetheless important to inquire whether one or the other was more advantageous from the perspective of fostering the eventual absorption of black communities into the American mainstream. In that respect, Washington's approach was manifestly the more significant, a fact symbolized by his appearing alongside George Washington Carver on official United States coinage by 1950.

It would count for far more, however, to place the endeavors of both approaches in the larger context of the evolution of political and institutional forms in general. For if it may appear that Du Bois played on more solid ground politically speaking, it is by no means evident that Washington did not hold powerful cards in that regard.

The European System

In 1648, the Peace of Westphalia set the course of modern politics—the politics of the nation-state. In doing so, it valorized the fifteenth-century principles of Machiavelli, vaulting politics above culture in determining the routine functions of civil life. That accomplishment, however, had the foreseeable consequence of rendering *raison d'état* superior to every other reason (politics above culture). What that means is that politics, which operates on the basis of power, would prevail over culture, which operates on the basis of influence (which is why George Washington declared that "influence is no government"). That formula, in turn, laid all civil life open to the inherent danger of oscillation between extremes of power. Culture once subordinated, politics could know no moderation other than that of the ephemeral in-between of swings from one extreme to the other. Machiavelli offered no solution to that problem.

Exactly one hundred years later, in 1748, appeared the magisterial work, *Spirit of the Laws*, which laid out a *programme* for operating on the principle of the nation-state without undergoing oscillations in extremes of power. It was a proposal to constrain power that would render the Machiavellian system compatible with moderation. This accomplishment was underscored in the general proclamation that there could be no crimes of mind. While it would require institutional forms strictly observed to prevent the exercise of excessive power, it was also necessary to delineate just what power was acceptable. That standard amounted to the declaration that power could extend no further than to permit or forbid deeds (and those of public import). Thus, *power constrained by conscience* is what made the nation-state workable. That is the reason that Montesquieu (author of *Spirit of the Laws*) declared Christianity (the foundation of conscience) the "greatest gift" to mankind. Nor was it an accident that he was the first modern thinker to provide a secular argument against race-based slavery and against the subjection of women.

What this all has to do with Du Bois and Booker T. Washington is fairly straightforward. In terms of the functions of modern civilization, there exist strict limits upon what can be accomplished by power (no "hate crimes," for example). Thus, there are limits to reform accomplished by means of coercion. Culture, which operates by influence rather than power, can extend well beyond the limits of politics. Thus, principles of indigenous development— education and moral formation—encompass a broader range of human possibilities. Now, when power is constrained, culture is given freer rein precisely because it lacks coercive force. That free rein can be used for good or ill, dependent on cultural context. Historically, the black church in the United States illustrated this quite well. As a result, it invites a contest for moral (and social) influence. In the context of this discussion, it can license racism (though not racist deeds) as readily as it can condemn racism. The question, however, is this: What in the actual situation of the

United States is the reality? What is the state of black America in the face of this quandary?

Putnam's *The Upswing*

It would be preferable if Putnam (and Alba, as well) had presented his findings in his own words. He could not be persuaded to do so. Accordingly, we must make do with our accounting, which we hope to do justly though we cannot do so comprehensively.

Putnam asked a simple question: What over the course of 130 years has been the path of development in the United States in relation to the relative status of blacks and non-blacks insofar as statistical evidence discloses it? He is concerned with relative economic (financial) status, relative political leverage, social cohesiveness (rates of social absorption), and communitarianism (cultural values). The answer he provides: "Better, then worse." His first figure, which is a template for all the findings in the book, along with the subsequent figure reporting trends in income inequality, tell the story in broad outline. (See Figures 1.1 and 1.2.) Putnam says of this result:

> In the mid-1960s the decades-long upswing in our shared economic, political, social, and cultural life abruptly reversed direction. America suddenly found itself in the midst of a clear downturn. Between the mid-1960s and today—by scores of hard measures along multiple dimensions—we have been experiencing declining economic equality, the deterioration of compromise in the public square, a fraying social fabric, and a descent into cultural narcissism...
>
> Since the 1950s we have made important progress in expanding individual rights (often building on progress made in the preceding decades), but we have sharply regressed in terms of shared prosperity and community values.[2]

Figure 1.1   Economic, Political, Social, and Cultural Trends, 1895–2015[3]

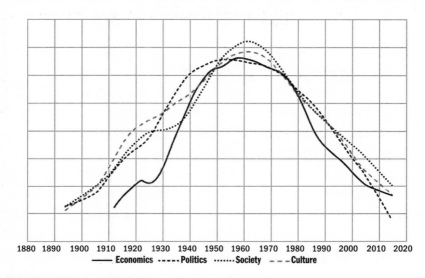

Note: Data LOESS smoothed: .2.

Figure 1.2   Income Inequality in the United States, 1913–2014[4]

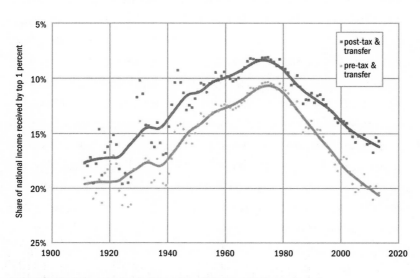

Source: Piketty, Saez, and Zucman, *QJEcon*, May 2018. Data LOESS smoothed: .2.

The significant and central observation deriving from this introductory analysis in *The Upswing* is that

> progress toward equality for American blacks didn't begin in 1965. By many measures, blacks were moving *toward* parity with whites well before the victories of the Civil Rights revolution, despite the limitations imposed by Jim Crow. And second, after the Civil Rights movement, that long-standing trend toward racial equality slowed, stopped, and even reversed.[5]

As he eventually phrases it, America took its "foot off the gas." What he terms the "I-we-I" curve purports to show that, while Americans were highly motivated by "communitarian values" (the "We" era), greater progress toward parity was made. In the "Robber Baron" era of the late nineteenth century, prevailing community values were "I" centered and, apparently, became so again post-1950. This account fails to deal with anomalies that we explain hereafter.

The "growth" and "regression" reflected in this analysis lies in lower "life expectancy," educational, wealth, and electoral outcomes for blacks in comparison with non-blacks. The modulation in the direction of equalizing distribution of wealth between 1950 and 1960 does not result entirely from economic change. It also has an attitudinal basis, which, interestingly, presents a picture contrasting strongly with the "I-we-I curve" that is the foundation of this analysis. That is, as we show in Figure 1.3, the period of "communitarian" growth corresponds with the period of greatest post-slavery repression; while the period of "individualistic" growth post-1950 corresponds with the period of diminished post-slavery repression:

Figure 1.3 Distribution of Wealth in the United States, 1913–2014[6]

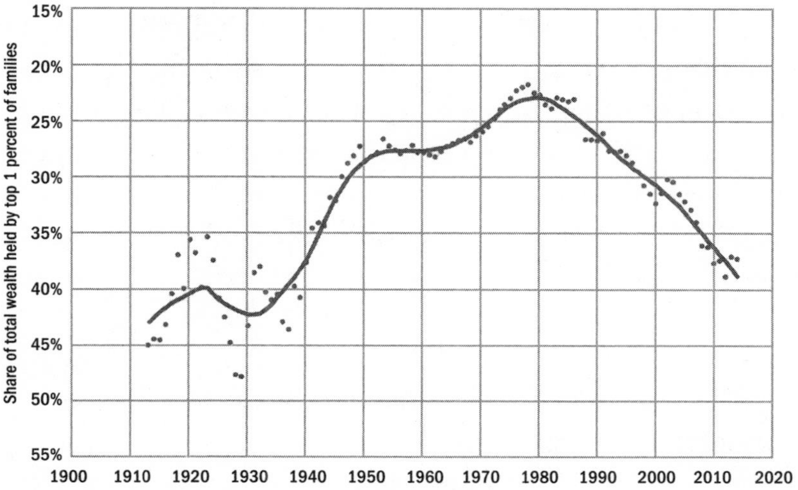

Source: Piketty, Saez, and Zucman, *QJEcon*, May 2018. Data LOESS smoothed: .2.

While Putnam argues (absent presentation of evidence) that this "upswing" in sentiment attenuated as the twentieth century closed, his argument hangs on the dying out of an older generation which, on this read, must have been replaced by a more racist, younger generation. For this, there is no evidence whatever. Moreover, no matter what the eventual analysis, the present analysis does not reflect a decline in community sentiment, insofar as racial acceptance is a fundamental element in the sense of community. This result would compel a conclusion that the state of black America confronts less racism today than it has ever encountered. The reason that conclusion is resisted by Putnam, as we shall later discuss, has to do with the mountaintop perspective that he takes and with his susceptibility to the criticism of critical race theorists.

As shown in Figures 1.4 and 1.5, the sharp drop in intergenerational economic mobility that began around 1955 mirrors growing economic inequality hinted at the same time but only settling in around the mid-1960s. These dynamics describe American society as a whole, but they contain a tacit reference to the condition of American blacks in the sense that the greater weight of the decline seems to have been borne by blacks (at least relative to the prior era of increasing "economic equality," a curious usage that elides wealth and income inequality). To disentangle such calculations, it is necessary to understand the context in which Putnam finds them meaningful. And that context is the prevailing "political sentiments" dominant in the country from one era to the next. (See Figure 1.6.)

When, therefore, Putnam lays out the advance of political agendas from the "progressive era" through the "civil rights era," he intends to measure the progress of absorption against the backdrop of political platform dominance. He interprets the dominance of the "progressive" platform as expressing a communitarian commitment (the "we" of the "I-we-I" curve) that is undermined by a "conservative" platform expressing an individualist commitment. (See Figure 1.7.) The one calls forth an era of purportedly common exertion across constituencies (absorption), while the other purportedly polarizes the society into competing and even mutually hostile groupings (apartness). On these terms, accordingly, the eligible explanation for varying degrees of economic and social advance among blacks and non-blacks in particular is to be found in the background effects of struggles for political power.

We should, however, take note in Figure 1.8 of the specific implication of the presentation of liberal and conservative representation in the House of Representatives (meant to indicate trends within the society): namely, that it reflects most dramatically not any clearly defined long-term trend (the terms "conservative" and

Figure 1.4   The Rise and Fall of Intergenerational Economic Mobility, 1947–2010[7]

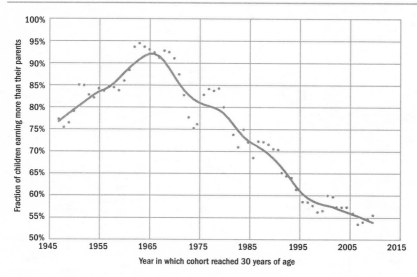

Source: Berman, "The Long Run Evolution of Absolute Intergenerational Mobility," Data LOESS smoothed: .25.

Figure 1.5   Economic Equality, 1913–2015[8]

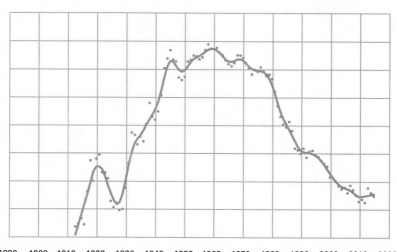

Note: Data LOESS smoothed: .1.

Figure 1.6   White Support for Selected Principles of Racial Equality, 1942–2011[9]

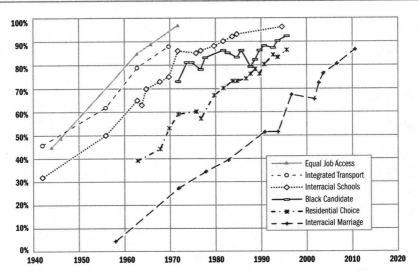

Source: Schuman et al., *Racial Attitudes*; Krysan and Moberg, *Portrait.*

Figure 1.7   Economic, Political, Social, and Cultural Trends, 1895–2015[10]

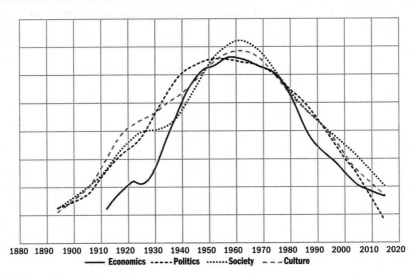

Note: Data LOESS smoothed: .2.

Figure 1.8 Asymmetric Polarization in the U.S. House of Representatives, 1879–2019[11]

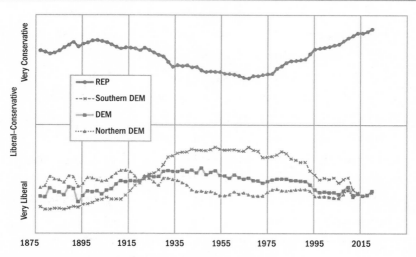

Source: Jeffrey B. Lewis et al., Congressional Roll-Call Votes Database (2019).

"liberal" having no real content in this particular presentation), while it does capture in a compelling manner the era of "massive resistance" that responded to the civil rights movement. In the period 1955–1975, we see movement toward the putatively liberal among Republicans and, taking the Democrats as a whole, a distinctive move toward the putatively conservative (driven, of course, by the huge swing among Southern Democrats). What this means, therefore, is that the terms "conservative" and "liberal" are here being used—but quite mistakenly—as proxies for racial animus. What they, in fact, reveal, insofar as they reveal any racial animus at all, is that the great weight of racial animus resided in the Democrat Party all along, including during the assumed periods of emphatic communitarianism. Now that is a great paradox. For how can the advocates of communitarianism be at one and the same time the hosts of the fund of racial resentment and separation? Here is how Putnam addresses the paradox:

Most interpretations of the 1960s are framed in terms of the political struggle between the Left and the Right, a struggle in which the initial victories of the Left (the Great Society and the Civil Rights revolution) triggered a conservative backlash, putting in power the Right, which has largely dominated American politics ever since. In Chapter 3 we acknowledged that narrative, but we also argued that the more durable and pervasive change was from communitarianism to individualism, a dimension that is conceptually and empirically distinct from the left-right spectrum. The shift in the Sixties was less from left to right (or the reverse) than from we to I, a shift that was entirely visible on both extremes, as the Old Right gave way to the New Right and the Old Left gave way to the New Left...

In short, the rapidly increasing salience of identity in American culture in the second half of the twentieth century began in young adult psyches far from race and gender and class and politics. Although identity was eventually reflected in those spheres, too, at its core it represented an emphasis on "I."[12]

However, when Putnam declares that "the emphasis on individual rights—civil rights, women's rights, gay rights, consumer rights, children's rights, and so forth...shows no sign of waning,"[13] he abstracts from the pervading reality that these were cultivated group rights, not individual rights. Here lies the Achilles' heel of his associational analysis; he abstracts completely from the perspectival treatment of the subject—looking from the mountaintop and ignoring the distorting effect of the lens.

When we correct for those distortions, we can discern the true significance of the findings in the data that he deploys. (See Figures 1.9 and 1.10.) Now, that distortion appears first in the discussion of "political comity," in which Putnam counterintuitively imputes greater comity (sense of community) to the era in which the repression of American blacks post-slavery was at its zenith!

Figure 1.9 Cross-Party Comity vs. Conflict as Reported in the National Press, 1890–2013[14]

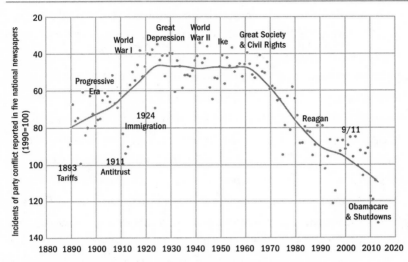

Source: Azzimonti, "Partisan Conflict and Private Investment." Data LOESS smoothed: .25.

Figure 1.10 Political Comity, 1895–2015[15]

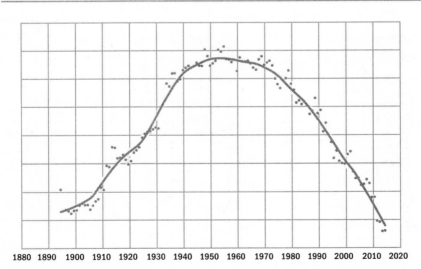

Note: Data LOESS smoothed: .20.

He has found, therefore, great momentum toward political comity at precisely the eras in which the greatest abuses of blacks post-slavery were in evidence! Lynchings reached their peak at the very era in which he begins his analysis and remained trenchant throughout the entire period (up to 1948), benefiting from no very powerful progressive effort to stop them prior to Harry Truman (there was lip service, to be sure, but no real political capital was expended). Even the avatar Eleanor Roosevelt, who gave voice to her opposition, was at the same time the biggest advocate of the claims of James Byrnes (the South Carolina segregationist) to succeed Franklin Roosevelt.

The inevitable question arises: What is missing in Putnam's account? The evident answer to that question lies in what has occurred in the valleys. That is revealed most profoundly not in the massaged statistics of census reports but in the general overview found at the surface of those reports. The singular fact is that black demography in the United States demonstrates compellingly that the growth slope of black absorption into the society of the United States has far more to do with the combined effect of a retardation of population increase among American blacks and massive immigration into the United States. Let's take a look at that census overview, shown in Table 1.1.

Table 1.1 Notes:

1 With the exception of 2010 social/economic characteristics data, all data is taken from the U.S. Census Bureau's Decennial Census Official Publications, found at https://www.census.gov/programs-surveys/decennial-census/decade/decennial-publications.1790.html.

The 2010 Decennial Census, adhering to the 1997 Office of Management and Budget (OMB) guidelines, relied on self-identification to classify by race and allowed individuals to self-identify with more than one race. All social/economic characteristics data from 2010 is taken from the Census Bureau's American Community Survey (ACS) and Current Population Survey (CPS), since the 2010 census did not report on these characteristics. All 2010 social/economic characteristics data on whites reflects "white only," whereas social/economic characteristics data on blacks reflects "black alone or in combination with other races."

2 This number reflects those who checked only the "white" box for the race question. Whites in combination with other races are not included in this number.

3 This number includes mixed white/non-white people who did *not* check the "black/African American" box for the race question.

4 Even where the numbers for the mixed black population are provided in census reports, they are highly unreliable, and they are not counted according to consistent methods across censuses.

5 Marriage data reflects the population 15 and over, with the exception of 1950 marriage data, which reflects the population 14 and over.

6 1950 marriage data for blacks also includes non-whites of other races, who make up 0.4% of the total population.

7 School attendance data for 1860, 1890, and 1920 reflects all persons 5–20 years, whereas school attendance data for 1950, 1980, and 2010 reflects *only* persons 5–13 years.

Table 1.1 Overview of the Black Population in the Decennial Census, 1790–2010

Census Overview, 1790–2010[1]	1790	1800	1830	1860	1890	1920	1950	1980	2010
Total U.S. population	3,929,326	5,305,666	12,858,670	31,443,321	62,622,250	105,710,620	150,697,361	226,545,805	308,745,538
Total black population	757,208	997,899	2,328,626	4,441,830	7,470,040	10,463,131	15,042,286	26,482,349	42,020,743
Total white population	3,172,120	4,307,001	10,530,044	26,922,538	54,983,890	94,820,915	134,942,028	189,035,012	223,553,265[2]
Blacks as % of population	19.27%	18.81%	18.11%	14.13%	11.93%	9.90%	9.98%	11.69%	13.61%
Whites as % of population	80.73%	81.18%	81.89%	85.62%	87.80%	89.70%	89.55%	83.44%	72.41%
Other non-white population	0	0	0	78,953	168,320	426,574	713,047	11,028,444	43,171,530[3]
Other non-white as % of total	0%	0%	0%	0.25%	0.27%	0.40%	0.47%	4.87%	13.98%
Mixed black population	N/A	N/A	N/A	588,352	1,132,060	1,660,554	N/A	N/A	3,091,424[4]
Mixed as % of total blacks	N/A	N/A	N/A	13.25%	15.15%	15.87%	N/A	N/A	7.36%
Mixed as % of U.S. population	N/A	N/A	N/A	1.87%	1.81%	1.57%	N/A	N/A	1.00%
% of blacks married[5]	N/A	N/A	N/A	N/A	55.01%	60.00%	63.21%[6]	46.60%	31.87%
% of whites married	N/A	N/A	N/A	N/A	55.42%	59.87%	67.06%	61.84%	54.01%
% of blacks divorced	N/A	N/A	N/A	N/A	0.37%	1.04%	2.29%	7.81%	10.92%
% of whites divorced	N/A	N/A	N/A	N/A	0.29%	0.67%	2.19%	6.04%	9.94%
% of blacks separated/spouse absent	N/A	N/A	N/A	N/A	N/A	N/A	10.40%	9.59%	5.92%
% of whites separated/spouse absent	N/A	N/A	N/A	N/A	N/A	N/A	2.73%	2.69%	3.31%
Black illiteracy rate	N/A	N/A	N/A	N/A	57.10%	22.87%	N/A	N/A	N/A
White illiteracy rate	N/A	N/A	N/A	N/A	7.66%	4.04%	N/A	N/A	N/A
Blacks as % of total illiterate	N/A	N/A	N/A	N/A	48.11%	37.35%	N/A	N/A	N/A
Whites as % of total illiterate	N/A	N/A	N/A	N/A	50.79%	60.96%	N/A	N/A	N/A
Black school attendance rate[7]	N/A	N/A	N/A	1.75%	31.96%	53.99%	80.87%	95.8%	97.40%
White school attendance rate	N/A	N/A	N/A	56.05%	55.41%	66.97%	81.94%	97.0%	97.05%

These numbers are so plain and so palpable that they escape the notice of sophisticated observers in search of occult explanation. It will perhaps aid in understanding if we relate an experience the senior author had in 2018, while leading forty-five school-teachers on a tour of civil rights movement memorials in the South. In Selma, Alabama, the group gathered in the sanctuary of Bethel AME Church ("Big Bethel"), the site at which voting rights protesters gathered to organize strategy before crossing the Edmund Pettus Bridge on the march to the capitol. While reviewing the dynamics of that historic march, the seminar leader paused mid-sentence, looked up at and around the sanctuary, and after a significant silence, inquired of the teachers, "Who do you think built this structure?" The point of the question was to direct attention to the obvious beauty and elegance of the architecture, erected in the first decade of the twentieth century. Surprised by the question, and pausing to reflect, someone eventually though tentatively offered, "The church members?"

She was right, of course, and the seminar leader emphasized that those American blacks worshipping in that sanctuary built by their own resources and industry, in the midst of the reign of lynching terror, Jim Crow, voting restrictions, and persistent oppression, an extraordinary monument to their resourcefulness and intelligence. It was clear that they could accomplish anything, given time and resources, no matter the traumatic stress to which they were subject. They were effective agents; they were not dependent or semi-dependent wards of others. While they, like all humans, required the protection of the laws ultimately to emerge in the fullness of civic participation, they required no assistance whatever to make their humanity manifest. To the further question, "Why do you suppose that you have always imagined American blacks of that era as semi-dependent wards of the state?" there was no reply. But there was a dawning consciousness of something very important having gone wrong in their education.

The numbers reported in these summary census reports stare at us just as blindingly as the beauty of Big Bethel stares at any soul sensitive enough to perceive. Looking at the rate of population increase alone (taking into account the pre-1860 and post-1860 distinctions regarding contributing factors) reveals much and nothing more importantly than the robust emergence of American blacks of the post-slavery era as people taking command of their lives. While growth rates can seem almost monotonic from 1800 to 1890, that would make the mistake of failing to account for the difference between importation and breeding up to 1830 (and still somewhat to 1860) and indigenous reproduction thereafter. That was the first sign of "upswing" in the post-slavery era, and it had no relation whatever to any policy pronouncements from the mountaintops of progressive-era custodial messaging.

Moreover, the effect is even more dramatic than it first appears if notice is taken that, unlike the population growth of the non-black population, population growth among blacks benefited from no significant infusion from immigration. That is, the growth rate was astonishingly higher than the growth rate of the non-black population when controlled for the effect of immigration. In an imagined universe in which the country had been closed to immigration post-1860, and the trend lines were extrapolated as they developed between 1860 and 1890, blacks and non-blacks would have approximated one another by 1950. That world, however, was not to arise, first because of the large-scale effect of immigration, and second (post-1950), the emergence of social dysfunction coupled with targeted abortion in black communities. In other words, a greater "upswing" was concealed by immigration, while a "downswing" was hastened through abortion and other practices.

Or again, consider the unprecedentedly dramatic change in literacy rates over the course of sixty years following the end of slavery. Albeit aided by generous initiative from charitable agents (largely from the North) contributing to this phenomenon, it is incontestably the case that literacy gains represent overwhelmingly the result of indigenous efforts on the part of American blacks themselves (and mainly in the South). We have referred to the dramatic infusion of Rosenwald schools above, and we note now that those schools receded into lesser prominence as a direct result of being co-opted into separate-but-equal public school systems that hobbled the dynamic energies of indigenous and spontaneous self-betterment. Here, again, we see an upswing before downswing sets in, an upswing that is quite independent of mountaintop public policy and even proves somewhat resilient when confronting the undermining influence of state-based public policy.

Finally, consider what is perhaps most dramatic in the surface statistics of the census reports—namely, how post-slavery American blacks attained rough parity with mainstream society with respect to the disposition to marry and form households (despite a legacy of family separations and abuse). The performance at the level of societal norms (taking non-black society as the norm) is nothing less than stunning. And it is no less stunning how rapidly the descent from that norm occurred post-1950. Here "upswing" was followed by "downswing" precisely in sync with the evolution of a full-throated custodial state officially assigning to American blacks the status of wards of a custodial state (protected classes).

If we will now reread the Putnam analyses in light of these observations, we should be able to draw certain general conclusions regarding the state of black America. To begin, it is manifest that American blacks have known great progress over the course of time since the end of slavery. At the same time, the rate of absorption of blacks as blacks into mainstream society has remained stubbornly low (we shall inquire why this is so in the next section). What we can observe is a stubborn refusal to regard American blacks *per se* as assuming full title to the status of bearers of the European tradition. As American blacks have largely shed characteristics of cultural distinctiveness, they have been postured all the more insistently as culturally distinct. In other words, in the "I-we-I" curve, the middle term is blank!

Alba's *The Great Demographic Illusion*

Why are American blacks still excluded from the "we" of American life? Richard Alba provides a handle for addressing that question most satisfactorily. For in revealing the hollowness of the myth of a future "majority of minorities" in the United States, what he actually accomplishes is to demonstrate how profoundly unwilling prevailing political sentiments are to recognize the emerging "we" of American life as insusceptible to the crutch of racial identification. The great question of the day, accordingly, and therefore, the question of the state of black America, is whether the tide of change that has been evidently sweeping the country since the end of slavery will eventually engulf it altogether or be aborted by the determined resistance of atavistic race-referencing.

Nor Black America; Nor White America

A first glance at *The Great Demographic Illusion* might tempt a reader to imagine an approaching end of the familiar distinctions of black and non-black Americans. The highlighted significance of an increasingly multiracial society ultimately implies a no-racial society (or perhaps we should say "no races"). We believe, however, that reading to be an oversimplification and by no means the most challenging reading. Rather, we shall submit, the implication is that with regard to "colors," a general fusion shall occur along lines of general paleness (that for mere reason of chemistry). Or, seeming "white" is all there is to being "white"! More importantly, however, what shall emerge is a form of national identification that will completely absorb all in the embrace of the European tradition, a thing that has not yet occurred. We repeat, as we said above, that is a life of politics above culture in which ties of blood, tribe, and religion will play no role in sorting power. In such a world, in which the individual must stand on character and accomplishment to advance, it may—and likely shall—still be prominent that communitarian values will rise and fall with political platforms. If that is to happen, however, it will have to be without the crutch of race or other non-relevant group identifications. In other words, a world in which the individual alone counts is not for all that a world in which individualism alone counts.

Let us see why this may be so.

The defect of narrative lies at the base of the demographic illusion. Alba himself falls victim to the defect of narrative, even as he labors (largely successfully) to correct the narrative. Before he can get to the critical data analysis, he must first take on the narrative of narratives driving political choices in ethno-racial terms. In his first two chapters, therefore, he develops a narrative of exploited "racial resentment" driving U.S. politics in the recent era, with extensive citation of one-sided, constructivist social science research and purportedly incendiary political rhetoric from one side of the political spectrum. At no point does he ever take up the question of any other content in the universe of political discourse that might materially affect political sentiments. The lack of evenhandedness discourages paying careful attention to the data analysis he goes on to provide. That failure therefore enables the comfortable assumption that Americans are being led into false apprehensions of a polarized ethno-racial future as a direct result of unprincipled actors. He takes this position in spite of having quite sensibly pointed out that triumphalist, race-referenced rhetoric about a future "majority of minorities" conveyed not only conceivably false interpretations of data but, more importantly, a stimulus of urgency. In short, even while rebutting central claims of the prevailing narrative, he nevertheless embraces the simplistic reductionism that narrative, rather than fact, shapes destiny.

The very first data table in *The Great Demographic Illusion* belies the tendency to simplify. Moreover, it underscores the conclusion we reached above concerning the context of black post-slavery demographics. The overall account of more than a century of immigration depicts a backdrop of dynamic pressures that would foster social and political uncertainty no matter what prior dispositions prevailed. The task here—relative to the state of black America—is to assess those dynamics independently of race-referencing as a precondition for the consideration of the effect of race as political and social determinant. (See Figure 1.11.)

Figure 1.11 Legal Immigration (Bars) and Foreign-Born Population (Line) by Decade, 1850–2017[16]

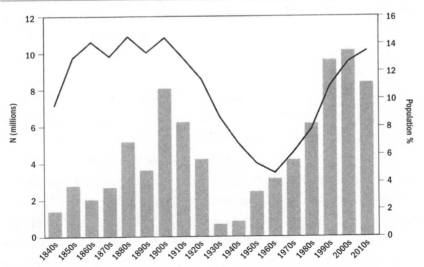

Note: Each point on the line indicates the foreign-born percentage at the end of the decade.

Sources: Office of Immigration Statistics, Yearbook of Immigration Statistics (various years); National Academies of Sciences 2015.

Now, this detailed account requires the analyst to ask the "but for" question: What would be the social/political dynamic of the United States but for race? The response must surely be that either pressures of absorption (assimilation and inclusion) or pressures of administrative cantonment and exclusion would ensue. Now, it has been the manifest purpose of Alba's life work to demonstrate precisely that fact. He has succeeded in redefining "assimilation" to reveal a standard that he terms "non–zero sum assimilation." That standard means, primarily, that social mobility occurs with minimal or no displacement effects. And the history of immigration in the United States demonstrates strongly that processes of absorption prevail.

The reason this is important is that the balance of *The Great Demographic Illusion* demonstrates precisely how that absorption occurs and why national discourse has so strongly closed its eyes to the reality. In a word, the dictum of Aristotle—that fellow citizenship requires intermarriage—describes *not diverging but converging populations* in the United States. The most important task for the analyst, therefore, is to determine where to locate the mean toward which the convergence will or must occur. That process, in turn, would dismiss the static analyses of a future "majority of minorities" and spawn a more serious inquiry into the evolving majority that will shape the social and political consensus. In short, the obsession with race-referencing specifically impedes thoughtful analysis not only of the state of black America but of the future of the United States.

Take special note that the slope of intermarriage, as shown in Figure 1.12, overlays quite well the rising slope of the "I-we-I" curve. However, as we shall observe, there is not a correlative downswing to match Putnam's "foot off the gas" metaphor in the socioeconomic realm. The implication is that much of the downswing is accounted for by occluding demographic elements

Figure 1.12 The Rise of Intermarriage since *Loving v. Virginia* (1967)[17]

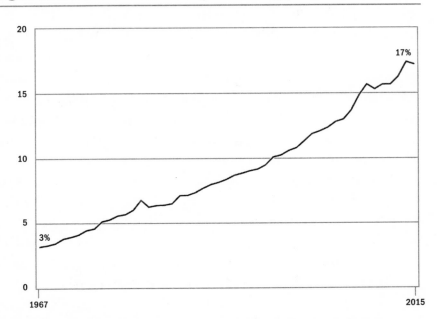

Note: The line shows the annual rate of marriage across the major lines of race and Hispanic origin among newlyweds.
Source: Livingston and Brown 2017, data courtesy of Anna Brown.

that are disappearing into the multiracial background. Accordingly, a fine-tuned analysis would require combining these two analyses into a common portrait.

As Alba recounts, much of the occluding effect is an artifact of official data reporting. Census Bureau and Office of Management and Budget procedure for recording and reporting racial identity actually serve to exaggerate racial distinctions, while inaccurately describing social dynamics. This was already evident in the treatment of Hispanics in the 1960s and '70s, when the convention of using "Spanish surname" as a racial identifier was revealed as completely misleading. That discovery led to the adoption of "non-Hispanic white" in an attempt to unveil intermarriage effects. That convention, in turn, has led to the no less non-sensible protocol of removing large numbers of "European origin" Hispanics from the category of "whites." Apart from the large-scale variations among persons of Hispanic descent, this urge to purify racial categories—all to preserve the practice of race-referencing—serves to render remote any realistic accounting of social dynamics in the United States. Add to that the residual effect of historically prior Hispanic-indigenous mixing and we inherit a mélange of categories that do not categorize to any useful purpose.

The foregoing account should suffice to portray the crisis of race reporting that characterizes present-day analyses. But the inherent fallacy of the entire edifice driving policy and discourse is made clearest by the observable evidence of present trends toward intermarriage across all ethno-racial identities.

Figure 1.13 on the next page shows trends of racial mixing by focusing on infant cohorts. Those dramatic changes reflect the pending emergence of a general society dramatically changed and in which it makes decreasingly little sense to speak in terms of race. Note particularly how the second generation so nearly approximates the overall slope, which indicates that the overall rate shall achieve increasing velocity over time.

Now when the reality of race mixing (which might just as well be termed "absorption") is looked at in relation to the variety of formations that occur on the basis of ethno-racial background (Figure 1.14), alongside the variety of formations according to income levels (Figure 1.15), it is clear that this phenomenon is concentrated around and below median income levels (contrary to the assumption frequently made that it is only the few college-educated and privileged who are really mixing). This statistical reality is also a plain reality to anyone who bothers to live "among the people." In short, what is being changed most rapidly and most profoundly is the broad social base.

In the face of these dramatic trends, it is to be expected that

Figure 1.13 Trends of Ethno-Racial Mixing among Infants, 1980–2017[18]

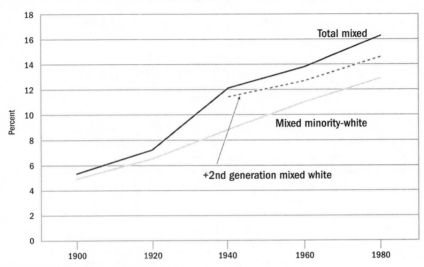

Note: Infants are defined as children under the age of one.

Sources: PUMS samples from the 1980–2010 decennial censuses and 2017 American Community Survey data, courtesy of IPUMS (Ruggles et al. 2019).

Figure 1.14 Rates of Parental Marriage for Infants from Different Mixed and Unmixed Family Backgrounds[19]

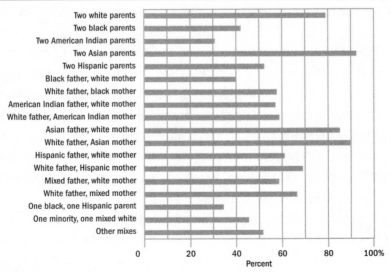

Source: National Center for Health Statistics, 2016 birth certificate data.

Figure 1.15 Median Combined Annual Parental Income of Infants from Different Mixed and Unmixed Family Backgrounds[20]

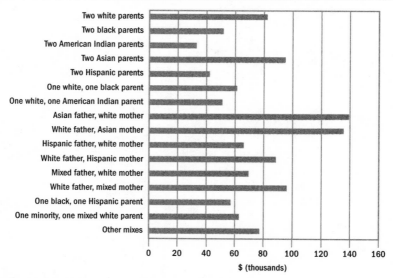

Note: Data restricted to infants with both parents in household.
Source: 2017 American Community Survey data, courtesy of IPUMS (Ruggles et al. 2019).

we will observe correlative trends in economic and educational status all converging toward the mean of mainstream society. And that is exactly what we observe.

Apart from the outlier effect of the Asian-based performance, what is most notable in Figure 1.16 is the clustered effect in levels of educational attainment across the various designations. And that outcome is still more dramatic across men alone than across women alone. Thus, we discover fewer distinctions across ethno-racial groupings in proportion to their presence in the overall population than we would otherwise be led to expect by the race-referenced narrative.

What these facts mean is that, while the process of absorption varies across ethno-racial designations, its direction is general across all. Moreover, the process seems destined in all designations to reflect the same dimensions that have heretofore been seen

Figure 1.16 Postsecondary Educational Attainment of Mixed (Expanded) and Unmixed U.S.-Born Men and Women Ages Twenty-Five to Thirty-Nine[21]

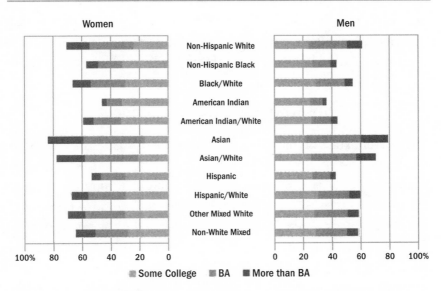

Note: To counteract selective reporting of mixed backgrounds on the race and Hispanic-origin census questions, these expanded mixed categories take into account ancestry data as well. See text discussion.
Source: 2017 American Community Survey data, courtesy of IPUMS (Ruggles et al. 2019).

to obtain generally among immigrant populations in the United States. The sole distinguishing question, therefore, is whether the circumstance of American blacks is anomalous, lagging, in the process of absorption, and if so, to what degree. In making this calculation, however, the trick is to remember that immigration reconfigures the base—the denominator—in such a way as to suggest retardation in a one-dimensional analysis where, in fact, multivariate swamping is the reality. That is, the size of the pool into which American blacks must jump increases proportionately to their progress! That factor is separate from and in addition to any effects of reproductive rates, household formation, and premature deaths. When Alba says the mainstream is expanding, he means that it is becoming more inclusive. However, it is apparent that it is also expanding in size relative to the positions of its constituent elements (which requires no overall increase in absolute number). Thus, insofar as the relations of blacks to non-blacks is the major distinction to be made, it matters that "blacks" are transmogrified through multiracial categorizations with the result of diminishing the record of "black" progress.

Absorption versus Cantonment

The current state of black America is a state of suspension between absorption and administrative cantonment. What we mean by administrative cantonment is the persistent policy of the government to treat with American blacks as separate and apart. American blacks are consistently recognized by the government first as black and only second as American. Whether this is the residue of slavery, which was certainly a form of political cantonment (a people permanently set apart to be governed by external structures), or a newly evolved form of cantonment (politically permeable), there can be little doubt that cantonment is the motif. This stands in contrast to the similar yet distinct reservation policy that was imposed on American Indians. The latter was accompanied with a fig leaf of sovereignty (that is, independence) which in no way applies to the cantonment of American blacks, who are treated as wholly dependent wards of the state (and not the "semi-dependent wards" the Indians were appointed to be in court decisions). Moreover, there are no territorial attributes of black cantonment (however much integral and/or ghettoized communities might have existed). Black life in the United States reflects still as it has heretofore the sufferance of the mainstream community.

Absorption, by contrast, means the complete permeability of all institutions, social and political. It derives from ease of transit across all social spaces physically and cognitively. The legal permeability that Justice Harlan prefigured in the notion of "colorblindness" meant precisely this. He perhaps did not realize, however, that "equality before the law" (legal permeability) was impossible without complete social and political permeability. The term "absorption," accordingly, conveys far more fully what was at stake in the concept of colorblindness. We shall see below that this is also the only possible meaning of "antiracism."

As a practical matter, however, it must be acknowledged that the standard of absorption remains an objective to be attained rather than a reality. This is so despite the society's evident capacity for absorption (as shown above). The reason for the disjunction between promise and reality lies mainly in the narratives that we embrace. The conscious refusal to embrace a narrative of absorption is the single greatest obstacle to its final realization.

The foregoing claim is made anecdotally apparent in an instructive story. A solidly middle-to-upper-class white community (except for a very small Mexican barrio) in California was once integrated without its knowledge. A music teacher, the daughter of an American Indian woman and an American black man, purchased a home in the center of town and lived there without incident for sixty years. After the initial decades of those sixty years, a prominent progressive real estate agent undertook to "integrate the town," conspicuously moving a black family into the community and trumpeting the progressive value it represented. Several years later, the same progressive real estate agent prevented a multiracial family from purchasing a home on the most prominent boulevard in the community, upsetting a signed contract for no reason other than to prevent the location of a black-based, multiracial family occupying so central and visible a space in the community. The same progressive real estate agent attempted to secure a similarly attractive property for the same family but met the conservatively principled refusal of the seller and suffered defeat as a result. Meanwhile, the music teacher who had been a longtime resident there, and who had taught the children of many of the most distinguished families, continued to live as assumedly "white." In fact, it was only toward the end of her life that she revealed to her black client (the persecuted property owner), who had become a very close friend, her ethno-racial background (very much to that client's surprise).

This was not an episode of "passing," as so well depicted in the novel of that title by Nella Larson. The spinster simply did not announce herself ethno-racially and therefore escaped the attributive cantonment that would have followed (she was not red-lined and had no trouble acquiring banking facilities). She benefited from the permeability that has generally characterized the status of American Indians, who do not have to be Indians unless they choose to be so.

Such personal stories constitute the elements framed by the public narrative that structures the cantoned environment. That is to say, cantonment is possible only to the extent that it is sustained by public policy, which licenses equally public and individual race-referencing as a legitimate basis for interacting with fellow citizens. The "progressive" real estate agent, whose real "racism" affected the lives of distinct individuals, was empowered to do so by the public preservation of race-referencing as legitimate. The "progressive" scholars Putnam and Alba, who are not racists, are no less subject to the influence of the patterned reactions engendered by race-referencing. As a consequence, they are intimidated by the discourse informed in that manner to profess innocence of any slights or negative inferences respecting any ethnic or racial background and, still more, to provide evident assurance of their commitment to an agenda of reform. Such moves are merely inverted forms of race-referencing, which interact in the larger universe of discourse in the same manner as the views of the "progressive but racist real estate agent" did.

It is for the reasons elucidated in the foregoing paragraph, therefore, that this analysis must take up—beyond the review of social science analysis—the current discussion of antiracism. For that discussion contributes mightily to reinforce the patterned policy of race-referencing, which, more than any other single contributing factor, affects the state of black America.

Kendi's Racism

Upon the death of George Floyd in the summer of 2020, if we take seriously the discourse that followed it, America experienced nothing less than a religious revival. Often described as an "awakening" or "reckoning," our national experience convicted many of sin, drew them to repentance, and established them on an apparent path to sanctification. But what is the content of this rekindled religious belief? Do all who claim to oppose racism really share a common faith?

In answer to these questions, apparent consensus formed around that version of the faith articulated most fully in the work of Ibram X. Kendi.[22] It is probably no exaggeration to say that Kendi's articulation of antiracism is more widely known and recognized by the general public than any other.[23] Any attempt to provide a positive account of "the state of black America" should at least contend with the core tenets of Kendi's thought and, if they are found lacking, suggest a better path forward.

What Kendi presents is no less than a total vision of reality that imposes a total claim on every soul. Our history, he says, is fundamentally a battle between racism and antiracism, and as peoples, we now poise on the precipice between them. At such a watershed moment, Kendi proclaims from the start, "there is no neutrality."[24] Every action, every idea, every policy—every person—serves the cause of either racist power or antiracist power. The only way to prove free of the mortal sin of racism is to become an antiracist: that is, to dedicate oneself to the lifelong struggle against racism in all its forms (which include biological racism, cultural racism, class racism, gender racism, queer racism, and antiwhite racism, among others). To merely insist that one is "not racist," as many Americans do, is in reality "a mask for racism."[25] How are we to reckon with such sweeping claims?

A small but vocal minority of intellectuals opted to reject them altogether. A cluster of black "heterodox" thinkers, including Glenn C. Loury, John McWhorter, Coleman Hughes, and Thomas Chatterton Williams, have presented sustained critiques of Kendi's thought, often in informal or journalistic contexts. Besides addressing perceived gaps or inconsistencies in Kendi's arguments, all these critics pay close attention to the religious character of Kendi's antiracism and of the antiracist ideology more broadly. Antiracism, they say, is dogma that demands unwavering faith, suppresses all dissent, and labels all people saints or heretics. In return, it promises what any good religion does: a sense of meaning and purpose, membership in a moral community, and the satisfaction of self-righteousness. Kendi's critics speak mainly from a secular perspective (whether atheist or agnostic), while differing in their valuation of religion as a cultural phenomenon. They agree that antiracism's religious quality is precisely the source of its danger. As John McWhorter remarks, the religion of antiracism is readily embraced by "secular, even pagan, mostly over-educated affluent whites" who nevertheless crave "a warm but inchoate sense of belonging…that often as not impedes rather than fosters social justice."[26] In this sense, the new antiracism represents a setback for genuine social progress. This echoes the phenomenon of "intimidation" that we recognize in the works of Putnam and Alba above. It is more than "white guilt" or "shame." It is a sense of the obligation to touch the "weak" with the expression of one's "love."

There is much to reckon with in both the ideology and the critique, but we highlight the biggest questions at stake, those concerning a faulty compromise between secularism and religious faith. Because the reigning version of antiracism is a false faith, it lacks power to heal a fractured nation and, conversely, bids fair to infect the wound gangrenously. Americans have a more promising source of unity than the antiracist creed. However, it is important to understand the false proffer in order collectively to respond to the challenges shaping the future of race relations and the future of America itself.

We begin that process by stating what is and is not racism, what is and is not systemic. Kendi's *performative definitions* (i.e., racism and antiracism are in the doing and not the thinking or feeling) fail to clarify real concepts that can be grasped by the intellect. A simple story may help to elucidate. The senior author, as a youth in a small, strictly segregated Southern town, once presented himself to the public library (a small thing, housing doubtless fewer titles than he currently holds in his personal library). He was no more than six or seven but long an avid reader, and he hoped perhaps to be provided something—anything—that he might read. The librarian informed him, however, that he was not permitted to enter because he was "colored." The usual narrative ends there, with the youth disconsolately walking away. On this occasion, however, the librarian said, "Sit down here" on the steps "and wait a moment." She returned promptly with a book and said, "You can read it here."

What does this story illustrate? First, and most emphatically, a racist system of public policy existed. No less manifestly, however, the toxemia it spreads does not necessarily reach to every heart subject to its domination. The librarian acted within the bounds of the law—and thus upheld racism—at the same time as straining against its intent and effects. In that sense she leaned into sentiments of humanity that may surely be termed counter-racist. This means, accordingly, that imposed racism and expressed racism are not colinear. Racism may be imposed where it is not felt, and significantly, it may be felt where it is not (or cannot be) imposed.

To move from anecdote to concept—testable proposition— we maintain that social codification is not colinear with social behavior (conformity). Therefore, it would necessarily follow that individuals may be racist in non-racist systems (retail racism) and non-racist in racist systems (wholesale racism). Inasmuch as the contradiction of that proposition constitutes the foundation premise of Kendi's "antiracism," however, Kendi's premise must fall under analysis—it is unfounded polemic rather than systematic argument.

Overview

How to Be an Antiracist is simultaneously memoir, history, political commentary, and spiritual handbook. By weaving together such diverse genres, Kendi unfolds a story about humankind in which a common conflict defines his personal experience, the history of the West, America's cultural and political landscape, and most crucially, everyone's soul. In each of the book's eighteen chapters, Kendi pairs a topical issue—power, ethnicity, class, sexuality—with an installment of his autobiography, inseparably intertwining his life and impressions.

As a descriptive account of the world, *How to Be an Antiracist* attempts to pin down the historical, cultural, and anthropological origins of racism. For Kendi, there is a distinct order of being when it comes to racism: Racist power precedes racist policies;

racist policies precede racist ideas. The history of racism begins with the sheer desire of *some persons* to dominate others. To accomplish this, the *former group* creates policies that codify a position of superiority over the latter. (Note the silent slide from an indefinite "some persons" to a definite "group.") Next, they justify the injustice on an abstract level by inventing racist ideas that artificially categorize "distinct individuals, ethnicities, and nationalities" as members of "monolithic races."[27] The impact of this is to "manipulate us into seeing people as the problem, instead of the policies that ensnare them."[28] Thus racist ideas exist to give the name of justice to whatever mechanisms preserve the dominance of the ruling group. The concept of race, despite its intellectual pretensions, is at root "a power construct," an ingenious social innovation for the expansion and preservation of self-interested power.[29] And it is effective, too, for *it produces every kind of inequity that exists among racial groups*. If race does not exist, strictly speaking, then any disparities in income, resources, health, crime and incarceration, education, political representation, or cultural influence must result directly from policies that have arbitrarily disadvantaged some to the benefit of others. Of course, even if this were true, it would not follow that the disadvantaging policy were racist.

A Flawed Conception of Political Life

That this is *only* a story and not a description of historical events is plainly evident in the fact that the empirical connectors in the story do not add up and, rather, elide crucial historical elements that must inevitably produce a different story. To understand why Kendi's work takes this turn, one must open his earlier work, *Stamped from the Beginning*.[30] That work is the foundation of *How to Be an Antiracist* and provides the analysis omitted in the later work. There, he explains that racism arose in fifteenth-century

Europe and acquired systematic form in the age of exploration. He conceives that the architecture of Europe was predicated upon the solidification of power relations with non-Europeans upon racial distinctions. In developing this analysis, he founds his reasoning upon the claim Jefferson Davis, president of the Confederacy, enunciated in his inaugural address. That claim was that black slavery was "stamped from the beginning" in the European settlement of North America. In relying upon this foundation claim for the defense of slavery, Kendi imitates those advocates who rely upon the argument of John C. Calhoun that slavery was a "positive good." That is to say that one and the other predicate an analysis of the United States on the defeated claims of slavery's defenders rather than the triumphant claims of those who ultimately abolished slavery. This incongruous analysis produces the result that the defeated argument is embraced as the true and proper characterization of the structure of power in the United States.

One reason this result occurs derives from Kendi's reliance on the ideological structures of Marxism—namely, the explanation of all political relations in terms of the relations between "oppressors and oppressed." In short, in order to analyze the United States consistently with the methodological imperatives of socialism, it is necessary to frame the discussion entirely in terms of a struggle for power rather than a struggle of ideas. The political system may only be understood as patterned relationships of power and submission (that is, social codification is read as compulsory, even when it is merely hypothetical). Since the very claim of the United States at its proper founding was to have transcended patterned relationships of power and submission, that claim is dismissed or discounted not by argument but by methodological necessity. Moreover, every element of the society so analyzed must conform to the required pattern. Thus, capitalism is merely an expression of the power relations in the society and, hence, strictly a matter of the material relations required to sustain race-based slavery.

This analysis, therefore, hangs entirely upon the misconstruction of the development of modern Europe as a bearer of race-based slavery. Not only does that perspective fail to discern the intrinsic and sometimes specific arguments against power relationships based on race (and gender, for that matter), it far more importantly fails completely to understand the true origins of modern Europe. That is ironic insofar as the fifteenth century not only submits Columbus, Marco Polo, and other exemplars of the age of exploration to review, but it also offers Machiavelli and his successors (upon whom Kendi does not reflect at all). Since it was precisely Machiavelli who developed power relations—not blood or tribe or religion—as the fundamental principle of political organization, the irony is all the more significant. For it means that Kendi failed to notice the anticipatory refutation of the Hegelian-Marxian analysis.

In a word, the Machiavellian move initiated the momentum that led Europe to develop a mode of civilization that eventually altered the basis of political organization throughout the entire earth. The focus on power relations produced successive attempts to concretize the idea of political power in a general account—most notably the Hobbesian account that replaced all other accounts of authority with positivism. The practical attempts to valorize political power eventually produced the systematic form of the nation-state as the basis of civilization itself. This achieved its consummation in the Westphalian settlement of 1648. However, that settlement produced the new and ultimately universal form of all political life without resolving the inherent problem of authority. The power thus established was arbitrary, inasmuch as theoretical notions of right were insufficient to direct claims of sovereign authority. Consequently, further reflection was required in order to elaborate a form for the nation-state in which the power that lay at its base could be understood as neither absolute nor arbitrary. That required the development of constraints on power in the service of liberty. Preliminary theorizing in that direction—by John Locke most notably—did not succeed in achieving the result. The Westminster constitutionalism that arose in the wake of the Glorious Revolution made Parliament legally sovereign, and therefore lacked the architecture to protect the liberty of citizens from arbitrary rule. Ultimately, therefore, progress was made with the influence of theorists such as Montesquieu, who inspired the creation of the American Constitution as the first truly contractual limit on government power. The constitutional nation-state, where power is deliberately constrained, arose from the development of European political thought.

What this means for our purposes is simply that the civilizational form that Europe eventually bequeathed to the globe is predicated precisely upon rejecting the claim that politics consists of the relations between oppressor and oppressed. Insofar as that has been accomplished to some degree, it is therefore false that the systematic form of politics establishes at its origins ("stamped from the beginning") racial or cultural attributes as components of political identity. Kendi's arguments, accordingly, are predicated upon misinterpretation of the forms and principles of political life itself.

Despite Kendi's failures in this regard, he advances his claims with the assertion that there is a perverse creativity to the putatively racist project. "Race makers" continually spawn "new forms of power: the power to categorize and judge, elevate and downgrade, include and exclude."[31] For example, whereas racism once appeared primarily in segregationist ideas about "genetic racial distinction and fixed hierarchy" (note that this is a late historical emergence in relation to Kendi's spurious account of the origins of racism), racism now takes the subtler form of assimilationist ideas, which "are rooted in the notion that certain racial groups are culturally or behaviorally inferior."[32] We must be attentive to the new masks that racism takes on as it adapts to the times. Even those who openly claim to oppose racism, Kendi warns, often do so in bad faith, and seemingly innocuous positions on race are the most dangerous of all.[33] In all this it is important to recognize that, although Kendi begins the analysis with "slavery," he sustains it with exclusive reference to "racism." This gambit serves to occlude the origins of the term "slave" as a reference to those Slavs, pinched between European powers and so oppressed as to make their very name the term for slavery—a distinctly non-race-based slavery. Kendi's silent move, accordingly, actually reinforces the current and inherited race-referencing, making it the peculiar tool of "antiracism."

This thought leads naturally to the book's prescriptive program. We overcome racism by piercing to the heart of the matter: the problem of power. Power created racism, and only power can uncreate it. In our society, power is reinforced by policy, which for Kendi encompasses "written and unwritten laws, rules, procedures, processes, regulations, and guidelines that govern people."[34] Hence, social codification. Since policies correspond with power, no policy is race-neutral: "Every policy in every institution in every community in every nation is producing or sustaining either racial inequity or equity between racial groups."[35] That is, every policy is founded in race-referencing, even if race is an artificial construct. Hence, the basic antiracist strategy is to take power from the racist policymakers and use it to institute antiracist policies, which will necessarily eliminate racial inequity. In short, "the only remedy to racist discrimination is antiracist discrimination."[36] The danger is that we lose sight of the plan, failing to match racist power with antiracist power and thus allowing justice to be trampled.

> *Antiracist power must* be flexible to *match* the flexibility of racist power, propelled only by *the craving for power to shape policy* in their inequitable interests. Racist power believes in by any means necessary. We, their challengers, typically do not…Anything but flexible, we are too often bound by ideologies that are bound by failed strategies of racial change.
>
> What if we assessed the methods and leaders and organizations by the results of policy change and equity? What if strategies and policy solutions stemmed not from ideologies but from problems? What *if antiracists were propelled only by the craving for power* to shape policy in their equitable interests?[37]

One of the "failed strategies" that Kendi addresses at length is that of persuasion. To channel all our efforts into persuading people that racism is false is an exercise in futility. This is because racists believe in racism not because it is *true*, but because it is beneficial to them. It is impossible to reason with their racist ideas, for their source is "not ignorance and hate, but self-interest."[38] Therefore, there is no common ground of truth which the powerful and the powerless can inhabit together—at least insofar as the powerful are committed to maintaining their position, which, we assume, is almost invariably the case. "The problem of race," Kendi concludes, "has always been at its core the problem of power."[39]

The entire argument, in short, hinges on the account of power relations in society, an account that, in fact, is manifestly contradictory to the evolution of modern power relations. We noted the historical development above. It is important, however, to reinforce the idea that the constitution constrained by liberty is a distinct form of power relations that expressly delegitimizes the relationship of oppressor and oppressed. That is the reason that, from 1776 onward, the unbending direction of political development in the United States has been defined by liberty rather than power. While it may seem to some to have taken an unseemly long time in getting from the promise of liberty to anywhere near the attainment of liberty, it is undeniably the case that the movement has been monotonic (if herky-jerky) in the form of the initial move toward abolition of slavery by degrees in the United States. That the Prince Halls, Benjamin Bannekers, and Richard Allens (among others) embraced the promise of liberty above power means that there is a different—and a superior—path forward than that projected by Kendi.

What is at stake, however, is Kendi's unproved assumption that this is a question of power, in the face of which no one may claim either immunity or indifference—the focus on the compulsory. A gun to the temple may well force a choice on those capable of choosing but will be an empty—if fatal—gesture regarding those not so capable as well as regarding those prepared for any eventuality (meaning the unscheduled choice of self-sacrifice). Kendi can see the matter differently not because his definitions make sense, but only because he rests his judgment on an ideological commitment that identifies racism and capitalism as a conjoined and ubiquitous political reality in the face of which effort must ensue to overturn it or all must succumb to it. That means, in light of *Stamped from the Beginning*, that the cause of antiracism is nothing less than the dismantling of the nation-state. At that point it is not difficult to see it as correlative with emergence of the Marxist universal world-state.

Since European civilization—and that is the proper name, not "white" civilization—takes its complete form of expression in the liberty-based nation-state (even if most of the nation-states existing have not yet found the way to a basis in liberty), then "antiracism" means "anti–European civilization." It is a demand for a new world order. While such a demand is coherent, it does not follow that it is predicated upon a coherent argument. Thus it is, for example, that it takes the argument against capitalism for Kendi to make his "intersectional" turn—while abjuring all class categorization (he dislikes terms such as "systemic racism")—in order to argue that salvation hinges uniquely upon overturning—not any particular policy—but capitalism itself.

At this point, therefore, the entire conceit of the book is lost. Neither racism nor antiracism is germane to the actual discussion. Only competent political and economic analysis can provide what is required to sustain this screed. And both competent political and economic analysis are completely absent. That should surprise none who perceive, in particular, that the references to capitalism assume without stating a specifically flawed economic principle: namely, that economies are founded in accidental or arbitrary policies. Think of Rousseau's suggestion that property rights originated simply by someone putting up a fence and someone else respecting it as a boundary. Perhaps Kendi should not be blamed too greatly for such intellectual confusion, for it is rare that anyone defines capitalism with clarity or offers any very serious account of economic activity.

To clarify matters, let us posit that capitalism is not intrinsically distinct from any other form of economic activity. All economic activity is founded in the human propensity to buy and sell (by whatever modality). As such, there is no possible economy apart from such foundation. However, economic activity is subject to varying degrees of regulation, from least (open rapine and exploitation) to greatest (totalitarian communalization). It is the same economic activity in either case but subject to varying degrees of accomplishment depending upon the varying exigencies of regulation. In this regard, it is fair to say that liberty begins (as the ancients observed) with poverty, when the little one may have poses no attraction to others, and slavery begins with wealth, for the opposite reason. The purpose of regulated economic activity, accordingly, is founded upon the benefit of assured title in one's possessions (as de Soto makes clear in *The Mystery of Capital*[40]). Beyond functional limits of assured title, regulation becomes counterproductive and replaces the rapine of banditti with the rapine of institutions.

In this context, to add racism—or antiracism for that matter—to dissimulating forms of institutional rapine produces no further meaning or definitional power. To claim, therefore, that capitalism emerged as the distinctive form of racism (or is it vice versa?—Kendi is not clear) and thus set it apart from human economic behavior in general is not only undefended but demonstrably absurd. The coexistence in history of the emergence of racism and the emergence of capitalism (loosely, and only loosely speaking) provides no foundation for the argument that Kendi makes in *How to Be an Antiracist*, nor in his earlier work.

For all intents and purposes, Kendi sees reconciliation between antiracists and their supposed opponents as simply impossible. Between the champions of justice and the champions of injustice there can only be a fight to the death. Kendi is careful not to draw the line between blacks and non-blacks, or even between Democrats and Republicans; the divide is more fundamental than that. Our nation is embroiled in a Manichean struggle between "the soul of justice" and "the soul of injustice."[41] As Kendi explains in an essay for *The Atlantic*:

> Opposing forces can dwell in a mind, in a nation. But can opposing forces dwell in a *soul*—if soul is elemental like breath? It is hard to imagine the enslaver and the enslaved being together in any

elemental sense. It is hard to imagine Trump and the survivor who voted against him being together in any elemental sense. But they have been battling in the same nation. There is a divide in America between the souls of injustice and justice: souls in opposition like fire and ice, like voters and voter subtraction, like Trump and truth.[42]

The line between justice and injustice is not only about racism. The soul of injustice perpetrates "genocide, enslavement, inequality, voter suppression, bigotry, cheating, lies, individualism, exploitation, denial, and indifference to it all," while the soul of justice advances "life, freedom, equality, democracy, human rights, fairness, science, community, opportunity, and empathy for all."[43] Yet, at least in our age, racism is the root of all evil. Like a metastatic cancer, racism

> has spread to nearly every part of the body politic, intersecting with bigotry of all kinds, justifying all kinds of inequities by victim blaming; heightening exploitation and misplaced hate; spurring mass shootings, arms races, and demagogues who polarize nations; shutting down essential organs of democracy; and threatening the life of human society with nuclear war and climate change.[44]

If racism continues to spread, it will spell utter ruin for humanity. Racists may believe they are racist for their own good, but racism in the end benefits no one, black or non-black: "White supremacist is code for anti-human, a nuclear ideology that poses an existential threat to human existence."[45] There is only one way to respond to the existential threat posed by the soul of injustice: Destroy it at all costs. Indeed, Kendi says, "There's no fighting for the soul of America. There's no uniting the souls of America. There is only fighting *off* the other soul of America."[46]

The heart of the matter, accordingly, lies in the preaching that American blacks may not—indeed, cannot—enlist in the fight "for the soul of America." This idea—the exclusion of black patriotism as an option, whose merit is its potential to save the nation itself—becomes accordingly the essence of the antiracism campaign and directly confronts the question of the "state of black America." In other words, the antiracism campaign means precisely to pose a demand for American blacks to peel away, to disengage from America. That particular move is viewed as the first move toward the eventual disestablishment of the European system in the United States and, ultimately, the world altogether. The utopian millennialism of this vision exists in some tension with the motives of self-improvement to which Kendi gives generous lip service.

Can We All Do Better?

If this plan sounds somewhat militant, Kendi also thinks the heart and soul of antiracism is a scrupulous and humble self-examination. Focusing too much on the racism of ideological opponents blinds us to the evil that lurks within us. For the heart is deceitful—who can understand it? Confessing his own deeply rooted patterns of racist thinking, Kendi challenges the notion that black people cannot be racist or that racism cannot be directed against white people. Just as a white person is not *ipso facto* a racist, neither is a black person *ipso facto* innocent of racism, for the simple reason that "Black people do have power, even if limited."[47] Whether we possess power, desire it, or are complicit with those who wield it, none of us can say that our hearts are uncorrupted. "Like fighting an addiction," Kendi says, "being an antiracist requires persistent self-awareness, constant self-criticism, and regular self-examination."[48] *Racist* and *antiracist* are not permanent identities, but "peelable name tags" that we alternate between in our struggle toward purification.[49] It is perhaps on this point that Kendi's religious sensibilities overwhelm his argument: "the heartbeat of racism is denial, the heartbeat of antiracism is confession."[50]

We ought finally to make clear the purported end goal of the antiracist project. Paradoxically, though Kendi thinks advocates of "race neutrality" pose the gravest danger to antiracism, his ideal is a society free from the artificial restrictions of racial categories—and from all other unjust impositions that divide and repress human beings. It is only that Kendi, because of his emphasis on the role of power, thinks that "terminating racial categories is potentially the last, not the first, step in the antiracist struggle."[51] Those who dismiss the relevance of race-referencing *now* evade the responsibility to correct the ongoing power imbalance caused by racialization. At this point in history the fight against evil still rages. But we can dream of the day when there is no hierarchy of racial groups; when there are no inequities of power or resources between them; when the cultural differences between them are celebrated, not judged (exactly what is a celebration without judgment?); and when integrated spaces foster "racial solidarity" amid diversity.[52] The other bigotries and oppressions that are historically intertwined with racism—capitalism, sexism, homophobia, transphobia, class-based prejudice, and ethnic prejudice—must be overcome, too. Kendi acknowledges that his vision may seem quixotic. Nevertheless, we must strive against injustice with our whole souls and lives, hoping against hope that justice will one day cover the earth. "Once we lose hope, we are guaranteed to lose. But if we ignore the odds and fight to create an antiracist world, then we give humanity a chance one day to survive, a chance to live in communion, a chance to be forever free."[53] In that world of communion and freedom, every individual would be equally valued and celebrated in all his uniqueness. For Kendi, this mission is a deeply personal one: "To be antiracist is to let me be me, be myself, be my imperfect self."[54]

What, then; shall American blacks wait for that far-off "one day"?

We confess that we do not review Kendi's work here because we expect to learn from it any substantive or concrete direction regarding the state of black America. Rather, we think his work poses a challenge that it does not and cannot answer: namely, what can American blacks do for themselves, here and now? What does Kendi's antiracism have to offer to American blacks in light of their legitimate interests? It should already be evident that Kendi's argument totters on shaky historical, economic, and philosophical foundations and, as such, does not deserve its status as gospel among progressive Americans. But we may go further and judge whether Kendi's influence is warranted by answering the question: *Is Kendi's thought worth the price of our attention?*

Our engagement with and weighing of ideas does not transpire in enclaves of pure reason, but is embedded in the context of individual human lives bounded by limits (of time, of finite intellectual resources, and of practical necessity). These limits are worth keeping in mind when we attend to questions of race, economics, and political power, which are not merely academic inquiries pursued for their own sake, but which bear upon us as aspects of the urgent question of how we ought to live together.

Kendi makes a hefty claim upon our attention, for he sets before us a quixotic goal of racial equity that, until accomplished, requires us to fixate single-mindedly on race. Consider Kendi's May 2021 article "We Still Don't Know Who the Coronavirus's Victims Were." Kendi paints the disparate impacts of the coronavirus on different racial groups as symptoms of a "racial pandemic" paralleling the virus itself. Although "dozens of states" have released data highlighting the pandemic's racial disparities over the past year, Kendi nonetheless contends that "the groups of people who suffered the most from COVID-19 in the United States did so almost completely out of the view of data"—since, for example, we do not know exactly how many American blacks died from the virus or how many white Americans received COVID-19 tests (presumably relative to American blacks). To shed light on shrouded groups, we must achieve "data equality" by building a comprehensive, uniform system of data that accounts for every individual in every racial group in the nation. This would require, among other things, "reporting every single variable of the identity of every single American every single time they receive medical care of any kind" and standardizing this data in conformity to centrally defined racial categories. Once we have an exhaustive mass of data at our disposal, we can make precise, informed policy decisions to correct racial inequities.[55]

We might point out the latent contradiction in Kendi's argument: We supposedly know beyond a doubt that severe racial inequities amounting to a "racial pandemic" have been perpetuated and exacerbated by the COVID-19 pandemic, yet our data is hopelessly inadequate to prove it. Consider the further irony that we do, indeed, know that at the time of this writing American blacks have volunteered for vaccination at half the rate of non-blacks. Does that express the operation of racial injustice or independent agency? This difficulty aside, the article reveals the impracticability of Kendi's proposal to rectify so-called inequity (it is a discussion beyond the limits of this work to explain why it is wrong to use "equity" as a substitute for "equality"). It is staggering to consider what this proposal would require. We are to obtain knowledge of the minute details of every individual's experience (classified by race) in any matter upon which racial inequity is deemed to bear. Through the mediation of a pristinely standardized national database, then, we will reach comprehension of the precise condition of each racial group in America, down to its very last member—and this for a population of over three hundred million. Such an achievement of collective omniscience, if it is even conceivable in an unwieldy world of complexity, human error, and constant flux, would require the mobilization of institutions on every level of society and a massive investment of time and resources. We can safely surmise that a society whose vital institutions devote themselves to this Sisyphean effort will have less time to attend to the real conditions of cultural health and prosperity. Such a society inadvertently flirts with suicide.

As people bound by limits, we cannot embrace a program that forbids our sparing any means (be they individual, social, or political) to reach a dubious end. For these are the terms upon which Kendi requires his argument be accepted. American blacks, as much as non-black Americans, should firmly reject such a totalizing imposition on our individual and collective attention.

So, in sum, how should American blacks take Kendi? We can sympathize with some of his sensibilities, perhaps find insights in the stories he tells. But ultimately we must bypass *How to Be an Antiracist* in search of a deeper understanding. So let us take up the quest again. We identify at a minimum the reality of responsibility for their own fate that lies in the hands of American blacks. It is no less true now than it has been throughout human history that peoples are always faced with the choice between persistence or migration, to stay or to leave. When choosing to stay, people experience multiple influences and/or motivations. But at least one such motive must be the same motive that almost exclusively moves people to migrate—namely, to find a better way. American blacks express resolve to seek the good in the United States by their very presence in the land. Moreover, they find strong justification in doing so in the very fact of the potentiality for self-government that has been from its inception the unique promise of the United States. In that sense, accordingly, the response to Kendi from American blacks is and must be identical to the response to America. And that response must be to say either yes or no to the United States. If the choice is to say yes, to affirm, then what follows of necessity is the obligation to contribute all that one has to assure that the United States will deliver its promise and will, therefore, survive the stresses of existence in a world ever encircled by political dangers. In the end, black patriotism is the only fit response to the siren of antiracism.

Conclusion: Black Patriotism and the American Future

We now see that antiracism, at least as it is formulated by Kendi, is no solution to our nation's ills. By making power the central reality of human life, by dismissing everyone who disagrees with his assumptions as a racist, and by giving a certain social and political program all the weight of a religion, Kendi only deepens the bitter division that threatens to fragment us. He can speak compellingly of unity, of justice, of peace—but he cannot show us the way there.

Correspondingly, Kendi's version of American history obscures, rather than illuminates, any path toward unity that might still remain. Kendi imposes on the American founding a radical division between the "wealthy white men" who secured freedom for themselves and the minorities who remained in bondage.[56] These two groups of people, because they were unequal in power, were fundamentally at odds with each other from the beginning—and they remain so today.

> Pundits talk of American disunity as if the divide is brothers and sisters fighting. This is a power divide. Let's not ask why the

master and the slave are divided. Let's not ask why the tyrant and the egalitarian are divided. Let's not ask why the sexist and the feminist are divided. Let's not ask why the racist and the anti-racist are divided. The reasons should be self-evident. There's no healing these divides or bringing these powers together.

America is the story of powerful people struggling to keep their disproportionate amount of power from people who are struggling for the power to be free.[57]

He actually believes (contrary to the prevailing views of the founders) that America is not free and never has been. Yet we are supposedly a nation defined by an ongoing struggle toward a future freedom (that is, not led from a principled beginning but pulled toward an explosive ending). And nothing poses a greater obstacle to this struggle, at least in our historical moment, than the illusion that this is not a struggle *for power*. "To save the Union, or, really, to create a conceptual Union, we must be saved from a myth as devout and destructive as American exceptionalism: that freedom comes before power."[58]

This is where we must consider the challenge that *How to Be an Antiracist* poses to the project of this volume. It is our purpose to inquire into the future state of black America, which necessarily involves an inquiry about the American future more broadly. Among those who see no cause to abandon the notion of America, our central concern is this: What makes us one people? For "America" to have any positive meaning, we must be more than a collection of individuals sharing a geographical space. We must be more, too, than a people of masters and slaves, bound together only by a mutual history of oppression and injustice.

To believe that we can be more than this, we must have certain foundational convictions about politics: namely, that a justly ordered society in which everyone participates in a common good is a human possibility. This is not to say that such a society can ever be perfectly achieved, only that there *is* such a thing as justice, and there *is* a good that all people can know—the good of self-government. Human nature is ordered such that the goal of the political community is justice, and justice benefits everyone. Thus, politics is not doomed to be a zero-sum struggle for power in which the strong benefit at the expense of the weak. In historical fact, this description is often apt. Indeed, we must expect the perennial presence of injustice. But there is a good order that transcends our disorder. By virtue of this, there always remains to us a better possibility for politics—one it is not foolish to pursue.

On some level, Kendi shares many of these intuitions. He presumes the existence of a universal justice which entails that racism is not ultimately good for anyone, even those who gain power by it. Racism, like other sins, corrodes the heart and corrupts the will of the guilty. If we could only replace the disorder of self-interested power with the order of love and justice, Kendi believes, we could have a society where no one is left out, where all people have the opportunity to flourish. Ultimately, however, Kendi can only grope blindly toward his goal: a justice that stands above and outside of the history of injustice.

How, then, do we propose to get there? We cannot avoid asking certain questions about religion. There is, of course, the purely psychological and empirical question posed by some of Kendi's critics: Can human beings live together peacefully without a shared faith? There is a long tradition of Western thought that maintains that we are religious creatures. Never content with a merely animal existence, we demand transcendence—and if we are denied it in the form of religion, we will seek to achieve it within history by means of politics. Evidence from the nineteenth and twentieth centuries supports this thesis. So, too, does the growing religious adherence of America's secular elites to the doctrine of antiracism. Coleman Hughes articulates the challenge this poses for us: If for many people antiracism is filling a "religion-shaped hole," what might we proffer to replace it?[59]

But more fundamentally, what does our religion (or lack thereof) say about the kind of world that we live in, and what does that mean for our politics? In the absence of faith in the transcendent, it becomes more difficult to justify our conviction that justice and peace are goods worth pursuing. Kendi's cynical overview of history should only reinforce this point. Why not admit that in politics, and in human history more generally, there is nothing that transcends power and slavery—that no possible arrangement could really secure a common good for human beings? Christianity offers a vision of reality as graciously ordered by God, in which suffering and injustice are never allowed the final word. It was with this vision in mind that the early Martin Luther King Jr. preached the "more excellent way" of love. His Christian faith convinced him of the possibility that Americans might "rise from the dark depths of prejudice and racism to the majestic heights of understanding and brotherhood."[60] But once we have lost the vision, can we still trust the plan? In short, we must ask whether the only alternative to a world ruled by providence is a world ruled by power.

Even if we cannot resolve these questions satisfactorily, it may be possible to forge a path forward. The empirical findings of Putnam and Alba, discussed previously, demonstrate that a practical solidarity is not only possible but likely in twenty-first-century America. Although we may not now be a people wholly united by a shared purpose, we are well launched on the journey to that destination (assuming we do not detour into cul-de-sacs of despair, one-way highways in which every mile traversed is a mile erased).

Putnam demonstrates that in the recent history of our own country, people united by common sense of purpose worked together to make American society more just and more prosperous. In the early to mid-twentieth century, the conditions of many improved, from the richest to the poorest and from the most historically privileged to the most historically marginalized. Even American blacks, although they faced immense and unique challenges, profited enormously during this period of history. Putnam provides extensive evidence that these improvements were largely the fruit of a widespread other-directedness and sense of social solidarity. What inspires this sort of political will in large swaths of the American population is difficult to say. But that it is possible, even where people differ as to the nature of justice and the destiny of humankind, seems evident from our past.

Likewise, Alba's research indicates that the zero-sum struggle for power is but one of multiple plotlines in the complex American story. Contrary to Kendi, Alba argues that assimilation has historically meant less a "whitening" than an absorption of minority groups and a reshaping of the mainstream; thus, it can constitute genuine social progress. Furthermore, race is only part of the story. As recently as the twentieth century, ethnic and religious conflicts were just as powerful as racial ones, yet in large part these have been supplanted by mutual respect and prosperity among ethnic and religious groups. What this ought to teach us is that the powerful and the powerless are *not* locked into a cycle of perpetual strife. Even as inequalities of power can never entirely be eliminated—and Alba openly acknowledges this point—we can indeed look to a more inclusive and united future. Alba sees evidence for this in the effects of racial mixing, which is starting to blur the boundaries between blacks and non-blacks and open up new vistas of American experience. Unfortunately, we find ourselves in a moment when a narrative of power and opposition dominates our collective psyche. But that narrative itself contributes to perpetuate racial conflict. If we recognize that it is not only counterproductive, but also factually inaccurate, we may be able to overcome our obsession with race-referencing and embrace the prospect of mutual cooperation.

All this should give us cause for hope. But it is not cause for complacency, for the moral and spiritual struggle remains. If we can only think in terms of power and division—if we cannot find the resources to transcend injustice both past and present—we will undermine the social capital we still have left. The bright possibilities painted by Putnam and Alba will not come to pass. To prevent a bitter end, it is certainly important that historians, social scientists, and economists, such as the ones represented in this volume, apply their expertise to illuminate new or forgotten sources of national unity. But it is also necessary for ordinary people to step back and think deeply about the whole. What kind of world do we live in? What assumptions about the human condition do our politics and policies presume? What are the fundamental requirements for obtaining the social and political goods we desire? It is time to pose these questions anew.

Is it not also time, once and for all, to make a commitment to the project of self-government in the United States? Might it not be conceivable that, without an upswing of black patriotism, the future of the United States cannot evade a downswing? It is clear: Yesterday, the state of black Americans was domination by a non-black majority; today, the state of black Americans is to chart their own course through the eddies of change coursing through the society; tomorrow, it is an open question whether there will be a state of black Americans or only a free America.

2

THE FOURTEENTH AMENDMENT AND THE COMPLETION OF THE CONSTITUTION

Abraham Lincoln and Reconstruction

Edward J. Erler

A braham Lincoln and the prime movers of the Republican Party viewed the Civil War as the second battle in the Revolutionary War. The Revolutionary War had vindicated the principle of the Declaration of Independence that the "just powers" of government must be derived "from the consent of the governed." Consent itself was a necessary conclusion from the "self-evident" truth "that all men are created equal." Equality and consent were reciprocal requirements for just government. The Revolution, however, had vindicated the principle of consent for some, but not all. As long as slavery continued to exist—and was protected by the Constitution—the American founding was incomplete; the principles of the Declaration were only partially implemented.

Representative Thaddeus Stevens, Radical Republican of Pennsylvania and a member of the Joint Committee on Reconstruction, addressed this question before the House on May 8, 1866, urging adoption of the Fourteenth Amendment:

I beg gentlemen to consider the magnitude of the task which was imposed upon the [Joint Committee on Reconstruction]. They were expected to suggest a plan for rebuilding a shattered nation—a nation which though not disseverd was yet shaken and riven...through four years of bloody war. It cannot be denied that this terrible struggle sprang from the vicious principles incorporated into the institutions of our country. Our fathers had been compelled to postpone the principles of their great Declaration, and wait for their full establishment till a more propitious time. That time ought to be present now.[1]

Senator Charles Sumner from Massachusetts, another Radical Republican, agreed with Senator Stevens:

Our fathers solemnly announced the Equal Rights of all men, and that Government had no just foundation except in the consent of the governed; and to the support of the Declaration, heralding these self-evident truths, they pledged their lives, their fortunes, and their sacred honor. Looking at the Declaration now, it is chiefly memorable for the promises it then made... And now the moment has come when these vows must be fulfilled to the letter. In securing the Equal Rights of the freedman, and his participation in the Government... we shall perform those early promises of the Fathers, and at the same time the supplementary promises only recently made to the freedman as the condition of alliance and aid against the Rebellion. A failure to perform those promises is moral and political bankruptcy.[2]

Sumner exhibited a profound understanding of the principles of the Declaration. He knew that compromises with slavery were necessary in order to secure approval of a Constitution that supported an energetic national government. The most thoughtful

Federalists understood that without a strong national government, the prospect of ever ending slavery was remote. On various occasions the slave states made veiled threats to bolt the Convention and establish a form of government unknown not only to the "principles of the Revolution," but to any kind of constitutional government properly understood: a "slaveholding republic."

Sumner pointed out that the Declaration posits equality as

> the first of the self-evident truths that are announced, leading and governing all the rest. Life, liberty, and the pursuit of happiness are among inalienable rights; but they are held in subordination to that primal truth. Here is the starting-point of the whole, and the end is like the starting-point. In announcing that Governments derive their just powers from the consent of the governed, the Declaration repeats again the same proclamation of Equal Rights. Thus is Equality the Alpha and the Omega, in which all other rights are embraced.

Sumner then noted that Madison, justly recognized as the principal theoretician of the Constitution, described the Declaration in the *Federalist* as the authoritative source of the Constitution's authority. "Madison," Stevens averred, "evidently inspired by the Declaration of Independence, and determined to keep the Constitution in harmony with it, insisted in well known words, that 'it was wrong to admit in the Constitution the idea of property in man.'" Stevens was quoting a famous remark Madison made during the Constitutional Convention. In *Federalist* 39, Madison noted that "the general form and aspect of the government [must] be strictly republican." "No other form," Madison warned, "would be reconcilable with the fundamental principles of the Revolution." Everyone would have recognized, of course, that those "fundamental principles" were announced in the

Declaration. If, Madison advised, the proposed Constitution is judged by the people, assembled in ratifying conventions for the purpose of accepting or rejecting the work of the Convention, as insufficiently "republican," they must reject it.[3] But Madison knew—even when he made his remarks at the Constitutional Convention—that the Constitution would have to recognize slavery and "property in human beings" in order for the Constitution to be accepted by the Southern states. Sumner, too, recognized that necessity, as did Stevens.[4]

The Declaration of Independence

There is no question that slavery is a clear violation of the central principle of the Declaration of Independence: the "self-evident" truth contained in the "Laws of Nature and of Nature's God" that "all men are created equal." The only question was whether the compromises in the Constitution that allowed the continued existence of slavery were absolutely necessary and just. Were they ultimately in the service of emancipation? Is it ever just to allow the continued existence of evil? Is there such a thing as a "necessary evil" in political affairs? And if so, does prudence or practical wisdom sometimes demand it be tolerated? Slavery presented an intractable problem to the founders and to republican statesmanship.

Statesmen are always presented with a world that they did not create. As such, they must work within the confines of the horizons which confront them. It is true, I say, that every generation has an obligation to improve the political life of future generations as much as it is possible to do so within existing conditions. I believe that America's founding generation did so to a greater extent than any other generation in history. Their efforts to change the political world had a profound impact. Not only were they the first to establish a nation on the basis of universal principles, but they made a supreme effort to put those principles into practice in the murky and ambiguous world of political life. The Declaration itself was a revolution in world-historical consciousness. Divine right of kings was replaced by *vox populi* or consent as the only legitimate basis for rule. Also firmly established in the natural right principles of the Declaration was the fact that the people possess ultimate sovereignty and, therefore, always retain the right—and the duty—to "alter or abolish" government when it is no longer willing or able to protect the "safety and happiness" of the people. The right of revolution, as it was frequently expressed at the time of the Revolution, was the right that guaranteed every other right. The principles of the Declaration revolutionized not only America, but eventually the world.

Republican Statesmanship

Republican regimes must operate within the boundaries of consent. The responsibility of republican statesmen is to shape consent or political opinion so that it will accept or approve what is right and just. The goal of republican statesmanship in a regime based on natural right is therefore to eliminate as much evil and injustice as possible, while it is possible, without destroying the basis in public opinion from which future evil and injustice can be eliminated. At times, republican statesmen must work by indirection, concealing the extent of their ultimate aims which (although just) may shock or repel public opinion. More than sixty years ago Professor Harry Jaffa wrote in his classic work, *Crisis of the House Divided: An Interpretation of the Issues in the Lincoln-Douglas Debates*, that

> Jefferson, in writing the Declaration, may have expressed no more than what he thought all believed. But it is also true that men in 1776 subscribed to propositions which had consequences

of which they were not fully aware and which they may not have accepted if they had been aware of them. That Jefferson intended the Declaration, or the philosophy it expressed, to have far more drastic consequences than were possible in 1776 is hardly open to question. And if the intention of the legislator is the law, then did not the historical meaning of the Declaration comprehend also its historic mission, and was not the mission the attainment as well as the promise of equality?[5]

Consider a simple, if not particularly revealing, example of the recognition of the tie between promise and attainment: Lincoln's opening remarks at the Fourth Debate with Douglas on September 18, 1858. Douglas, of course, had called Lincoln a "black Republican" who desired to bring about the complete equality and amalgamation of the races. "I will say then," declared Lincoln, "that I am not, nor ever have been in favor of bringing about in any way the social and political equality of the white and black races—that I am not nor ever have been in favor of making voters or jurors of negroes."[6] Notably absent from Lincoln's statement was that "he would *never be in favor*." Any thoughtful observer of Lincoln's position, however, knew that his principles—the principles of the Declaration—when implemented to their fullest extent would embrace the whole panoply of rights and privileges for black men and women. Had he said that publicly in Illinois in 1858, his future as a politician would have been over. He concealed the full extent of his principles in order not to shock or destroy the basis in consent from which further progress could be made. The full implementation of those principles would require a second Revolutionary War—a Civil War. For the time being, however, it was still necessary to speak of the sole purpose of the war as the preservation of the Union.

At the time of the founding there was widespread agreement

that the Declaration of Independence supplied the moving principles of American political life. Although the people accepted the natural right principle that "all men are created equal," they were unwilling to consent to the immediate emancipation of slaves. Slavery, of course, was a manifest violation of natural right and what Madison termed "the rights of human nature." It is easy to agree in principle that slavery is unjust and contrary to the laws of nature and natural right. But when racial prejudice and private interests are at stake, principles are easily ignored or postponed—or as we might say today, "re-imagined." It is difficult, if not impossible, for statesmen and founders to translate political theory into political practice, especially in regimes grounded in the consent of the governed. In Plato's *Laws*, the Athenian Stranger gives the laws to a new Cretan regime. Aristotle tells us that Crete is the place Socrates would have gone had he taken the advice of his friends and fled his conviction and sentence of death. Although it was illegal to escape a criminal sentence, it was not uncommon and even expected in cases where death was the penalty. Socrates, of course, refused to break the law. The Athenian Stranger was a philosopher who endeavored to create a city in deed, unlike Socrates in the *Republic*, who created a city in speech. But in order to create a city in deed, a "second best city," the philosopher needs a young and energetic tyrant by his side to translate his speech (i.e., his theories) into practice. Republican statesmen cannot translate republican principles into republican practice tyrannically. They must rely on persuasion to move public opinion in the right direction—in the direction of fulfilling the natural right principles of the Declaration. It cannot be done at one fell stroke. Public opinion is stubborn, slow to move, and sometimes immune to reason. But republicanism has no alternative if it remains true to republican principles.

"I know the better and I do the worse," although strikingly

un-Platonic, is a difficulty that all human beings have experienced. If the framers had abolished slavery all at once at the time of the founding, they would have done so without the consent of the governed. They would have therefore purchased the freedom of the slaves at the expense of enslaving the free by acting without their consent. They would have perpetrated an act of tyranny which, in fact, would not have liberated the slaves but subjected them to tyranny along with the rest of the American people. All would have been forced to live in a regime that was not based on the consent of the governed. Thus we see that politics always deals with a choice between the lesser of two evils—it never (or rarely) deals with a choice for the best, except in "imagined republics."

Politics is always tragic. This has always been known to competent political philosophers. The best that republican statesmanship could do under the circumstances of the American founding was to create the constitutional ground that would eventually lead public opinion and consent to accept the moral commands imposed by the Declaration. Once the principle was accepted that slavery is unjust because it violates natural right, then moral appeals could be made for practice to live up to that principle. "The thought is the father of the deed" are words that Abraham Lincoln might have spoken. Without the thought, the deed will never follow; the thought must always precede the deed. And Lincoln *did, in fact, say* that the "self-evident" truth that "all men are created equal," the thought that is at the center of the Declaration, is the "father of all moral principle" among us.[7]

The Constitution and the Declaration of Independence

The Constitution never uses the terms "slave" or "slavery," preferring to employ circumlocutions (Article I, Section 2, "three fifths of all other persons"; Article I, Section 9, "the migration or importation of such persons"; Article IV, Section 2, "person held to service or labor").[8] As Abraham Lincoln argued, the framers intended to put slavery in "course of ultimate extinction,"[9] and once the thing itself disappeared, there was no need for anything to remain in the Constitution to remind us of its existence. This simply shows that slavery had never been a part of the Constitution's principles (as opposed to its "compromises"). The Constitution treated slavery as in principle wrong—a necessary evil—to be tolerated only as necessary and to be eliminated as soon as politically possible. In his "Address at Cooper Union," February 27, 1860, Abraham Lincoln utterly refuted Chief Justice Taney's dictum in the *Dred Scott* case that Congress had "the power coupled with the duty" to pass a slave code for the territories. Lincoln remarked that it was hardly possible to argue that it was a "plainly written" command of the Constitution or a "plainly written" constitutional right belonging to the slaveholding states when the word "slave" or "slavery" never appeared in the Constitution, nor was the word "property" used in connection with any of the abovementioned "circumlocutions."[10] The chief justice, nevertheless, had held that "the right of property in a slave is *distinctly* and *expressly* affirmed in the Constitution."[11]

The provisions in the Constitution dealing with slavery are compromises, that is, departures from the Constitution's principles that serve the ultimate purpose of supporting or upholding those principles.[12] If we read only the text of the Constitution, we find no grounds to rank its various provisions. There are no superior or inferior parts; every part must be judged to have equal authority. Those provisions protecting slavery thus have the same authority as those protecting freedom. But if we follow Lincoln (and Madison) and say that the Declaration provides the ends for which the Constitution serves as the means, then it is possible to distinguish the principles of the Constitution from its compromises.[13] In this light, the "circumlocutions" dealing with slavery are clearly "compromises" and not principles; they are not essential to the Constitution, but temporary departures from what is essential. But are these compromises necessary and are they just? That is, do they serve in any way the cause of emancipation that is ultimately demanded by the Declaration?

Abraham Lincoln's most penetrating explanation of republican statesmanship as it related to the Declaration and the Constitution appeared in a critique of the *Dred Scott* opinion in his "Speech at Springfield, Illinois," June 26, 1857. This was just a year before Lincoln was nominated to be the Republican candidate to oppose the incumbent, Stephen A. Douglas, for Senate. By June 1857, the contest with Douglas had already reached full stride (it would culminate a year later in the Lincoln-Douglas debates). Lincoln demonstrated with Euclidian precision that Chief Justice Taney's opinion in *Dred Scott* rested on errors of constitutional construction as well as errors of fact. But the most egregious error pointed out in Lincoln's analysis was Taney's argument that blacks of African descent, free or slave, were not included in the language of the Declaration. "Chief Justice Taney, in his opinion in the Dred Scott case," Lincoln recounted,

> admits that the language of the Declaration is broad enough to include the whole human family, but he and Judge Douglas argue that the authors of that instrument did not intend to include negroes, by the fact that they did not at once, actually place them on an equality with the whites. Now this grave argument comes to just nothing at all, by the other fact, that they did not at once *or ever afterwards*, actually place all white people on an equality with one another. And this is the staple argument of both the Chief Justice and the Senator, for doing this obvious violence to

the plain unmistakable language of the Declaration. I think the authors of that notable instrument intended to include *all* men, but they did not intend to declare all men equal *in all respects.* They did not mean to say all were equal in color, size, intellect, moral developments, or social capacity. They defined with tolerable distinctness, in what respects they did consider all men created equal—equal in "certain inalienable rights, among which are life, liberty, and the pursuit of happiness." This they said, and this meant. They did not mean to assert the obvious untruth, that all were then actually enjoying that equality, nor yet, that they were about to confer it immediately upon them. In fact they had no power to confer such a boon. They meant simply to declare the *right*, so that the *enforcement* of it might follow as fast as circumstances should permit. They meant to set up a standard maxim for free society, which should be familiar to all, and revered by all; constantly looked to, constantly labored for, and even though never perfectly attained, constantly approximated, and thereby constantly spreading and deepening its influence, and augmenting the happiness and value of life to all people of all colors everywhere. The assertion that "all men are created equal" was of no practical use in effecting our separation from Great Britain; and it was placed in the Declaration not for that, but for future use. Its authors meant it to be, thank God, it is now proving itself, a stumbling block to those who in after times might seek to turn a free people back into the hateful paths of despotism.[14]

The chief justice argued that while the language of the Declaration was capacious enough "to include the whole human family," the actions of its authors revealed their intentions more clearly than their words. The fact that they did not emancipate the slaves all at once indicates that they did not, in fact, believe that blacks of African descent were included in the phrase "all men are created equal." Had they believed it to be a "self-evident truth," they would have treated it as a categorical imperative and emancipated slaves regardless of the consequences. Since they did not, the inference is inescapable: They didn't believe it. Indeed, these

> men who framed this Declaration...high in their sense of honor, and incapable of asserting principles inconsistent with those on which they were acting...perfectly understood the meaning of the language they used, and how it would be understood by others; and they knew that it would not, in any part of the civilized world, be supposed to embrace the negro race, which, by common consent, had been excluded from civilized government and the family of nations, and doomed to slavery. They spoke and acted according to the then established doctrines and principles and the ordinary language of the day, and no one misunderstood them.[15]

Had these honorable men believed that blacks were created equal without acting to free the slaves immediately, they would have been vulnerable, as Lincoln noted, to the base charge of "hypocrisy." In Taney's mind, this was unthinkable.

Lincoln deftly points out the illogic of Taney's argument: He has also "proven" that the Declaration does not include whites by the mere fact that not all white people were equalized all at once. Thus, according to the faulty logic of the "categorical imperative" employed by Taney, whites could not be considered as having been "created equal" by the framers of the Declaration any more than blacks of African descent. Of course, as Lincoln rightly noted, there was "no such power" to equalize blacks and whites, nor to equalize all whites. The only power possessed by the framers of the Declaration was to create a "standard maxim," a guide for future enforcement of the principle of equality.

Lincoln also pointed out factual errors in Taney's decision, most notably those referred to in Justice Benjamin Curtis's *Dred*

Scott dissent. Justice Curtis successfully rebutted Taney's claim that blacks of African descent were no part of the people who framed and adopted the Constitution when he pointed out that free blacks

> in at least five of the States...had the power to act, and doubtless did act, by their suffrages, upon the question of its adoption. It would be strange, if we were to find in that instrument anything which deprived of their citizenship any part of the people of the United States who were among those by whom it was established.[16]

Curtis also points out that Taney's categorical statement that the framers would have freed the slaves all at once had they believed "all men" included blacks ignores the fact that the framers did not have the power to accomplish such a feat. In short, it ignores the necessary element of statesmanship in the framers' view of republican politics. "My own opinion," Justice Curtis asserts,

> is, that a calm comparison of these assertions of universal abstract truths, and of their own individual opinions and acts would not leave these men under reproach of inconsistency; that the great truths they asserted on that solemn occasion, they were ready and anxious to make effectual, wherever a necessary regard to circumstances, which no statesman can disregard without producing more evil than good, would allow; and that it would not be just to them, nor true in itself, to allege that they intended to say that the Creator of all men had endowed the white race, exclusively, with the great natural rights which the Declaration of Independence asserts.[17]

Lincoln had declared in his critique of the *Dred Scott* decision that "I could no more improve on McLean and Curtis, than [Douglas] could on Taney."[18] McLean had also filed a stinging rebuke of Taney's majority decision which, as much as Curtis's dissent, emphasized the Declaration and founding principles. It is evident that Senator Douglas was unable to improve on Taney's woefully flawed analysis—his impossible contention that the phrase "all men are created equal" meant only that British subjects in America were equal to British subjects born and resident in Great Britain at the time converts Taney's "categorical imperative" into high comedy.[19] But it is clear to any intelligent observer that Lincoln did improve substantially on the dissents of McLean and Curtis.

Although it has not been widely recognized, Chief Justice Taney in his opinion in *Dred Scott* was an early exponent of the "historical consciousness" that later became an important element of progressivism. He argued that the framers of the Declaration were merely expressing the dominant opinions of their day. Even the greatest statesmen are unable to transcend the orthodoxies of their time. Thus, an accurate assessment of their work must take into account the climate of opinion in which they operated. Nothing they did or said was revolutionary or transcended the authoritative opinion of their time. Taney was thus an early adherent of historicism. All thought is relative to the era in which it is produced, even the thought of the most far-sighted thinkers and statesmen. The Declaration was not revolutionary, nor was it a call for revolution, even though its framers might have deluded themselves into thinking it was. The language of the Declaration, when considered in the context of prevailing opinion, shows, Chief Justice Taney asserts, "that neither the class of persons who had been imported as slaves, nor their descendants, whether they had become free or not, were then acknowledged as part of the people, nor intended to be included in the general words used in that memorable instrument."[20]

Taney described what he thought was the regnant opinion of the founding era: For more than a century, he avowed, this class of persons have

been regarded as beings of an inferior order; and altogether unfit
to associate with the white race, either in social or political relations; and so far inferior, that they had no rights which the white
man was bound to respect; and that the negro might justly and
lawfully be reduced to slavery for his benefit.[21]

The enlightened opinion of the civilized world at that day regarded
blacks of African descent as mere articles of property to be "bought
and sold, and treated as an ordinary article of merchandise and
traffic wherever a profit could be made by it."[22] And since these
were not only the most enlightened opinions of that day, but
shared by the most sophisticated and learned people, they were
undoubtedly shared by the framers of the Declaration—who,
regardless of their capacity to speak the language of the timeless
truths of natural right, were merely reflecting the most powerful
orthodoxies of their time. Their belief that the principles of the
Declaration were applicable to all men everywhere and always
was simply a self-willed delusion.

All Men Are Not Created Equal in All Respects

The equality of the Declaration must be understood in terms
of natural right or "the rights of human nature." It is a self-
evident truth that "all men are created equal" because no one is
so superior by nature as to occupy the position of a natural ruler,
having been marked by God or Nature's God to rule. It is also
a "self-evident" truth that "all men are not created equal in all
respects." As Lincoln noted, men are not created "equal in color,
size, intellect, moral developments, or social capacity." They are,
however, created equal in the natural rights to "life, liberty, and
the pursuit of happiness." None of the qualities in which men are
created unequal establishes a claim to rule others by nature. Size
or strength may give one the power to rule, but not the right to

rule by nature. Superior intelligence or wisdom might initially seem to qualify as a natural claim to rule. As Jefferson noted in a famous letter, however, "because Sir Isaac Newton was superior to others in understanding, he was not therefore lord of the person or property of others."[23] Natural inequalities in the capacity for moral or social development, which most certainly exist, are subject to the same criticism.

The most puzzling quality Lincoln mentions is inequality of "color." Color, of course, is an accidental feature of the human persona; it is not part of the essence of human nature. Certainly there cannot be a natural inequality of color, such as exists with respect to size, intelligence, and moral and social capacity. Distinctions of color are arbitrary, having no connection with nature or natural right, and Lincoln's mention of color first in the list seems to emphasize this. Inequality of "color" can exist only by convention, never by nature, as slavery itself exists only by law or convention and never by nature or natural right. From a slightly different point of view, one could say that the inequality between God and man is so great that whatever inequalities exist between human beings would be insignificant (indeed nonexistent) in the eyes of God. One could easily argue that the equality doctrine of the Declaration is one of natural law as well as divine law (the "Laws of Nature and of Nature's God").

It is clear that Taney wholly misunderstood the founders' view of statesmanship. Lincoln argued that the "abstract truth" at the core of the Declaration served no practical purpose in effectuating independence from Great Britain. But, Lincoln contended, it was not put there for that purpose; it was for future use, "to set up a standard maxim for free society," serving as a goal or *telos* as well as a gauge to measure progress toward the fulfillment of that *telos* adumbrated in the Declaration. Without a standard maxim, how could we know where we are, where we are going, or how far we have progressed? What is more, the goal ("aug-menting the happiness and value of life to all people of all colors everywhere") is so lofty as almost certainly to be unattainable. It is a goal that can be approximated, and progress can move ever closer to perfection, even if perfection is never attained. Without a standard maxim, republican government has no direction, no goal, and no manner of measuring progress toward the goal.

Lincoln saw Douglas's appeal to popular sovereignty as an attempt to take the issue of morality out of the slavery ques-tion. Douglas said that local majorities in the territories should decide whether or not to have slavery. If it was in their interest, Douglas said, they should "vote it up." If not, they should "vote it down." It was simply a question of majority rule, a matter of whose interest was served; no moral questions were involved. Douglas frequently called this "the great principle of popular sovereignty" or "the fundamental principle of self-government."[24] But we know that according to the natural right principles of the American founding, majorities are limited to exercising the "just powers" of government. Not every majority that assembles is just; it is authorized to decide only within the boundaries of the "Laws of Nature and of Nature's God."

Jaffa argued that the question that divided Lincoln and Doug-las was the same one that divided Socrates and Thrasymachus in the first book of Plato's *Republic*.[25] Thrasymachus argued that justice was always the "interest of the stronger" and that whatever laws were promulgated by the rulers were therefore just. In oligarchy, the rich are the stronger and the laws made in their interest are just. In democracy, the majority is the strongest, and when it makes laws in its interest, those laws must be pronounced just. "What if the rulers make mistakes," Socrates queries, "and instead of passing laws for their interest they mistakenly pass laws in the interest of the weaker?" Doesn't Thrasymachus's definition presume wisdom in the majority? The argument is too well known to need further elucidation. Douglas clearly argues with Thrasymachus that the interest of the majority should prevail in a democracy—hence the doctrine of popular sovereignty. Lincoln argues that majority rule must be informed by wisdom—the wisdom of the Declaration. Lincoln always viewed the Kansas-Nebraska Act, insofar as it repealed the Missouri Compromise of 1820, as effectively a repeal of the principles of the Declaration. The Missouri Act was a compromise: It gave up some territory for slavery, but banned slavery "forever" in vast tracts of land from which new free states were expected to join the Union. The compromise upheld the principles of the Declaration while it yielded to compromise in order to advance those principles.

Reconstruction and the Separation of Powers

Reconstruction became a contest between the executive and the Congress. This rivalry was exacerbated after Lincoln's death. Lincoln always signaled his willingness to cooperate with Congress, and even though Andrew Johnson evidenced some early signs that he would follow his predecessor's plans for Reconstruction, he quickly disappointed Republicans in Congress. The failure of Reconstruction can be traced to the bitter competition that developed between Republicans, who dominated Congress after 1865, and Johnson, whose states' rights sympathies and general sympathies with the plight of the South became increasingly clear. The wholesale pardoning of rebels and the restoration of their confiscated property was an immediate retreat from congressional Reconstruction. Later, his high-handed vetoes of the second Freedman's Bureau Act in 1866 and his veto of the Civil Rights Act in the same year signaled that the war between presidential Reconstruction and congressional Reconstruction would make Reconstruction as Lincoln had envisioned it impossible.

While the Civil War was in progress, the advantage belonged to the executive for the simple reason that in the scheme of the separation of powers, the authority to wage war is lodged in the president. Military necessity was the justification for the first acts freeing slaves. Slaves who made it to Union lines could be declared "contraband" at the discretion of military commanders, who simply would not return them to their masters when it was demanded. The first Confiscation Act, passed in August 1861, provided that any slaves employed in labor for the military in support of the rebellion could be confiscated, and those claiming their services forfeited any right to their labor. The law did not declare the slaves to be free, only that their labor used to support the rebellion was confiscated. A provision to declare their freedom was rejected by Congress, presumably in consideration of the delicate political situation of the border states.

Militia Act

On July 17, 1862, two important pieces of legislation were passed, both undoubtedly in response to General George McClellan's disastrous failure in the Peninsular Campaign. On July 1, 1862, Lincoln had asked the state governors for 300,000 additional troops. The Militia Act empowered the president to institute a militia draft if this quota was not met. The new act amended the 1795 act to permit the enlistment of blacks of African descent. And according to Section 13 of the act, regarding the slave of a master who has borne arms against the United States who serves in the militia, "he, his mother, wife and children, shall forever thereafter be free, any law, usage, or custom whatsoever to the contrary notwithstanding." Since this law was justified by military necessity, it did not address the case where the master was a loyal slave owner. The call for black soldiers was a great success and not only provided much-needed manpower for military campaigns but paved the way for citizenship for blacks. During an important point in the debate, Senator Jacob Howard of Michigan, who later became instrumental in crafting the language of the citizenship clause of the Fourteenth Amendment, said that any slave who

> takes his musket or any other implement of war and risks his life to defend me, my family, my Government, my property, my liberties, my rights, against any foe, foreign or domestic, it is my duty under God, it is my duty as a man, as a lover of justice, to see to it that he shall be free...If we are to emancipate these slaves according to the policy sketched by the President of the United States, then we all know that justice will be done to every loyal owner whose slave may be employed in defending the Government.[26]

This last statement suggests compensation for loyal slave owners. Howard doesn't mention citizenship, but it surely was on his mind as he gave this impassioned speech. Senator James Harlan, Republican of Iowa, followed Howard with a short but equally impassioned speech. "I do not think an individual, a slave, that may have been armed and mustered into the service of the United States," he stated, "will ever again be fit for slavery. I think that is the history of the whole world on this subject. I do not remember a single example since civilization commenced, when slaves have been mustered into the armed service of a country and again attempted to be returned to slavery." He concluded, "If the slaves of loyal masters are mustered into the service of the United States, we ought to provide for their liberty."[27]

The idea of emancipation as a reward for militia service was controversial enough, and candid admission that citizenship could also be a recompense for service was too dangerous to be openly suggested. But Professor Herman Belz recognizes that it was a logical consequence of militia service—as Senators Howard and Harlan almost certainly did—when he remarks,

Given the American tradition of the citizen-soldier and the fact
that military service was regarded as an obligation and privilege
of citizenship, enlistment in the Union army appeared to be a
way for blacks to establish a claim on U.S. citizenship...Although
military service would not by itself be legally conclusive of citizenship, citizenship was seen as involved in the question of army
enrollment.[28]

Second Confiscation Act

The other significant legislation passed on July 17, 1862, was the
second Confiscation Act, which declared the freedom of the slaves
of all persons committing treason or supporting the rebellion as
well as all slaves within Union lines, escaping to Union lines, or
captured by Union troops whose owners were engaged in insurrection. Both Congress and Lincoln were drawing ever closer
to the inevitable conclusion that military emancipation was the
only way to save the Union after the failure of the border-state
representatives to accept the offer of compensated emancipation proffered in March 1862. According to Professor Belz, the
Confiscation Act of 1862 "was designed to confirm the de facto
emancipation that was taking place with the advance of Union
armies, aimed principally at placing black manpower at the service of the Union."[29]

The president followed the progress of the Confiscation Act in
Congress closely and sent a draft of a veto message to Congress
when it was nearing a final vote. His main concern was that the
Confiscation Act in cases of treason "declares forfeiture, extend-
ing beyond the lives of the guilty parties." As Lincoln pointed
out, the Constitution commands that "no attainder of treason
shall work corruption of blood, or forfeiture, except during the
life of the person attainted." While quickly noting that there was
no formal attainder involved, he nevertheless argued that such

punishment could not be constitutionally supported "in a different form, for the same offence." The president vowed to veto the legislation because, in his opinion, the forfeiture provisions were unconstitutional. He also believed the act was unconstitutional in allowing *in rem* proceeding against abandoned or seized property of traitors and those who aided and abetted rebellion. Due process demands reasonable notice and time to appear.[30] This would mean that slaves emancipated by the Confiscation Act would not become legally free until trials were held after the war. Congress responded to the president's veto points at least enough to satisfy his most pressing objections.

Lincoln, however, was unwilling to move as quickly as Congress wanted. He believed that the confiscation of property, even for military necessity, was constitutionally suspect; with respect to slaves, he always preferred compensated emancipation, with the decision to be made by the states and not the national government. He never wavered in his belief that the national government had no power to interfere with slavery in those states where it already existed. That was his assurance to the slaveholding states in his First Inaugural: "I have no purpose, directly or indirectly, to interfere with the institution of slavery in the States where it exists. I believe I have no lawful right to do so, and I have no inclination to do so."[31] Lincoln did believe, however, that the federal government had the power to keep slavery from entering federal territories, thereby preventing new slave states from ever joining the Union. But as we have already seen, Chief Justice Taney's decision in *Dred Scott* had issued the infamous mandate that Congress had "the power coupled with the duty" to pass a slave code for the territories. In fact, as we have seen Lincoln argue, Congress had neither the power nor the duty to pass such a code, and Taney and the Supreme Court had no constitutional authority to suggest such a duty. A year after *Dred Scott*, Lincoln forcefully argued in his "House Divided" speech that there was no longer any ground for compromise on the issue of slavery; he predicted that the country would become all slave or all free. Taney's analysis—which was a direct attack on the 1856 Republican Party platform—gave the slaveholding states the first constitutional ground, however illusory and tendentious it might have been, for secession, and we can say with certainty that his opinion in *Dred Scott* was the proximate cause of the Civil War.

The Question of Colonization

Section 12 of the Confiscation Act authorized the president to make provisions for the voluntary colonization "in some tropical country beyond the limits of the United States, of such persons of the African race, made free by the provision of the act...with all the rights and privileges of freemen." Although the act freed slaves, it did nothing to protect their rights and liberties during the continuance of the war. As Belz pithily notes:

> Perhaps most significant, in authorizing colonization, albeit voluntary, it failed by implication to secure the right of remaining within the American republic. Only in a foreign country were Republicans—sensitive to the demands of politics and the strength of race prejudice—willing to make a promise of equal rights for emancipated slaves.[32]

Congress subsequently appropriated money to finance colonization and President Lincoln considered it an obligation to consider how plans to do so might be executed. Projects that emerged centered on locations in Central or South America. Colonization had a long history in America, and leading statesmen—Jefferson, Madison, Monroe, Henry Clay, and Lincoln, among others—could advance the cause of emancipation without shocking the prejudices of those who feared amalgamation and large-scale integration with blacks by nominally supporting colonization. Colonization gave these statesmen rhetorical cover to advocate for gradual emancipation of slaves, if not immediate emancipation. Their goal, however, was always to draw public opinion and consent ever closer to the principles enunciated by "the Laws of Nature and of Nature's God." During his earlier campaigns in Illinois in the 1850s, when Lincoln had to contend with deep-seated antipathy toward blacks, he used colonization as rhetorical cover on several occasions to create space for his antislavery arguments. At times, while professing to favor colonization, he nevertheless expressed doubts about its practicality.

Politics and Emancipation

Lincoln was cautious, but determined. He would not violate the Constitution, but he would suppress the rebellion and use every constitutional tool at his disposal. He was well aware that while soldiers would fight—and fight courageously—to preserve the Constitution and the Union, they were reluctant, even unwilling, to fight to emancipate slaves. If the widespread perception developed that the purpose of the Civil War had turned from the preservation of the Union to the emancipation of slaves, there would be a political reaction in some of more volatile Northern states, to say nothing of the reaction that was certain to take place in the border states, all of which would be a severe blow to the war effort. Lincoln was in the delicate situation of having to convince the political world that emancipation of slaves would serve a purely military necessity in preserving the Union.

On July 12, 1862, Lincoln had written an "Appeal to Border State Representatives to Favor Compensated Emancipation." In the appeal, he reminded the border-state representatives that had they "voted for the resolution in the gradual emancipation message of last March, the war would now be substantially ended." On March 6, 1862, Lincoln had recommended that Congress adopt a joint resolution proposing that the United States would cooperate with any state that would "adopt gradual abolishment of slavery, giving to such State pecuniary aid, to be used by such State, in its discretion, to compensate for... such change of system."[33] The resolution that had been passed by Congress, but was not adopted by any state, was now renewed by Lincoln. The appeal was accompanied once again by the promise of voluntary colonization for the emancipated slaves.

Lincoln urged the border-state representatives to accept compensation now because the progress of the war, he said, will render the slaves in the predictable future without any value. It is not reasonable, Lincoln pointed out, to reject the force of this argument. But the passions of all those who were tied to the interests of slavery prevented them from being persuaded by reason, even by the simplest calculations that appealed to their self-interest.[34]

On August 22, 1862, Lincoln wrote a letter to Horace Greeley in response to Greeley's open letter, "The Prayer of Twenty Millions," published in the *New-York Daily Tribune* three days earlier. Greeley had been exceedingly critical of Lincoln's enforcement of the Confiscation Act, arguing that any concessions made to influence the border states only strengthened the treason that divided the nation. He also complained that Lincoln had countermanded General C. Fremont's proclamation in Louisiana emancipating slaves within his command in September 1861 (before the Confiscation Act), as well as General David Hunter's similar decree on May 9, 1862 (also before the Confiscation Act) covering the Sea Islands off the coast of Georgia, Florida, and South Carolina. Lincoln can hardly be accused of not enforcing the provisions of the Confiscation Act before it was passed. Lincoln had used the occasion of his "Proclamation Revoking General Hunter's Order of Military Emancipation" to remark that

> whether at any time, in any case, it shall have become a necessity indispensable to the maintenance of the government to exercise such a supposed power, are questions which, under my responsibility, I reserve to myself, and which I can not feel justified in leaving to the decisions of commanders in the field. These are totally different questions from those of police regulations in armies and camps.[35]

Lincoln did, as Greeley charges, allow General Henry Halleck's controversial General Order No. 3 prohibiting fugitive slaves from being admitted to Union lines within his command (which at the time was the Department of Missouri).[36] Lincoln may have reasoned that it was a question of whether Halleck's command could handle the influx of refugees and thus a matter of "police regulation" best decided by military commanders. Lincoln, however, later came to rue his decision.[37]

The most famous lines from Lincoln's letter to Greeley are surprising to the contemporary mind, although we must bear in mind the fact that at the time he wrote them, he had already written a draft of the Emancipation Proclamation and awaited only a propitious occasion to release it. "My paramount object in this struggle," Lincoln said, "*is* to save the Union, and is *not* either to save or to destroy slavery. If I could save the Union without freeing *any* slave I would do it, and if I could save it by freeing *all* the slaves I would do it; and if I could save it by freeing some and leaving others alone I would also do that." Lincoln knew, as any military strategist did (or almost anyone who looked at a map), that the border states were crucial to the war effort and could not be as casually dismissed as Greeley thought. Lincoln closed with this peroration: "I have here stated my purpose according to my view of *official* duty; I intend no modification of my oft-expressed *personal* wish that all men every where could be free."[38]

The Preliminary Emancipation Proclamation

The preliminary Emancipation Proclamation was issued exactly one month later on September 22, 1862. It contained no moral arguments or exhortations of any kind. One Radical Republican complained that it was written in the "the most dry routine style," and other Radicals concurred with John A. Andrews, governor of Massachusetts, that it was "a mighty act" at the same time that it was a "poor document."[39] Lincoln, of course, intended to produce a "poor document," one that would excite as little controversy as possible on a topic that was highly controversial. Lincoln had spent the decade of the 1850s, including the Cooper Union speech, his only campaign address in the election of 1860, engaged in the task of vindicating the principles of the Declaration of Independence and arguing for the moral evil and injustice of slavery. According to Jaffa, the Great Emancipator exhibited a single-minded purpose from 1854 (when he delivered his Peoria speech) until his inauguration in 1861 that the Missouri Compromise of 1820 must be restored. The Missouri Compromise Act had prohibited slavery "forever" in the remaining unorganized portions of the Louisiana Purchase Territory. The Missouri Compromise was repealed by the Kansas-Nebraska Act of 1854, whose principal architect was Lincoln's arch–political rival, Stephen A. Douglas. As Jaffa cogently remarks: "Every political speech that Lincoln delivered" in the period between the Peoria speech and his inauguration had the restoration of the ban upon slavery as its leading purpose. All of Lincoln's arguments culminated in a plea that slavery not be permitted to *extend* itself into *new* lands, such as those from which it had been prohibited by the Missouri Compromise (and, earlier, by the Northwest Ordinance). Never did Lincoln argue for any political action against slavery in any state. Never did he argue for a construction of the Constitution that might have accomplished such interference indirectly as by denying the competence of the federal government to pass fugitive-slave legislation or by maintaining the competence of the federal government, under the commerce clause, to interfere with the interstate slave trade.[40]

Lincoln certainly knew that if the Missouri Compromise restrictions could be restored, the territories would remain free, and from the free territories, free states would be admitted to the Union. Lincoln's goal was accomplished, at least formally, on June 19, 1862, when federal legislation abolished slavery in all territories then possessed by the United States and all future territories that might be acquired. Regardless of the ultimate outcome of the war, whether slavery survived in some or all parts of the Union, there would be no future slave states admitted from any territories of the United States.

The Emancipation Proclamation declared that "the war will be prosecuted for the object of practically restoring the constitutional relation between the United States, and each of the states, and the people thereof, in which states that relation is, or may be suspended, or disturbed." The president also noted that at the next meeting of Congress he would again recommend the voluntary acceptance of either immediate or gradual compensated emancipation for the slaveholding states and colonization with the consent of the freed slaves. Those recommendations were presented in his annual message to Congress as three constitutional amendments on December 1, 1862. The rest of the Proclamation declaimed that the military would not under any circumstances return fugitive slaves, and announced that the provisions of the Confiscation Act regarding fugitive slaves would be rigorously enforced. At the same time, the Proclamation promised compensation for losses to those who had remained loyal throughout the rebellion, including compensation for the loss of slaves.

Both praise and blame were provoked by the Proclamation. The mercurial Horace Greeley, whom we heard earlier giving the "Prayer of Twenty Millions," now shifted his gaze to the heavens in praise of Lincoln: "God bless you for the great and noble act," he implored. The Proclamation is the "beginning of a new life for the nation [and] one of those stupendous facts in human history which marks not only an era in the progress of the nation, but an epoch in the history of the world."[41] Ralph Waldo Emerson, formerly a critic of Lincoln, writing in the *Atlantic Monthly*, now saw fit to rank the Proclamation alongside the Declaration of Independence as one of the great documents of history.[42] Even abolitionists and Radical Republicans jumped on the bandwagon of praise for Lincoln, rarely qualifying their hyperbole with even a hint of dissent. Criticism was rampant, too, especially from Northern Democrats. Many saw in the language of the Proclamation an invitation to slave insurrection that would lead to the mass slaughter of women and children who were left behind by soldiers serving in the Confederate armies. The military, they pointed out, was charged with recognizing and maintaining the freedom of "all persons held as slaves" in those states where the people were still in rebellion and must "do no act or acts to repress such persons, or any of them, in any efforts they may make for their actual freedom." "Any efforts," it was alleged, could easily encompass servile insurrection and race war if they were intended to effectuate "actual freedom."

Democrats had already decided to make emancipation an issue at the upcoming congressional elections in October. The New York Democratic Party platform denounced the Emancipation Proclamation as nothing less than "a proposal for the butchery of women and children, for scenes of lust and rapine, and of arson and murder." The party's nominee for governor, Horatio Seymour, hysterically declared that if it was necessary to abolish slavery to save the Union, "then the people of the South should be allowed to withdraw themselves from the government which cannot give them the protection guaranteed by its terms." Similar sentiments were expressed by Ohio and Indiana Democrats in reaction to the Proclamation.[43] Democrats wielded the Proclamation as a club to bludgeon the Republicans in the October 1862 elections. In Ohio, Democrats won fourteen House seats to five for Republicans; and in Indiana, Democrats won seven of the eleven contested congressional seats and won a majority in the state legislature. The parties divided the Pennsylvania House seats evenly, but Democrats won a majority of the legislature in New Jersey as well as the governorship of New Jersey and New York. In all likelihood, only the fact that gubernatorial elections were not held in Ohio, Pennsylvania, Illinois, and Indiana prevented Democrats from being elected in those states. Overall, the election returned a net increase of twenty-seven Democratic congressmen to Washington. Democratic political appeals were openly racist, frequently proclaiming that freed slaves would flock to the North, displacing white labor and generally degrading the level of civilized life. Michael Burlingame references the *New-York Daily Tribune*'s report that in the fall 1862 campaign

> Democrats relentlessly employed their customary appeal to "cruel and ungenerous prejudice against color which still remains to disgrace our civilization and to impeach our Christianity." Their

race-baiting was especially virulent in Ohio and Indiana. The Cincinnati *Commercial* justly complained that "the prejudice of race has been inflamed, and used by the Democratic Party with an energy and ingenuity perfectly infernal."[44]

Constitutional Questions

Lincoln was always troubled by doubts about the constitutionality of the "military necessity" justification for the confiscation of property, including slaves. His main concern was that courts would declare unconstitutional the freedom that had been granted to slaves, particularly in the Confiscation Act and the Emancipation Proclamation, and order them to be returned to their owners. We have already pointed out that the clear implication of the Confiscation Act—due to modifications made in response to Lincoln's complaint about its *in rem* proceeding against abandoned property—was that the freedom of slaves would become legal only after trials at the end of the war. His concerns seemed to be confirmed when former Supreme Court Justice Benjamin Curtis, whom we have seen Lincoln praise highly for his dissenting opinion in the *Dred Scott* case, published a pamphlet shortly after the preliminary Emancipation Proclamation was announced arguing that it was unconstitutional because it could not be supported by the president's claim that it was grounded in "military necessity."

First of all, Curtis argued, the preliminary Proclamation was itself not issued to meet a "military necessity," but simply an announcement that there would be an executive action of that character

> three months hence, thirty days after the next meeting of Congress, and within territory not at present subject even to our military

control. Of course such an executive declaration as to his future intentions, must be understood by the people to be liable to be modified by events, as well as subject to such changes of views, respecting the extent of his own powers, as a more mature and possibly a more enlightened consideration may produce.[45]

Thus a proclamation that announces an intention to act in response to military necessity three months in the future is not itself justified by "military necessity," which can only be an immediate, not a remote or future, necessity. The events of war change far too rapidly to predict what measures will be required that far in advance. There is time for deliberation and public discussion, even discussion of "his own constitutional power to decree and execute them."[46] Curtis continued:

The Constitution has made it incumbent on the President to recommend to Congress such measures as he shall deem necessary and expedient. Although Congress will have been in session nearly thirty days before any executive action is proposed to be taken on this subject of emancipation, it can hardly be supposed that this proclamation was intended to be a commendation to them.[47]

Curtis's main objection, however, was to the Proclamation's provision that by executive decree on January 1, 1863, persons held as slaves within designated states or parts of states "shall cease to be lawfully held to service, and may by their own efforts, and with the aid of the military power of the United States, vindicate their lawful right to personal freedom." Curtis alleged that the provision was unconstitutional because it was an attempt to repeal valid state laws which regulate the domestic institutions of the states. Curtis pointed out that the national government is limited to exercising only delegated powers.[48] Lincoln, of course, did not disagree with Curtis on this point. As he clearly stated in his First Inaugural and the Message to Congress in Special Session, July 4, 1861, he had no authority under the Constitution to interfere with slavery in any of the states where it already existed, nor did he intend to do so. By the same token, Lincoln insisted, there could be no constitutional right to secession—the Union was perpetual. Any attempt to destroy the Union would, if necessary, be met with force, which, contrary to the animadversions of President Buchanan in 1859, is a constitutional obligation of the federal government.[49] The slaveholding states could hardly advance the right of revolution as a justification for secession because the right of revolution is a doctrine of natural right which derives from the principle that "all men are created equal." Any justification based on the right of revolution would, at one and the same time, be an irrefutable argument in favor of emancipation. Slavery, as we have repeatedly noted, exists only by convention or force, not by nature or natural right. Slavery is *contra natura*: It violates every principle of human nature because it contradicts the first principle of human nature, the "self-evident truth" that "all men are created equal." This is a truth that the slaveocracy—following its philosophical architect John C. Calhoun—denied, because its whole existence depended on the suppression of that truth.

All the offers of compensated emancipation—whether gradual or immediate—that were extended to the slaveholding states were voluntary. When the states in rebellion refused these offers and chose to remain at war, the Proclamation promised, as we have seen, the recognition and maintenance of the freedom of those slaves who could "by any effort" gain "actual freedom" in those states in rebellion against the United States. Presumably the states in rebellion were technically still in the Union, but they could hardly complain about the interference with their domestic affairs when they were engaged in an effort to destroy the Constitution that guaranteed states' rights. The military necessity to prevent the destruction of the Constitution and ensure the preservation of the Union was the express rationale for the war for the North. If the protection of the freedom of slaves who obtained their freedom or who were captured by Union forces hindered the ability of rebel armies to conduct military operations, then the president's powers as commander in chief were justified in invoking military necessity.

Curtis had similar complaints about the suspension of the writ of habeas corpus that Lincoln issued just two days after the Proclamation. Curtis argued that it had been "generally" and perhaps "universally" admitted "that Congress alone can prohibit the courts from issuing the writ." Thus, Curtis charged Lincoln with another dangerous violation of the separation of powers in prosecuting the war effort.[50] It is true that the restrictions on issuing writs of habeas corpus appear in Article I, Section 9, of the Constitution, the section which generally contains limitations on the powers of Congress: "The Privilege of the Writ of Habeas Corpus shall not be suspended, unless when in Cases of Rebellion or Invasion the public Safety may require it." Does its placement in Article I mean that only Congress has the power to suspend the privilege? In his Message to Congress in Special Session, July 4, 1861, Lincoln anticipated this question. Noting that it had been decided that a state of rebellion did exist and that public safety did require the suspension of the privilege, Lincoln said that "now it is insisted that Congress, and not the Executive, is vested with this power." He continued:

> But the Constitution itself, is silent as to which, or who, is to exercise the power; and as the provision was plainly made for a dangerous emergency, it cannot be believed the framers of the instrument intended, that in every case, the danger should

run its course, until Congress could be called together; the very
assembling of which might be prevented, as was intended in this
case, by the rebellion.[51]

It would be difficult to dispute Lincoln's constitutional construction, especially the point about the presence of an imminent
danger when Congress is not in session or is prevented by the
danger itself from assembling. Surely in those circumstances
the executive (or even the courts) have the power to suspend
the writ. The danger may even be merely anticipated. The rebellion or the threat to public safety does not actually have to be
in motion if the government can act to forestall the emergency.
It is impossible to think that the authors of the clause intended
that the suspension of the writ must wait until the danger was
present and fully developed before it could be invoked. In any
case, Lincoln's suspension of the writ on September 24, 1862, was
ratified by Congress in the Habeas Corpus Act of March 3, 1863,
which allowed the president to continue using the suspension
power until the end of the war.[52] Lincoln never responded to
Curtis, although he certainly took his objections seriously—not
because he believed they were true, but because he thought they
might carry weight in the courts.

Second Annual Message to Congress

In any case, most observers must have been surprised when
they learned of the contents of Lincoln's Second Annual Message, delivered to Congress on December 1, 1862, in which he
fulfilled his promise made in the Proclamation to recommend at
the next meeting of Congress practical measures to implement
compensated emancipation and colonization. But hardly anyone
could have anticipated Lincoln's proposal for three constitutional

amendments to accomplish that purpose. How could amendments to the Constitution be practical under the political circumstances that existed in December 1862? Did Lincoln's optimism outrun his sense of political reality? Did he misjudge political circumstances? Neither of these seems likely. Did Lincoln conceal his real intentions? The Message is certainly complex and the peroration most striking. It deserves greater attention than we will give it here.

The first constitutional amendment proposed by Lincoln specified that every state where slavery then existed that chose to abolish slavery, either immediately or gradually by January 1, 1900, would be compensated by the United States through the issuance of interest-bearing bonds. The second amendment guaranteed that all slaves who enjoyed "actual freedom" from the "chances of war" before the end of the rebellion "shall be forever free" and that loyal slave owners of slaves having gained actual freedom would be compensated. The third proposed amendment would order Congress to appropriate funds to colonize "free colored persons" with their consent outside the United States.[53]

After introducing the amendments, Lincoln indulged a simple observation: "Without slavery the rebellion could never have existed; without slavery it could not continue." Yet, as he had reminded us earlier when he quoted his own First Inaugural address, this simple observation teetered on the precipice of a great moral divide: "One section of our country believes slavery is *right*, and ought to be extended, while the other believes it is *wrong*, and ought not be extended. This is the only substantial dispute." With the Proclamation, the great moral divide had been crossed—slavery was wrong and ought not to be extended. Emancipation and preservation of the Union had become inextricably bound together into one purpose. But could the people become reconciled to that purpose? Could Americans ever become one people, united once again by its ancient faith that "all men are created equal"? Lincoln repeated his geopolitical argument from his First Inaugural that the territory occupied by the United States was suitable for one people only, that a border between North and South would be impracticable. But the question of how Americans might become one people again after the intractable moral divisions caused by the existence of slavery seemed almost impossible to answer. Lincoln had argued throughout the 1850s that Americans became one people because of their dedication to the principles of the Declaration of Independence. The defense of slavery drove the slaveocracy to reject those principles. Would they ever be reconciled to them as the price of becoming once again part of the American people? Reuniting the people must require sacrifices on both sides. There would be compensations for the sacrifices; but could the compensations be equal or even proportional? This would certainly be a requirement of justice.

Justice and Compensations

The extended period allowed for compensated emancipation in Lincoln's proposal would naturally disappoint those still bound to servitude, who would have no guarantee of immediate freedom or even prospects of gaining freedom in their lifetime. But the lack of immediate freedom, Lincoln argued, would be compensated by the knowledge that their posterity would enjoy freedom. By the same token, those who advocated perpetual slavery would be disappointed by the abolishment of slavery by compensated emancipation; but their disappointments would be mollified by the long grace period in which slavery would continue to exist. The sacrifices, of course, are not equal or proportional. On the one hand, delayed freedom for slaves, many who would have no chance of ever being free; on the other hand, the grudging sacrifice of slavery, softened by compensation and a thirty-seven-year grace period: This simply does not balance on the scales of justice. It wouldn't seem to provide much common ground, but would afford many sources for festering resentments on both sides that would in all likelihood extend well beyond thirty-seven years.

Masters and slaves would supposedly benefit by the fact that the status of both classes would not suddenly be disrupted by wholesale emancipation. Slaves would not be left destitute; masters would have time to become accustomed to the loss of their privileged status and the fact that they eventually would have to treat their former slaves as fellow citizens with privileges and immunities equal to their own. Yet surely this could not happen in thirty-seven years or in three generations. And the sacrifices asked on the part of the two classes were still grossly disproportional.

The money to pay for the compensation of slaves was to come from taxes paid in part by the North. But the people of the South, Lincoln argued, were not more responsible for introducing slavery into America than the people of the North. And the people of the North were not hesitant to use the products of slave labor imported from the South, so it is hardly accurate to say that the South had been more responsible for the continuance of slavery than the North. The injustice of slavery must be shared in common by the nation as a whole. Compensated emancipation was therefore a common object of the nation and all sections should share the common charge associated with it. Making this a common cause might help unify the nation, although this seemed to be a rather thin reed in such tumultuous times and could become yet another source of resentment.

Lincoln Questions Colonization

A curious part of Lincoln's Message involves the third proposed amendment on colonization. Lincoln says that he "cannot make it better known than it already is that I strongly favor colonization." He then proceeds to give a powerful argument *against* colonization, saying that "there is an objection urged against free colored persons remaining in the country, which is largely imaginary, if not sometimes malicious." The argument that Lincoln wants to rebut is one, as we have seen, that was widely circulated by Democrats in their successful campaigns in Ohio and Indiana in the fall 1862 elections. Free blacks, it was said, would emigrate North and displace white workers because they were willing to work for cheaper wages. Lincoln responds to this popular argument by remarking that

> in times like the present, men should utter nothing for which they would not willingly be responsible through time and in eternity. Is it true, then, that colored people can displace any more white labor, by being free, than by remaining slaves? If they stay in their old places, they jostle no white laborers; if they leave their old places, they leave them open to white laborers. Logically, there is neither more nor less of it. Emancipation, even without deportation, would probably enhance the wages of white labor, and, very surely, would still have to be performed; the freed people would surely not do more than their old proportion of it, and very probably, for a time, would do less, leaving an increased part to white laborers, enhancing the wages of it.

Colonization, Lincoln continues, would reduce the supply of labor and increase the demand and wages for white labor.

Lincoln then queries whether free slaves will swarm forth and cover the entire land. Are they not already in the land? he answers. Liberation will not make them more numerous. Will free blacks flee North when there is no longer anything to flee from? Free labor will replace slavery, and the interests of former slaves and former masters will be engaged. The entire plan offered in the

Message, Lincoln notes, is economic. It will secure peace more speedily and maintain it more permanently than force alone, and it will be less expensive. Most importantly it will cost no blood! It cannot be doubted that the plan proposed would shorten the war. But Lincoln was aware that the difficulties of passing the plan were almost insurmountable: two-thirds of both houses of Congress; three-fourths of the states to ratify (including seven slave states). Nevertheless, Lincoln proclaims, "the dogmas of the quiet past, are inadequate to the stormy present. The occasion is piled high with difficulty, and we must rise with the occasion. As our case is new, so we must think anew, and act anew. We must disenthrall our selves, and then we shall save our country." These sentences could well have served as the peroration of the Message, but Lincoln added another one which for its beauty and pathos rivals anything that Lincoln wrote.

Second Peroration

In thirteen terse sentences, Lincoln warns his "Fellow-citizens" that "*we* cannot escape history." As we learn in short order, it is beyond question that Lincoln includes slaves in the address "Fellow-citizens." After all, what does he mean by writing in the tenth sentence that "In *giving* freedom to the *slave*, we *assure* freedom to the *free*" except that the fate of the two races is bound together in the fate of America itself? This common destiny requires a common citizenship. The Civil War—"the fiery trial through which we pass"—has put "this Congress" and "this administration" on the world-historical stage which "will light us down, in honor or dishonor, to the latest generation." The central sentence intones, "We know how to save the Union," followed by "the world knows we do know how to save it." It is tyrannical to enslave human beings and hold them as articles of property; those who hold such property engage in the unbridled use of force that is driven by unrestrained passion. Any nation that tolerates slavery as a permanent feature itself becomes less free by its willingness to tolerate the degradation of the rights of human nature in fellow human beings. If it is argued that slave owners have an interest in protecting property rights, then interest becomes the standard and measure of rights. But as we have already seen Lincoln argue against Douglas's popular sovereignty doctrine, it will always be in someone's interest to profit from the suppression of the rights of others. Today, it might be blacks of African descent; tomorrow it will be any number of religious minorities or other racial and ethnic minorities who cannot vindicate their rights by majority vote. This is how a nation becomes less free by tolerating slavery. It is impossible to tolerate slavery without preparing the ground for one's own slavery. Majority rule gives the illusion of freedom, but as Lincoln was able to demonstrate over and over again, the idea that interest—not nature and natural right—was the only ground of rights meant that everyone's rights, majority as well as the minority, were in danger.

We know how to save the Union. Free the slaves and make them citizens. This will preserve the freedom of all Americans. "We shall nobly save, or meanly lose, the last best, hope of earth... The way is plain, peaceful, generous, just—a way which, if followed, the world will forever applaud, and God must forever bless."

The Southern slaveholders ignored Lincoln's appeal to reason at the time of his First Inaugural; it was hardly to be expected that they would listen to him twenty-one months later when passions had elevated to an even greater pitch. Indeed, they did not.

Final Emancipation Proclamation

On January 1, 1863, the final Emancipation Proclamation was

issued, designating the states and the parts of states where the people were still in rebellion. Within those areas, the Proclamation declares slaves shall be free and the executive department of the government, including the military forces, will recognize and maintain their freedom. The president declared the Proclamation to be "an act of justice, warranted by the Constitution, upon military necessity." He thereupon invoked "the considerate judgment of mankind, and the gracious favor of Almighty God." Lincoln is reported to have said that the final Proclamation had "knocked the bottom out of slavery," although he didn't expect sudden results.[54] Thus ends 1862, the most active legislative year concerning the nation's posture toward slavery and emancipation. Lincoln, of course, knew despite his heroic public persona, there would be grave problems for reunifying the nation, particularly in regards to emancipated slaves.

Third Annual Message to Congress: Proclamation of Amnesty

Lincoln appended a "Proclamation of Amnesty and Reconstruction" to his Third Annual Message to Congress delivered on December 8, 1863. It allowed for the restoration of rebellious states when a number of voters equal to 10 percent of those who voted in the election of 1860 took a loyalty oath to the Union and pledged their willingness to accept emancipation. Several classes of rebels were excluded from amnesty: military and government leaders, those who had resigned commissions in the U.S. military or federal legislative and judicial posts to join the rebellion, and those who had mistreated captured black soldiers or their white officers. Those who were willing to take the loyalty oath would have their rights restored. This loyal 10 percent could then hold a constitutional convention to write a new constitution which abolished slavery and established a state government that was republican in form. This government would be recognized by the president, although "whether members sent to Congress from any State shall be admitted to seats, constitutionally rests exclusively with the Houses, and not to any extent with the Executive." The states must recognize the permanent freedom of the emancipated slaves and "provide for their education, and which may yet be consistent, as a temporary arrangement, with their present condition as a laboring, landless, and homeless class." Thus, the freedmen would not realize any substantial change in their immediate daily lives. They would continue as a laboring, landless, and homeless class. Lincoln stressed that this was a temporary condition, perhaps calculating this might induce more rebels to surrender.[55]

First Freedmen's Bureau Act 1865

The plight of the freedmen remained a constant concern of Lincoln and leading Republicans. However, it wasn't until March 3, 1865, that a bitterly divided Congress passed the first Freedmen's Bureau Act and the president signed it on the same day—the last major legislation Lincoln would sign. The purpose of the act was to provide relief for freedmen and refugees. It was to operate for the duration of the war and for one additional year, providing food, shelter, clothing, medical services, and land to displaced white loyalist refugees and newly freed slaves. The act also provided for the establishment of schools, supervision of contracts between freedmen and employers, and management of abandoned or confiscated land. Early in the congressional debate, the assumption was that the relief would apply exclusively to freedmen to assist them in making the transition from slavery to freedom. The greatest fear, warned Representative Thomas Eliot,

Republican of New York, was that there would be a revival of slavery with its "odious features" but "without its name."[56] The objection arose from several quarters that this would discriminate against white refugees who were equally in need of relief. Senator Sumner called this a "strange complaint" but agreed to include white refugees as the price for passing the act.[57] Senator John Henderson of Missouri responded:

> I do not wish now to draw any comparison showing the distinctions that are made here between freedmen and the white refugees from the southern States. There are today in my State thousands of individuals from the State of Arkansas, and from the southwest part of Missouri who are refugees from their homes in consequence of the fact that they were Union men. These are just as poor as the freedmen.[58]

Others argued that government largess handed out to freedmen and refugees would create dependent classes that would have no incentives to become free from the massive government bureaucracy that would be created to minister to these newly created classes. Representative William Kelley, Republican of Pennsylvania, was certain that the "future welfare of the freedmen demands . . . they must not be permitted to contract habits of idleness, indolence, and vagrancy. The welfare of the people of the North demands it. They need the commodities yielded by this territory."[59] The fact that the Bureau would extend only one year beyond the end of the war was of little assurance to those suspicious of what came to be known in later ages as "big government" and "welfare dependency." Others argued that simple justice and compassion demanded action to relieve the suffering of both freedmen and refugees and that any unanticipated consequences could be dealt with after the immediate emergency was met.

Second Freedmen's Bureau Act 1866

The Freedmen's Bureau Act was renewed on July 16, 1866, after another protracted battle. Congress was able to forge enough agreement to overcome President Andrew Johnson's veto. The Bureau Act was debated at the same time as the Civil Rights Act of 1866, also vetoed by Johnson, but passed by a supermajority in Congress on April 9, 1866, in what was becoming a struggle for the soul of America. Both bills were passed on the authority of the Thirteenth Amendment, which had been ratified on December 18, 1865. Section 2 gave Congress "the power to enforce this article [the Thirteenth Amendment] by appropriate legislation." Both the Civil Rights Act and the Bureau Act were objected to vigorously by Democrats on constitutional grounds. The passage of the Fourteenth Amendment certainly dispelled any constitutional objections retroactively. In any case, some intelligent constitutional commentators have argued that it is a mistake to concentrate on the Civil Rights Act because

> the Republicans who framed the Second Freedmen's Bureau Bill understood that judicial action could not eradicate slavery...Legislation was necessary to provide former slaves with various goods and services, the precise provision of which depends on local circumstances and changing conditions. Given the need for a high degree of nimbleness in the managing of the transition, Congress, rather than the judiciary, had to play the lead role in removing all badges and incidents of slavery in American constitutional life.

The author of this analysis argues that Republicans who passed the Bureau Act "interpreted congressional power under Section Two of the Thirteen Amendment in light of what they believed to be a fundamental constitutional commitment to a national government strong enough to provide for the general welfare."[60]

Thus, according to this constitutional commentator, the Bureau Act was designed principally to protect the welfare of freedmen. Welfare—the elimination of the badges and incidents of slavery—rather than the security of rights and liberty, the principal purpose of the Civil Rights Act of 1866, was the best way to integrate freedmen into postwar social and political life.

Representative James A. Garfield of Ohio, debating the second Bureau Act, said that

> in the solemn words of the great proclamation of emancipation, we not only declared the slaves forever free, but we pledged the faith of the nation "to maintain their freedom"—mark the words, "*to maintain their freedom*" ... [Liberty] is the realization of those imperishable truths of the Declaration "that all men are created equal," that the sanction of all just government is "the consent of the governed."

The peroration to his speech was rousing: "The spirit of slavery is still among us; it must be utterly destroyed before we shall be safe."[61]

The most commonly repeated refrain during the debates was that the purpose of the Bureau was to prepare the transition from slavery to freedom. The most commonly voiced complaint from Democrats was that the Bureau would create a permanent welfare bureaucracy. It is difficult to believe that the main intention of the framers of the second Freedmen's Act was welfare as opposed to the protection of rights and liberties. An original intent understanding of the congressional debate compels the conclusion that protecting individual rights and liberties was the central purpose of the Freedmen's Act. But once the administrative state transformed the purpose of government from the protection of liberty to the security of the welfare of the community, it was incumbent upon constitutional scholars to reject original intent jurisprudence and transform it into a jurisprudence that was more ideologically compliant. The congressional debate had to be reinterpreted to emphasize the welfare implications of its drafters rather than its rights-securing purposes. The general welfare clause was never invoked as a constitutional ground for passing the act as our commentator suggests. Rather, the Thirteenth Amendment in conjunction with the Civil Rights Act of 1866 proved authoritative; both of these focused on securing natural rights. The Freedmen's Bureau wasn't about easing the transition from slavery to freedom after all, we are told by the modern-day revisionist defenders of the welfare state; it was about welfare. And as we now understand, progressive thought requires the subordination of the rights of individuals to the welfare of the community.[62]

Civil Rights Act of 1866

The citizenship of freedmen was finally recognized in the Civil Rights Act of 1866, passed just months before the Bureau Act. What was implied in the Militia Act of 1862 as a matter of natural right and justice was brought to fruition in the Civil Rights Act that extended the same rights to blacks as are held by white citizens: rights to own property; to make and enforce contracts; to sue; to give evidence; to inherit, purchase, lease, sell, hold, and convey real and personal property; and to enjoy the full and equal benefit of all laws and proceedings for the security of person and property. Senator Lyman Trumbull, principal author of the Civil Rights Act, said it was based on Congress's power to act under the Thirteenth Amendment, which in turn, he said, was an expression of the principles of the Declaration of Independence:

> Of what avail was the immortal declaration "that all men are created equal; that they are endowed by their Creator with certain inalienable rights; that among these are life, liberty and the pursuit of happiness," and "that to secure these rights Governments are instituted among men," to the millions of the African race in this country who were ground down and degraded and subjected to a slavery more intolerable and cruel than the world ever before knew?[63]

The basic premise of the Civil Rights Act was clear from its plain language: Blacks have the same rights and protections as whites. Equal protection of the laws and the rule of law will not tolerate racial class distinctions. The grant of U.S. citizenship carried with it automatic citizenship in the states where the newly enfranchised citizens resided. This would be made explicit later in the Fourteenth Amendment, but it was assumed in the Civil Rights Act, otherwise the states could prevent federal protection of civil rights and immunities of state citizenship by withholding state citizenship. I believe there can be little doubt that the framers of the Civil Rights Act and the Fourteenth Amendment intended the federal government to have the power to enforce the rights, privileges, and immunities that attached to both U.S. citizenship *and* state citizenship. As mentioned, the bill was vetoed by President Johnson on March 27, 1866. In his message to the Senate, the president said that his primary objection was that the bill's protection of the rights of federal citizens intruded on the police powers of the states in "matters exclusively affecting the people of each State," including the expediency of discriminating "between the two races."[64] In an impressive display of unity, Congress passed the Civil Rights Act over the president's veto and it became law on April 9, 1866.

Origins of the Fourteenth Amendment

Many members of Congress, however, had second thoughts about whether the Thirteenth Amendment provided adequate constitutional grounds for such sweeping legislation and whether a simple legislative act could overturn the *Dred Scott* decision. In addition, there was the stark realization that future Congresses could repeal the act by simple majorities. These considerations provided the impetus for the Fourteenth Amendment. The protections embodied in the Fourteenth Amendment centered on the privileges and immunities of federal citizenship. Representative John Bingham is justly considered the author of the first section of the amendment, with the exception of the citizenship clause,[65] and he argued throughout that the privileges or immunities clause was the essential feature. In his final remarks in the Fourteenth Amendment debate, Bingham said that "hitherto" the Constitution had a glaring defect "which the proposed amendment will supply." Congress has never had the power "by express authority of the Constitution... to protect by national law the privileges and immunities of all citizens of the Republic and the inborn rights of every person within its jurisdiction wherever the same shall be abridged or denied by the unconstitutional acts of any State."[66] Bingham understood privileges or immunities comprehensively, including "natural rights," the "rights of human nature," "fundamental rights," and constitutional rights, including the provisions of the Bill of Rights. As a matter of constitutional jurisprudence, the privileges or immunities clause of the Fourteenth Amendment was effectively rendered null and void by the Supreme Court in the *Slaughterhouse Cases* (1873), the first decision to consider any provision of the amendment. After the privileges or immunities clause fell into desuetude as a result of the *Slaughterhouse* decision, courts turned to the due process and equal protection clauses as a substitute for privileges or immunities. Those two clauses, however, were never intended to carry the weight or the substance of privileges or immunities.[67] The result has been a constitutional impasse that still remains to be sorted out on a satisfactory basis. The prospect of reviving the original purposes of privileges or immunities seems remote despite Justice Clarence Thomas's best efforts.

In December 1865, Schuyler Colfax was elected speaker of the House of Representatives for the thirty-ninth Congress. A few weeks before the first session began, Colfax remarked in a speech delivered in Washington, D.C., that terms for restoration must be accepted by the rebellious states. In addition to repudiating the various ordinances of secession and ratifying the Thirteenth Amendment—"extinguishing slavery, that the cause of dissension and rebellion might be utterly extirpated"—the states formerly in rebellion must agree to

> other terms upon which I think there is no division among the loyal men of the Union, to wit: That the Declaration of Independence be recognized as the law of the land, and every man, alien and native, white and black, protected in the inalienable and God-given rights of life, liberty, and the pursuit of happiness.[68]

And in his acceptance speech upon election as speaker, Colfax said it was the responsibility of Congress to "afford what our Magna Charta, the Declaration of Independence proclaims is the chief object of government, protection to all men in their inalienable rights."[69] This was, I believe, Colfax's attempt to set the terms for the coming debate in the House. The Republican Party can be fairly said to have taken this suggestion as their architectonic guide for Reconstruction. After Congress passed the Fourteenth Amendment in June 1866, Colfax gave a speech that revealed a profound understanding of the meaning of the amendment. Praising "Abraham Lincoln, that great and good man—would to God he were to-day in the Presidential chair," Colfax lamented, "But while he is gone, and although God buries his workman, his work still goes on, and we are to finish the work that Abraham Lincoln began." Colfax quoted Section 1 of the Fourteenth Amendment and remarked:

> I stand by every word and letter of it. It is because it is the Declaration of Independence placed immutably and forever in our Constitution. What does the Declaration of Independence say?— that baptismal vow that our fathers took upon their lips when this Republic of ours was born into the family of nations. It says that all men are created equal, and are endowed by their Creator with certain inalienable rights, among which are life, liberty and the pursuit of happiness; *and that to secure these rights governments were instituted among men.* That's the paramount object of government, to secure the right of all men to their equality before the law. So said our fathers at the beginning of the Revolution. So say their sons to-day, in this Constitutional Amendment, the noblest clause that will be in our Constitution.[70]

This was indeed Lincoln's vision, as it was the ultimate vision of the founders. Colfax recognized the Fourteenth Amendment—as Lincoln most certainly would have—as the formal completion of the founding. The translation of principle into practice would require continued republican statesmanship. But there was no longer any constitutional barrier to the vindication of individual rights in the states. Now that "equal protection of equal rights" was enshrined in the Constitution as the basis for the rule of law, the privileges and immunities of U.S. citizenship must meet "equal protection" and "due process" standards. Senator Jacob

Howard, Republican of Michigan, who became floor manager
in the Senate for the Fourteenth Amendment when the chairman of the Joint Committee on Reconstruction, Senator William
Fessenden, was unable to preside because of illness, gave the
most complete explication of Section 1 before the addition of the
citizenship clause. Senator Howard conveyed the Joint Committee's expansive understanding of what constituted the privileges
and immunities of U.S. citizens. They included, not only those
implicated in Article IV, Section 2, of the Constitution, but the
provisions of the Bill of Rights as well. Thus, the provisions of
the Bill of Rights were understood by the Joint Committee to be
included as an essential part of the "privileges or immunities"
clause and not, as in later years, a piecemeal accretion added or
"incorporated" by Supreme Court decision to the Constitution
through the "due process" clause. Section 5 for the first time
gave Congress the constitutional power to enforce privileges
and immunities against state interference. States' rights could no
longer be used to argue the autonomy of states to regulate their
own domestic institutions.

Senator Howard continued by expressing the Joint Committee's view that the equal protection and due process clauses

> disable a State from depriving not merely a citizen of the United
> States, but any person, whoever he may be, of life, liberty without
> due process of law, or from denying to him the equal protection
> of the laws of the State. This abolishes all class legislation in the
> States and does away with the injustice of subjecting one caste of
> persons to a code not applicable to another. It prohibits the hang-
> ing of a black man for a crime for which the white man is not to
> be hanged. It protects the black man in his fundamental rights
> as a citizen with the same shield which it throws over the white
> man ... Ought not the time to be now passed when one measure of

justice is to be meted out to a member of one caste while another and a different measure is meted out to the member of another caste, both castes being alike citizens of the United States, both bound to obey the same laws, to sustain the burdens of the same Government, and both equally responsible to justice and to God for the deeds done in the body?[71]

Equal protection of the laws means that the law cannot be based on racial or class divisions. Rights belong to individuals, for men are created equal, and nature does not create caste or class distinctions. Once it is understood that individuals possess rights—not classes and especially not racial classes—then the rule of law can become the rule of reason because the arbitrary factor of race will be excluded. When those who are created equal are treated unequally, then natural right is violated and injustice will undermine the rule of law. There is indisputable proof that the framers of the Fourteenth Amendment sought to ground the Constitution in the natural right principles of the founding and the rule of law that flows from those principles.

Afterword: An Incomplete Attempt at "Giving Accounts"

I have spent my entire academic career defending the principles of natural right and natural law as they relate to the American founding and the American Constitution. I was always guided by Abraham Lincoln, who saw the importance of understanding the Constitution in light of the principles of the Declaration of Independence. In this I almost always followed the work of Harry Jaffa, most particularly his *magnum opus, A New Birth of Freedom* (2000). I recognized some years ago that the Fourteenth Amendment was an explicit attempt on the part of its framers to complete the regime of the founding by making the Constitution conform to the principles of the Declaration of Independence. The Civil Rights Act of 1964 was, I believed, a perfect legislative expression of this idea—the idea that Senator Howard had expressed on behalf of the Joint Committee on Reconstruction in 1866 that was quoted *in extenso* immediately above. The command of the Civil Rights Act of 1964 as originally written was that rights belong to individuals rather than racial classes and that race cannot be a factor in hiring, firing, or advancement in employment, and that public accommodations must be free from racial discrimination. Almost immediately upon its adoption, however, the courts and administrative agencies transformed the act from one that prohibited discrimination on the basis of race into one that *required* discrimination on the basis of race. This was called "affirmative action," which its proponents assured a skeptical world was only a temporary measure to be employed in the service of genuine equality of opportunity. One generation, it was said, would suffice to overcome the lingering effects of past discrimination; then the "playing field" would be level and the temporary discrimination, the euphemistic "goals and timetables," would no longer be necessary. It should have been easy to predict that once racial class entitlements became a part of the law by administrative and judicial fiat, it would be extremely difficult to end them. Today what was originally called "affirmative action" and justified as "racial class remedies" for historic racial class injuries is now called "equity." "Equity" no longer requires justification; it doesn't need one because it is an open revelation of what affirmative action has always been—a racial class entitlement.

When the Civil Rights Act of 1964 was passed, almost everyone seemed optimistic that the final vestiges of race consciousness had been removed from the laws of the nation. It seemed to be the culmination of a long campaign to banish race, color, and ethnicity from the law. Its purpose was noble and its reach was extensive. The focus was on the rights of individuals; its promise was the equal protection of equal rights. It seemed that the dream of a color-blind Constitution had at long last been recognized, if perhaps not fully realized. The Civil Rights Act, along with the Voting Rights Act passed the next year, had finally put the destructive genie of race securely in its bottle; there were now legal remedies available for racial injustices. But as soon as that old racial genie had been secured, new prophets arose and said: "We can teach that old genie new tricks. We can teach him to give up his evil ways and be a force for good. We will turn him loose to do the work of racial reparations and racial equity." Others with longer memories and further vision warned: "Don't do it! That evil genie is incapable of learning new ways; history has proven that he will always be a force for evil. He is a trickster: He will promise good things, he will promise equality, but he will never be satisfied with equality under the law. He always seeks superiority; he wants to rule; he wants to dominate; he will destroy. Have we not learned our lesson? Don't let him loose again. You will regret it. That evil genius is willing to work every deception on those of good will, and in the name of equality he will destroy equal protection of the laws and racial equality." Are not these words of warning proving to be correct?[72]

Narrative and Rational Discourse

"Identity politics" has replaced the regime of individual rights that inspired the framers of the Fourteenth Amendment and the Civil Rights Act. Individuals look to their racial, ethnic, sex, sexual orientation, transgender, or a myriad of other groups to assert their public identity and legal status. Each identity group creates its own "narrative" to justify its own separate status and grievances against society and government. Narrative has replaced reason in public discourse, and narrative does not require the same attention to fact and historical truth that reason does. Sometimes we hear that reason itself is "white supremacy" or "colonialism," a way of expanding Eurocentric control. Thus, narratives can pick and choose what facts and what "truths" are convenient. Narrative "truth" is not truth in any real sense; it is more akin to ideology, an attempt at justification that uses selective historical facts and skewed logic to reach a predetermined conclusion. The claim that Abraham Lincoln was a "racist" is an outrage to any reasoning person. But the hysteria that drives narratives leads some to say, "Because Lincoln was white, he must have been a racist." This is an assertion without logic. Perhaps the whole idea of the American founding that a regime could be based on "universal principle" and could therefore govern itself by "deliberation and choice" put too much demand on the human capacity for reason. Perhaps human nature was incapable of living up to such high standards.

When I say "All lives matter," I am called a racist! But when I ask my Black Lives Matter friends, "Why it is racist to say such a thing?" the answer is always, "Because it is racist to say so." When I respond, "Since black lives are included in all lives, along with every imaginable race or ethnicity, how can it be racist?" the reply is the same: "That is racist, too." "But," I continue to ask, "the statement 'all lives matter' is a colorblind statement; how can it be racist?" Here I hit on the nub of the problem. "Black lives matter" is itself an assertion of privilege, a statement of racial superiority. "All lives matter" suggests subordination of "black lives" in "all lives." Although it is a logically correct proposition that black lives are included in "all lives," it doesn't give black lives preeminence. Now we can understand why Western logic is "racist." It doesn't credit a simple assertion of racial superiority.

Were equality and equal protection all along a utopian dream? Do people prefer privilege to equality; do they desire to rule? Did the evil genie understand something that I didn't—or something I thought could be overcome? Perhaps equality itself inspires both the desire to rule and the desire for privilege. If everyone is equal, then everyone is equally a ruler and has an equal right to rule. Why should the egalitarian impulse to rule be suppressed by a social compact that imposes obligations enforceable by government even if it is based on reason and consent? The narrative of Western civilization is met by this narrative: "Hey Hey, Ho Ho, Western Civ has got to go!" This may have been something taught by our "trickster" friend. How did our trickster know that it would be so appealing? Because it had a tricky rhyme? As a chant it has a tribal charm? Was it a sufficient negation of Western reason? Our trickster has shown vastly greater sophistication and seriousness with his "black lives matter" appeal; he has seen how easily his charm and guile work. Our trickster may soon prophesize new gods, and if so, we know these new gods will demand great sacrifices; he may even have heard of Heidegger!

It was the dedication to a universal principle that "all men are created equal" that became the foundation of America. It has been bandied about and widely accepted at the highest levels of government and education that this is simply an expression of "white supremacy." Its negation (or cancellation) will require some form of nonuniversal thinking—if that is possible. More likely its negation or cancellation will rest on simple assertion or some test of ideological purity that resembles tribal belief more than it does reasoned discourse, which it has rejected in advance. It won't be that easy to destroy Western reason. It can't be done by reason or logic (or even ideology)—it has to be done by force or assertion. I won't give up because I know for certain that tribalism is the worst of all possible forms of social organization, for within it, justice is left out of public discourse (since justice requires reasoned discourse). The founders and Lincoln were not racist, and Western reason (or reason *simpliciter*) is not racist. Our future is still with the founders and Lincoln—and the Fourteenth Amendment, if properly understood.

3

THE LAST GENERATION OF RADICAL REPUBLICANS

Race and the Legacy of Reconstruction in the American South, 1877–1915

Robert D. Bland

On February 26, 1900, South Carolina's senior Democratic Senator Benjamin Tillman stood before the upper chamber of Congress and offered a stunning assessment of the violent overthrow of Reconstruction. "We have done our level best. We have scratched our heads to find out how we could eliminate every last one of them [black voters]," Tillman exclaimed. "We took the government away," he went further. "We stuffed ballot boxes. We shot them. We are not ashamed of it."[1] Referencing his own role in the violent events in South Carolina's Upcountry during the summer and fall of 1876, Tillman's unvarnished account of the role that he and his political party played in the violent "redemption" of South Carolina's government was met with little fanfare in the mainstream press of the time. Politicians on both sides of the aisle had come to the agreement that while the campaign of terror wielded by South Carolina's paramilitary groups was excessive, Reconstruction, as a political project by then popularly understood to have been led by corrupt white Northerners and ignorant freedpeople, was best left to the dustbin of history.

While the bulk of the fin de siècle Republican Party found Tillman unseemly but essentially correct in his assessment of Reconstruction's illegitimacy, some in the party sought to reclaim the legacy of Reconstruction. In a January 1902 interview with the *Boston Herald*, former slave, Civil War hero, and late-nineteenth-century congressman Robert Smalls challenged the negative account of his state's Republican Party. "South Carolina had the most brilliant galaxy of colored leaders of any state in the South," Smalls argued, "and the negro never had such opportunities to prove his ability to exercise high official authority and to vindicate his race."[2] That same year, at a Grand Army of the Republic meeting in Washington, D.C., Smalls turned the "'pow wow' of earnest and thoughtful men" into a moment where the black veterans "learned from one another the race's way out of the exasperating plight" that was their current valley moment in the arc of African American history.[3] Far from accepting the growing consensus around the failure of Reconstruction, Smalls, a man now in his late sixties, continued to operate as if the hopeful message of the party of Lincoln and Grant could find a receptive audience.[4]

While black Americans navigated the perils of the shifting American political landscape under their feet during the last decades of the nineteenth century, many, like Robert Smalls, argued that the Republican Party's recent defeats were a temporary setback in a larger struggle. Having fought during the 1880s to both preserve bastions of political power at the local level and defend the Republican Party's accomplishments in the black press, Republican leaders in the South entered the final decade of the nineteenth century with a sense of optimism. Hoping to pass a new federal elections bill, and confronted by a series of Southern state legislatures that were calling constitutional conventions to disfranchise black voters, Southern Republicans continued to confront the Democratic Party's antiblack policies. That these

Southern Republicans lost these battles and entered the twentieth century facing a world shaped by widespread disfranchisement hides an important fact: Black Republican leaders and voters continued to organize within the GOP and believed that their participation in the party of Reconstruction could make a meaningful difference in their lives.

Historians have long understood the late-nineteenth-century era as a low tide moment of formal political activity in black America. Historians have argued that black Americans, confronted with disfranchisement and a national Republican Party no longer committed to using the federal government to protect the Fifteenth Amendment, retreated from party politics and placed their attention on institution and community building. By the turn of the century, the number of black voters in South Carolina had dwindled, dropping from 91,870 in 1876 to 13,740 in 1888.[5] While some attention has been paid to the late career of Frederick Douglass as a Republican Party operative, the political story of late nineteenth century is largely framed around betrayal and abandonment.

And yet, even in the midst of this harrowing political moment, black leaders and black communities did not lose faith in the project of Reconstruction. Despite the shrinking number of avenues to pursue electoral politics, Reconstruction-era black leaders and their constituents continued to engage in debates around major policy issues, shape the Republican Party at every level of the party's structure, and vote in places where their access to the ballot box was not completely obstructed. In doing so, they not only built a rival political world during the late nineteenth century but also established a coherent political vision that could be used to defend the promise of the Fifteenth Amendment.

This essay examines the efforts of black Americans to craft a defense of Reconstruction and make meaning out of the Republican Party during the last decades of the nineteenth century. Confronted with a Democratic Party that instituted state laws that drastically reduced the black electorate, and a national Republican Party that was now distancing itself from the once-popular "bloody shirt" politics of deploying the memory of the Union cause, the handful of black Republican officeholders and party leaders who were still alive fought to reverse the party's retreat from Reconstruction. Emphasizing two of the remaining bastions of black Stalwart Republicanism, the South Carolina Lowcountry and Washington, D.C., I argue that the demise of Radical Republicanism was not immediately apparent to those living through the late nineteenth century.[6] While the old guard of leaders recognized that they did not have the same support from the national GOP as their predecessors, and that the Southern Democratic Party was resurgent, they understood these shifts as temporary. Most importantly, they believed that they stood on a powerful moral argument related to voting rights and the meaning of the Civil War and Reconstruction that could ultimately win the day in the public sphere.

Put another way, while some in the Republican Party no longer wanted a prolonged fight over voting rights in the South, black political leaders like Robert Smalls remained committed to the ideals they believed to be at the core of the Republican Party. Sensing that they were entering the political wilderness, these Stalwart Republicans echoed Frederick Douglass's 1872 clarion call that "the Republican Party is the ship and all else is the sea."[7] Keenly aware that they were out of step with where the party was heading—and where many new black leaders saw as the proper direction of black political life—the old guard politicians believed that they were a major political victory away from securing a return to Reconstruction.

Challenging the standard interpretations of black politics in the post-Reconstruction era, this essay charts a new path for understanding how black Americans understood the Republican Party in the late nineteenth century. I move beyond the standard post-Reconstruction interpretation of African American political history, which has emphasized how, in the wake of Republican Party's abandonment of black Southerners following the Compromise of 1877, black Americans were left with only the marginalized realm of symbolic politics. This interpretation, I argue, obscures the fact that after the Reconstruction there was still considerable storm and stress within the remaining bastions of black politics over the meaning of the Republican Party. Far from representing isolated or exceptional places in the black world, the South Carolina Lowcountry and Washington, D.C., both served as "living archives" of an earlier era's political history. While unable to reverse the larger shift toward disfranchisement, the late-nineteenth-century black leaders who struggled over the meaning of the Republican Party built a counter memory that helped keep the political vision of the Reconstruction alive during the Jim Crow era.

The Birth of Southern Republicanism

On March 21, 1867, members of the Lowcountry's Union League gathered in Charleston to create a proposal for a new state constitution. The Union League was a secretive, paramilitary organization that emerged in the postbellum South to provide protection and political education for freedpeople. Charleston's Union League would call the meeting a "Union Republican" convention, and from its deliberation in the sea coast city came the framework for the 1868 state constitution. Five days later, the first chapter of the Republican Party would be founded in the nearby town of Beaufort. By the end of the decade, the clandestine grassroots chapters of the Union League had been replaced across the former Confederacy by official chapters of the Republican Party. Bringing together white Northerners, white Southerners opposed to the former planter class, and black Southerners, the South's GOP would steward the political project of Reconstruction.[8]

Over the next decade, Republicans in the South would write new state constitutions that guaranteed universal manhood suffrage, establish public school systems for black and white children, invest in public works and railroads, expand access to asylums and poor relief, and eliminate debtor's prisons. The Republican coalition in the South offered the country—and the world—its first glimpse of multiracial democracy. Looking back on the accomplishments at the end of the decade, one of South Carolina's most prominent black politicians argued, "We had built schoolhouses, established charitable institutions, built and maintained the penitentiary system, provided for the education of the deaf and dumb, rebuilt the ferries. In short, we had reconstructed the State and placed it upon the road to prosperity."[9]

Such a fundamental reversal of the social and political order was met with a fierce and violent backlash. The first iteration of the Ku Klux Klan emerged in 1866 as a vehicle to terrorize Republican voters. Killing a still-unknown number of black *and* white Republican voters in the South during Reconstruction, the Klan enacted a reign of terror that threatened the promise of biracial democracy from its onset. In response to these acts of political violence, the federal government deployed federal troops to formally occupy the former Confederacy and created what would become the modern Department of Justice to prosecute Klan members with the newly created Enforcement Acts.[10]

Though the Reconstruction was initially supported by both radical and moderate Republicans, support slowly dissipated during the 1870s. Financing its expansive policy goals through property taxes, a reversal from the regressive head tax system that existed in the antebellum South, the Republican Party in the

South sparked fierce opposition from the former planter class, who believed that the new system of taxation was a scheme to transfer wealth from the region's white landowners to freedpeople and their white allies. The new tax system, coupled with the fact that black Southerners could now both exercise the franchise and hold office, proved to be an overwhelming assault on the racial ideology of the region's white elites. First attacked by the Ku Klux Klan, black and white Republicans in the South faced a second wave of violence during the 1870s by an assortment of white paramilitary groups seeking to redeem the South for white rule. One by one, Republican-led state governments began to fall, until the presidential election of 1876, when massive violence and voter fraud cast doubt on the election returns in the states of Louisiana, Florida, and South Carolina and left the control of the White House in limbo. Recognizing that many Northern Republicans had grown exhausted with Reconstruction—and were embracing the arguments made by white Southerners against it—the Democratic Party struck a grand compromise with the Republican Party that secured the removal of federal troops from the South.[11]

While the Republican Party began to fade in large portions of the American South in the two decades following the end of the federal government's military occupation, the GOP did not completely disappear. In the upper Piedmont and Mountain South, white yeomen remained loyal to the party of Lincoln. In nascent urban centers of the New South such as Atlanta, Nashville, and Durham, Republican Party candidates were elected to municipal offices such as the city council and the school board. Finally, in black-majority regions of the rural South, robust chapters of the Republican Party, fueled by freedpeople and black Northerners who had moved to the South during the Reconstruction era, continued to keep the GOP alive in the South and pushed the national party to protect the Fourteenth and Fifteenth Amendment rights of the South's black citizens.[12]

The Afterlife of the South Carolina Lowcountry's Republican Party

Nowhere was this struggle more visible than in the South Carolina Lowcountry. Despite the removal of federal troops in 1877, the Republican Party remained an active—albeit diminished—political force in South Carolina. In 1878 and 1880, Republican candidates were able to compete for and contest three out of the state's five congressional districts. When the 1880 census demonstrated that South Carolina was entitled to two more congressional seats due to population growth, the state's conservative leaders put forward a plan that would gerrymander the state in such a manner that the state's black majority would only be able to affect elections in one district. At a special session of the state legislature that convened on June 7, 1882, state senator J. F. Izlar of Orangeburg introduced a bill dividing the state into seven congressional districts. Samuel Dibble, a Democratic congressman from South Carolina, was the plan's architect. Hoping to ensure Democratic control in six of the seven new districts, Dibble drew the boundaries so as to concentrate a full 25 percent of the state's black population into a single district, the new Seventh Congressional District, thereby diluting black voting strength in the other six districts.[13]

Though the gerrymandering effort tilted the political landscape in favor of the state's Democratic Party, it did not break South Carolina's Republican Party. The state party continued to meet and select delegates from across the state to send to the party's national conventions. The national party continued to appoint black men to federal positions in the state's post offices, lighthouses, and custom houses. Most importantly, the South Carolina Lowcountry housed the most robust of the remaining bastions of Southern Republicanism. The political and civic institutions in the newly created Seventh Congressional District, the birthplace of wartime Reconstruction, would preserve the legacy of the Civil War–era Republican Party in a way that would serve as a beacon for those who still believed that the Thirteenth, Fourteenth, and Fifteenth Amendments were the cornerstones of the party's moral vision.[14]

A place where free-born black Northerners and Southern-born freedpeople had offered competing visions of political power and citizenship since emancipation, the post-Reconstruction Lowcountry continued to serve as a battleground for the future of black America during the late nineteenth century. "We are, indeed, worthy of the name 'Africa' that is, as far as holding offices are concerned," a Beaufort resident proudly informed black readers in the black press. For those nineteenth-century black Americans who had been born free and received an education in the North, the postbellum Lowcountry was one of the few remaining places in the country where black men could hold office and exercise political influence. In order to preserve this site of ambition and racial destiny in the decades that followed Reconstruction, some would argue for educational limits on the franchise to preserve a respectable image of black politics. "With all due respect to Sumner, Thad Stevens, and those other leaders of the majority, I must say it was a mistake to confer suffrage as soon upon the freedmen," argued William J. Whipper, a Northern-born attorney and Republican politician based in Beaufort. While not representative of the larger Republican Party, his conservative vision of voting rights highlights how the vision for the future of black politics in the South was always contested.[15]

For Southern-born black South Carolinians, the Lowcountry

represented a more practical vision of citizenship. Union occupation and Reconstruction-era tax policies created a class of small landowning farmers that retained economic independence well into the twentieth century. The political culture that emerged in the Lowcountry boasted numerous civic organizations, regular mass meetings, and a large concentration of veterans from the United States Colored Troops, all of which fostered a rich participatory democracy in the region. In turn, this culture fostered a deep sense of accountability to black voters among the region's political leaders. "Dey says dem *will do* dis and dat," remarked one black voter in Beaufort County after hearing an 1878 speech from a Democratic Party candidate. "I ain't ax no man what him *will do*—I ax him what him *hab done*."[16] Most importantly, the region's black majority offered a safety valve for black South Carolinians fleeing persecution and ongoing political violence in the state's Upcountry region. "I hardly think it probable that any prisoner [in Beaufort County] will ever be taken from jail by a mob and lynched, let his color or offense be what it may," Smalls boasted.[17] As economic and political opportunities dwindled in other parts of the state, and as acts of violence went increasingly unpunished, the Lowcountry offered black South Carolinians an opportunity to shape the Republican Party and hold its leaders accountable to a practical and forward-looking vision of black freedom.

Robert Smalls built the second act of his political career as the defender of this grassroots vision of the Republican Party. A Stalwart Republican, he continued to support the national Republican Party after the Compromise of 1877 and campaigned with Ulysses S. Grant when the former president sought a third term in 1880. When the new Seventh Congressional District was created in 1882, Smalls not only used the new gerrymander to highlight the ongoing disfranchisement efforts on the part of the

Democratic Party in the South but also used the hypervisible black district as an example of racial progress. A "black political mecca," this district captured the national imagination and was heralded in the black press as an example of what was possible if Northern Republicans remained committed to the advancement of civil rights.[18]

As the Seventh Congressional District was the last holdout from the Reconstruction era, its political races during the 1880s served as a referendum on the current state of black politics. Robert Smalls, who was immensely popular among Union veterans in the North and freedpeople in the Lowcountry, struck some as out of step with the direction of post-Reconstruction black politics. Self-educated and Gullah-speaking, Smalls was attacked by his opponents as a man who degraded the level of black political discourse as opposed to raising it to loftier heights. "We fear that the defeat of Mr. Smalls was due in part to the belief that he entertained that no colored man was entitled to represent that District but himself," argued one Northern newspaper.[19] The younger generation of men not only had a problem with Smalls as a relic of the past but also rejected his deployment of bloody shirt rhetoric that emphasized the violence wrought by slavery, the Confederacy, and redemption.

To these claims, Smalls and his allies would retort that the young men of ambition failed to understand the Lowcountry's particular political landscape. "We have a great deal of sympathy for men with swelled heads for those of our race," Bampfield mocked, "who, because they enjoyed the benefits and privileges which were denied the greater number of us in antebellum days of getting 'eddycashum,' boastfully allude to ignoramuses who are intelligent enough to outgeneral them and make their heads ache very very badly." Despite his perceived political liabilities, Smalls understood how to run a Gilded Age political machine—

which required doling out patronage to friends and punishing enemies—and how to frame the recent past to craft a political narrative that united disparate constituencies.[20]

Smalls, like other Southern Republicans, had to confront splintering factions within his party and resurgent Democratic opposition seeking to topple his bailiwick in Beaufort County. Once satisfied to leave the Seventh District to black voters and Republican Party politicians, South Carolina's Democratic Party began contesting the Seventh District's congressional seat by the middle of the decade. When Smalls ultimately lost his seat in an 1886 midterm election to a scion of one of the Lowcountry's most prominent families, a new round of recriminations erupted. Contesting the election before the House of Representatives, Smalls and his lawyers charged the Democratic Party for numerous irregularities, such as failing to register eligible voters, reducing the number of polling places in the district, not opening polling places on election day, and throwing out eligible ballots. At the same congressional hearing, his Democratic opponent argued that black Democrats in the district had been intimidated and ostracized by Smalls and his constituents. While these claims of voter intimidation on the part of Robert Smalls were proven to be frivolous, many of his opponents latched on to the narrative created by the Democratic Party to support their own claims that Smalls was out of step with the current moment in black politics.[21]

Though he lost his contest before Congress, largely because the Democratic Party controlled the White House and House of Representatives, Smalls used this high-profile battle over voting rights to raise the alarm over the nature of elections in the South. Highlighting the precipitous drop in voter participation in the decade that followed Reconstruction, Smalls used his fame and political success to highlight how South Carolina's post-Reconstruction political history had been "a continued series of murders, outrages, perjury, and fraud."[22] Detailing the litany of new obstacles to voting that had been erected in the years since Reconstruction, Robert Smalls sought to make Northern Republicans aware not only of the extent to which South Carolina's Democratic Party would go to hollow out the Fifteenth Amendment but also of the continued sacrifices black South Carolinians would make in support of the party of Lincoln and Grant. "At any election in South Carolina when the votes shall be counted as cast," Smalls argued, "it will be found that the negroes of the South are as true and as loyal to the principles of Republicanism as they were to the flag of this great country when treason sought to blot it out."[23] Drawing a direct comparison between the Union cause and the post-Reconstruction Republican Party, Robert Smalls offered a hopeful message to Northern Republicans, suggesting that all was not lost in the South and that black Southerners were still steadfast in their support for the GOP.

Washington's Republican Party

While local Republican Parties remained active in other pockets of the black-belt South, the epicenter of post-Reconstruction black political life had shifted to the nation's capital. Similarly to Beaufort, Washington experienced black freedom much earlier than other regions of the country. After Congress offered compensated emancipation to the district's slave owners on April 16, 1862, the nation's capital not only became the first place to witness the permanent destruction of slavery during the war but also became a beacon for freedpeople in nearby Northern Virginia.[24]

In the decade after the war, black Washingtonians briefly held the franchise, served in local government, and built a number of civic, educational, and political institutions that prepared a generation of political leaders. The city witnessed a rapid expansion of its black population during and immediately after the Civil War, as well as a brief period of black political activism following the passage of the 1867 District of Columbia Suffrage Act. The plethora of educational institutions and high-status federal positions in Washington made it the beacon for black ambition and uplift in the 1880s. Howard University had emerged as the preeminent institution for black higher education and the largest producer of black attorneys in the country. The M Street School, which would later become the Paul Lawrence Dunbar High School, was the most prestigious black high school in the country and attracted talented black students from across the country. The Metropolitan African Methodist Episcopal Church served as the intellectual center of the AME Church in the United States, and its reading and lecture circle, the Bethel Literary and Historical Society, stood atop a larger world of exclusive social clubs in the city.[25]

As Washington became the new capstone of the post-Reconstruction black world, the political leaders who had flocked to South Carolina Lowcountry in the previous decade now established new lives in the nation's capital. Francis Lewis Cardozo, a Charlestonian who had left the Lowcountry to pursue higher education at the University of Glasgow and returned to his home state to become involved in Republican politics (and eventually to become the secretary of state), now served as the principal of the Colored Preparatory School. Richard Cain, who had once overseen AME missions in South Carolina and was elected to the U.S. Congress while residing in Charleston, moved to the District of Columbia to serve as the AME bishop over the Mid-Atlantic States. Richard T. Greener, who had been a professor at the University of South Carolina and a leader in the Union League, now worked as a law clerk for the Treasury Department. Whitefield McKinlay, a member of Charleston's Brown Fellowship who had been educated by Cardozo and served in the inaugural class of black state legislators, moved to the District of Columbia to become inspector of the Port of Washington; he would also become a wealthy real estate agent and a de facto kingmaker in Republican politics.[26]

No figure was a more important interlocutor in the debate over black America's political past and future than William Calvin Chase. Born free in antebellum Washington, he split time during the Reconstruction era working for local newspapers and holding minor positions in the federal government. In 1882, he founded the *Washington Bee*, a periodical that would occupy the center of the black political world. Mirroring Chase's commitment to the Stalwart wing of the Republican Party, the *Washington Bee* mythologized the Reconstruction-era heroes who now lived in the city and regularly traded barbs with the new generation of writers and political leaders who criticized the GOP for failing black voters during the Hayes and Arthur Administrations. T. Thomas Fortune, editor of the *New York Freeman* and the *New York Age*, was a particular target of Chase's ire. He was a self-proclaimed independent who sought to encourage other black Americans to abandon the party of Lincoln. "The Republican politicians used our votes and flattered self-esteem just so long as our votes held out," Fortune argued. "When we no longer had votes with which to help them to win victories, they made issues of our misfortunes, not to assist us, but to boost their fast waning power."[27] Rejecting Fortune's claim about the failure of the Republican Party, Chase argued that "the negro has not weakened and will not weaken in his allegiance to the Republican Party and that desertions are mainly due to spite or the desire and hope of office."[28] In his full-throated defense of the Republican Party and its ideals, Chase demonstrated the ongoing importance of electoral politics broadly, and the

Republican Party more particularly, as a vehicle for black freedom in the post-Reconstruction era.

Where Chase spoke for a nascent vision of black politics directed by race's "best men," Perry Carson would come to represent a more working-class vision of the Republican Party's future. Born free in antebellum Maryland, Carson assisted fugitives on the Underground Railroad in Baltimore as a teenager before moving to Washington during the Civil War. Learning politics under the tutelage of Alexander Shepherd, one of the most powerful machine politicians of the late nineteenth century, Carson would go on to run his own political patronage network in the nation's capital. Standing six feet six inches tall and weighing more than 250 pounds, "the tall black oak of the Potomac" organized Washington's black working-class citizens at a moment when the city's elite leaders began pursuing a more elite-driven vision of racial uplift. His primary organization, "The Blaine Invincible Republican Club," boasted being the oldest black political organization in the city and having a membership that numbered in the hundreds. The sole Republican delegate from Washington for the party's national conventions between 1880 and 1900, Carson had access to Republican Party elites and thus could offer his supporters federal positions, audience with key figures in the Republican Party, and rich and robust political space where working-class Washingtonians' concerns over civil rights, police brutality, and labor issues would be heard.[29]

Paralleling Robert Smalls's political base in South Carolina, Perry Carson's working-class base upset the black community's elite power brokers, who held on to a more whiggish notion of political power. Labeled a "disgrace" by Chase, Carson's working-class constituents were considered obnoxious and uncouth by Washington's black strivers. The struggles over class, race, and political culture were most visible in the city's April Emancipation Day celebrations. A secular high holiday in Washington, Emancipation Day was filled with parades, barbecues, and political speeches. At a moment when the greater nation's eyes turned toward the nation's capital to think about the story of Emancipation, especially as it related to current questions of racial progress, any and all actions by the city's black parade goers became a referendum on the entire race. Following the 1888 Emancipation Day celebration, one leader proclaimed that the parade "showed no advancement of the race in this city" and was "void of dignity, uniformity and respectability."[30] The offensive parade goers, citizens who would have been represented more by Perry Carson than by William Calvin Chase, saw Emancipation Day as a moment to be seen and represented in a political world that, while still offering opportunities to engage in Republican politics, increasingly did not have many spaces for working-class black Americans to shape the direction of the party. To this end, Carson sought to make the concerns of the city's poorer wards and residents seen and heard. "He may not suit the dandies of the colony," one observer remarked about Carson, "but he suits the bone and sinew."[31]

The End of the Republican South

By the last decade of the century, the Republican Party in Beaufort still wielded significant power, but was badly wounded by factional divisions and a growing generational rift between Smalls's machine and the younger politicians who hoped to guide the party in a new direction. Sensing that the political winds were changing, Smalls began partnering with Beaufort County's white elites to divide local offices between members of his political clique and local Democrats. This arrangement, known as fusionism, was a strategy used in other parts of the South where conservative members of the Democratic Party partnered with moderate black Republicans to block a surging Populist movement from capturing office. In 1888, Smalls successfully orchestrated a fusionist arrangement that secured the positions of sheriff, clerk of court, school commissioner, and coroner for Republicans while granting probate judge, count commissioner, and state senate to Democrats.[32] While such a fusionist arrangement required making deep concessions to their longtime political opponents, this pragmatic approach to the shifting terrain of the New South's political landscape allowed the Lowcountry to remain a place where black Southerners could continue exercising the franchise and where black officeholders could continue fighting for the Republican Party's future in the region.[33]

The fusionist strategy to preserve some Republican power in South Carolina, however, came at a great reputational cost. Accused of abandoning the Republican Party by several of his former allies, Smalls was brandished a traitor to the Republican cause in the national press. Although Smalls was once "the idol of the Republicans of this county," Whipper argued that he "was now accused of going into the very arms of the bloodstained Democracy that he has so long, so often and so roundly denounced."[34] Seeking a federal appointment from Benjamin Harrison's incoming administration in 1889, Smalls defended his recent action before the black press by arguing that he was the true heir to the Republican Party and that his opponents and critics in the Lowcountry were "men of the lowest degree of character" and represented "the carpetbagger and the rum element."[35]

Most vocally represented in the state of South Carolina by Benjamin Tillman, the Populist movement sought to mobilize white yeomen against both the wealthy white elites and black Republican politicians. "The fact is the Negro vote is a frozen serpent," Tillman warned his constituents.[36] While greatly diminished across the state, the Republican Party in South Carolina was still sending black men to represent the "Black Seventh" during the Fifty-First and Fifty-Second Congresses, and black voters in the Lowcountry were still electing Republican officials to the state legislature and county government. Thus, the Lowcountry's Republican establishment was seen as a threat to a united white political party. Hoping to finally close the chapter on the Reconstruction era, South Carolina's Democratic Party once again gerrymandered the state to eliminate the Seventh Congressional District. In 1894, the Democratic Party swept every congressional district and narrowly won a statewide referendum for a constitutional convention. Modeling this convention after the 1890 Mississippi Constitutional Convention, Tillman hoped to emulate the clauses added to Mississippi's constitution that effectively disfranchised black voters by implementing a literacy test, property and residency requirements, and a poll tax. Most dangerous was a new "understanding clause," which allowed the registration official to assess a voter's comprehension of the Constitution—adding another subjective barrier that could be used to disqualify black voters who met all other state requirements while also creating a loophole to prevent poor whites from being disfranchised by the new literacy test.[37]

The only individuals standing against the constitutional convention's effort to enact the near-complete disfranchisement of South Carolina's black voters were six Republican delegates from the Lowcountry. Led by Robert Smalls, the delegation also included his onetime political opponents William J. Whipper and Thomas E. Miller. Over the course of the convention, the six men made powerful arguments in defense of Reconstruction and the Republican Party's legacy in the state. "In the convention of 1868 there were less than a dozen negroes and less than a dozen white men engaged in the work done there," William J. Whipper said. "I am proud of the work done in that convention," he continued. "The way it has stood the test has shown that there was nothing dangerous in it."[38]

Recognizing that they were outnumbered and fighting a losing battle, the delegates from Beaufort called on the Democratic Party to enact literacy tests or property qualifications without the nefarious understanding clause. "In behalf of the 600,000 Negroes in the State and the 132,000 Negro voters all that I demand is that a fair and honest election law be passed," Smalls exclaimed. "We care not what the qualifications imposed are: all that we ask is that they be fair and honest and honorable, and with these provisos we will stand or fall by it."[39] Willing to concede broader democratic principles in the name of "good government," the delegates from Beaufort highlighted the moral shallowness of the disfranchisement effort by showing that despite the arguments to the contrary, the new state constitution left the Reconstruction-era document largely intact.

Despite the significant blow of disfranchisement, the Republican world built by the older generation of leaders did not completely disappear. The *Washington Bee* championed the heroic efforts of the Lowcountry's politicians and called on the national Republican Party to remain engaged in future struggles over black voting rights. The Blaine Invincible Republican Club continued to meet well into the early twentieth century and advocated for a broader vision of Republican politics. Robert Smalls continued to participate in Republican Party politics in the state of South Carolina and would vote in local and statewide elections well into the twentieth century's second decade.[40]

The Republican Party would continue to drift away from its black constituents, but the last generation of black Republican leaders held on to the world they had built in the decade after the Civil War. Armed with a knowledge of what Reconstruction had meant, and still able to wield levers of power and patronage, the last generation of Republican figures made voting rights a central issue in Republican Party politics when many of the party's top leaders no longer had much stomach for that fight. When the figures of this generation began to pass away in the first decades of the twentieth century, the knowledge of this world that they had built began to disappear. The party of Grant and Lincoln would continue to have adherents during the first decades of the twentieth century. It even maintained a bastion of Republican Party power into the interwar period in Illinois's First Congressional District on Chicago's Southside and in the robust Republican Party political machine in Memphis, Tennessee, which thrived under the stewardship of Robert Church Jr. and George Lee. But the more expansive vision of what the party could accomplish faded with the deaths of the Reconstruction generation. Upholding an optimistic vision of the Republican Party's past and a hopeful view of its future, the old guard figures like Robert Smalls, William J. Whipper, William Calvin Chase, and Perry Carson represented an important but lost history of the late nineteenth century. Still committed to a version of the Republican Party that supported and protected the voting rights of black Southerners, the last generation of Reconstruction politicians preserved a moral vision of the GOP that spoke to voters at all levels of the party and offered a radical vision of what was still politically possible at the dawn of the Jim Crow era.

4

COMPETING VISIONS

W. B. Allen

The image most frequently employed in the Bible to convey the idea of felicity in this world invokes the eudaemonia of repose under "one's own vine and fig tree." That image powerfully conveys the full measure of the means and fruits of economic endeavor. Taken as a suggestion of undisturbed enjoyment (peace and prosperity), it is only partly correct. To take the full measure of the promise, one must reflect on the special importance of the reference to the vine and the fig.

Harvesting the fruit of the vine and the fig tree requires, first of all, undertaking the rigorous labor of planting, cultivating, and tending. God, in other words, did not promise to provide material security. He promised rather to reward the effort to merit material security, while endowing us from the beginning with the power to exert such effort. It should be well known that the development of grapes and figs in the abundance fit to provide secure enjoyment demands, first, a labor that will require as long as five years before the plantings will bear the fruit that is wanted. Therefore, in order to enjoy repose under one's own vine

Originally published under the title "Race and Economics," in *Race and Covenant: Recovering the Religious Roots for American Reconciliation*, ed. Gerald R. McDermott (Grand Rapids, MI: Acton Institute, 2020). Permission to reprint granted by the Acton Institute.

and fig tree, one must first work to make the vine and fig tree fruitful—which takes a long time.

This understanding of the biblical promise relates directly to our approach to capture the measure of economic promise in the contemporary world, and especially in the context of race and economics. For it is arguable that in no other dimension of current economic thinking has common opinion been more misguided. Indeed, I would say further that in no other dimension of current thinking has common opinion been more deliberately misled. In a word, we have experienced the persistent and distorting teaching that the effective use of liberty depends upon the prior guarantee of material security. That teaching has been systematically inculcated by influential leaders from Franklin D. Roosevelt through Lyndon Johnson and Martin Luther King Jr. Although the theoretical foundations of the teaching originate with the progenitors of neo-progressive ideology in the early twentieth century, the effective dissemination of the teaching flowed from the efforts of later icons of reform.

Roosevelt set the tone beginning with his 1932 Commonwealth Club address,[1] and continuing through his State of the Union messages of 1941[2] and 1944. In this series of public statements he developed the arguments that

1. True individual freedom cannot exist without economic security and independence: "Necessitous men are not free men."[3]
2. Certain economic truths have become accepted as self-evident: "We have accepted, so to speak, a second Bill of Rights...a new basis of security and prosperity."[4]

Roosevelt's reformulation of the meaning of human rights for the United States attained its consummate formulation in the 1948 United Nations Declaration of Human Rights, which bore his direct imprint: "The right to a standard of living adequate for the health and well-being of oneself and of one's family, including food, clothing, housing, medical care and necessary social services" (Article 25). This version of every man under his own vine and fig tree inverts the biblical order, making eudaemonistic enjoyment a prerequisite for the free exercise of one's powers of labor (without indicating any purpose for which to labor!).

These prescriptions for modern life were captured in Lyndon Johnson's 1965 declaration that, in order for "20 million Negroes" to have

> the chance...to learn and grow, to work and share in society, to develop their abilities—physical, mental and spiritual—and to pursue their individual happiness, equal opportunity is essential, but not enough, not enough. Men and women of all races are born with the same range of abilities. But ability is not just the product of birth. Ability is stretched or stunted by the family that you live with, and the neighborhood you live in—by the school you go to and the poverty or the richness of your surroundings. It is the product of a hundred unseen forces playing upon the little infant, the child, and finally the man.[5]

Implicit in this argument is the mistaken hypothesis that economics is not color-blind, with the result that racial variations in economic performance can be traced to the systemic dynamics of the economic system. That hypothesis is false. While people are not color-blind, economics is. When people divert economic dynamics to the harm of disfavored minorities, it is human intervention rather than economics that is at fault. We see this plainly in the transition from Theodore Roosevelt's initial attempts to desegregate the federal workforce to Woodrow Wilson's aggressive resegregation of the federal workforce. The fact that Wilson's neo-progressivism was deliberately coordinated with the legally imposed practice of Jim Crow had far more to do with stunting black economic progress than anything intrinsic to free market economics. When neo-progressives subsequently blamed the economic system, this only obscured the real cause of the frustrated dreams of American blacks in general.

King's "Dilemma of the Negro Americans"

One casualty of this misdirected suspicion proved to be Martin Luther King Jr., who was incontestably the foremost public figure in the United States at the time he broached the most important question confronting the nation. This was the question of his book *Where Do We Go from Here: Chaos or Community?*[6] In raising that question as he did, he implied that he would deliver what the nation most needed at that moment. King's judgment was that community was the appropriate answer to the question. Arguably, every significant issue of race and culture that Americans have since discussed was raised at some point by King. My contention is that, if in the meantime we have inherited chaos rather than community, we must ask whether it has something to do with the responses he provided to his own question. In other words, if the economic lot of blacks in America today is far less than what it should be, we might look at the ways that King answered the question.

Several possibilities confront us. Either (1) King responded correctly with an adequate view of community, and his wisdom went unheeded; or (2) King responded incorrectly and his error passed for wisdom in the nation, entailing natural consequences; or (3) variations of each of these came to pass and intersected with other cultural forces.

King looked for moral strength in a mystical and mythical "capacity for hardships" in American blacks to forge the path toward the end of full integration into American society. "It is on this strength that society must now begin to build."[7] At that point he jettisoned any potential for the claims of freedom and self-government as sufficient to ground the appeal for wholesale inclusion in American society: "This is no time for romantic illusions and empty philosophical debates about freedom. This is a time for action."[8] His explanation for this was pragmatic: The difficulties American blacks faced in 1967 (when he wrote) were cultural and inherited, he believed, and only liberation from the weight of that inherited tradition could supply the life change that American blacks needed. The discovery of a cultural or institutional basis for black disadvantages provided for King the "most optimistic" part of the story. By his lights, culture could be turned from the work of destruction to the work of reconstruction.

> The causes for [the black community's] present crisis are culturally and socially induced. What man has torn down, he can rebuild. At the root of the difficulty in Negro life today is pervasive and persistent economic want. To grow from within, the Negro family—and especially the Negro man—needs only fair opportunity for jobs, education, housing and access to culture. To be strengthened from the outside requires protection from the grim exploitation that has haunted the Negro for three hundred years.[9]

This "optimistic" conclusion comes eight pages into an analysis which opened with the observation that the "dilemma of white America is the source and cause of the dilemma of Negro America."[10] King's two Americas, setting the tone for the 1968 Kerner Commission Report,[11] relate to one another only as "oppressor" and "oppressed" are related to one another. For the American black, the connection between his pain ("the central quality" of his life) and his hopes is a necessary intervention from "outside" to transform oppression into salvation. Without that intervention, there would be no escape from America's lack of true community.

"Being a Negro in America means being scarred by a history of slavery and family disorganization," King wrote, weaving the reality of three hundred years into an accumulated burden in 1967 and presenting an account of the abstract "Negro family" as if it were an autobiography.[12] In these early pages, the reader cannot escape the obvious implication that, respecting "negroes," the "content of their character" is a product of suffering, impotence, and impoverishment. Neither in recounting the tales of woe nor the magical survival of American blacks does King ever turn to any intrinsic human capacities or strengths, either in explanation of past achievements or in projecting future achievements. Culture, it seems, is the only force that has formed black character—and the only force that will liberate blacks.

Since for King the warp of cultures in America is color, one might anticipate that the weave would be character, as in the expression that people are to be judged "not by the color of their skin, but by the content of their character."[13] That would mean that the cultural change one seeks is not so much color-blindness (which would be merely a consequence of paying primary attention to character) but rather that sensitivity to character which would merge two cultures into one. To change the culture, one must teach the society how to make judgments of character. According to King, however, American blacks cannot take on that task themselves, for they live under the spell of "color shock"—the concept that their rejection is due to something they cannot change.

> It constitutes a major emotional crisis. It is accompanied by a sort of fatiguing, wearisome hopelessness. If one is rejected because he is uneducated, he can at least be consoled by the fact that it may be possible for him to get an education. If one is rejected because he is low on the economic ladder, he can at least dream of the day

that he will rise from his dungeon of economic deprivation. If one is rejected because he speaks with an accent, he can at least, if he desires, work to bring his speech in line with the dominant group. If, however, one is rejected because of his color, he must face the anguishing fact that he is being rejected because of something in himself that cannot be changed.[14]

Famously, each of King's hypotheticals served in the earlier part of this century as the catechism black families carefully rehearsed in their children (including, I dare say, the family of the elder King who instructed King Jr.). For example, they were surely taught the value of advancement through education. The conclusion, however, that skills and character which one might change have been subordinated to the overriding importance of "color shock" relegates the earlier catechism to a second-order necessity. A day may come when one can counsel poor men to "try harder," if ever the society can rid itself of "color shock."

Paradoxically, King seemed to believe, that would not happen. As long as blacks were mired in poor education, poverty, and social disadvantage, these things "proved" that color shock was a long way from being eradicated. So in the meantime, "wearisome hopelessness" was inevitable for blacks. It would be impossible for them to attempt cultural or economic improvement as long as they were poor and disadvantaged. Their poverty and disadvantage were proofs of white racism, which showed that color shock was deeply entrenched. It was a vicious circle: Black disadvantage proved white racism, which made black efforts to escape disadvantage futile, while lack of effort reinforced white perception of black inferiority, which in turn only reinforced white racism. King's remedy actually perpetuated the problem.

King wrote little about character in American blacks except to exculpate crimes by citing the "environment" and "victimization."

It may be a dramatic illustration of the path taken in his book (and life) that he focused, as did many others, on the disproportionate number of American blacks who served in Vietnam as an injustice, while saying nothing of blacks' disproportionate heroism, their disproportionate sense of duty, and their disproportionate inclination to volunteer.

But King did not neglect character entirely. When he enumerated five recommended responses to "the Negro's dilemma,"[15] he began with his closest invocation of character, "a rugged sense of somebodyness." To overcome a "feeling of being less than human, the Negro must assert for all to hear and see a majestic sense of his worth."[16] Naturally, mere self-assertion is not a substitute for solid accomplishment. Moreover, it may be the case that a premature self-assertion may subvert the genuine foundations of accomplishment, which alone engender self-respect.

Nonetheless, King evidently means in this appeal to inculcate a sense of need for such fundamental virtues as industry, courage, and moderation. In this regard, it is impossible to explain why his spirited defense of real life in the ghetto (where there are "churches...as well as bars," "stable families...as well as illegitimacies," and "ninety percent of the young people...never come in conflict with the law"[17]) did not provide him substantial opportunity to sermonize on opportunities for emulation in the pursuit of "somebodyness." Praiseworthy elements of character must surely inform the "striving" and "hoping" which he described in that context. It appears that he did not enlarge on these themes because they did not support the ultimate response he had fashioned for the main question.

The remaining responses to "the Negro's dilemma" are "group unity," a "constructive use of the [limited] freedom we already possess," union "around powerful action programs," and "enlarging the whole society and giving it a new sense of [progressive] values."[18] These prescriptions for "social change" merge in a single consideration, which King developed in his final chapter, "The World House." There he describes the emergence of a political movement transcending the United States and animating a global movement toward social democracy.[19]

That ultimate political movement is the international analogue to the indigenous political movement he envisioned for United States, where he would nurture a five-point program that argued, "More and more, the civil rights movement will have to engage in the task of organizing people into permanent groups to protect their own interests."[20] As described, it would consist of blacks, Northern liberal Democrats, labor unions, and an ever-widening circle of oppressed peoples. King was convinced that "there is a need for a radical restructuring of the architecture of American society."[21] The word "architecture" was deliberate, for King had in mind a new design based on fundamental principles rather than incidental circumstances.

King said little else about character, for three reasons. First, he placed no faith in the character of American whites. Second, he expected no rewards for exertions of character by American blacks. He was not interested in a "new black middle class" and never counseled the poor to follow the middle class. Third, a focus on character within a given community would be inconsistent with his mission to transcend that community for the sake of a new community built on entirely different grounds.

Although King acknowledged that "we are also Americans," that was a decidedly subordinate moral consideration in the analysis. The fact that "our destiny is tied up with the destiny of America"[22] did not commit American blacks to an American destiny which was intrinsic to its foundation. For King, American racism could be negated ultimately only by the negation of the moral soil from which it sprouted. It was as if racism was native to America's soil rather than an excrescence of that soil, and it would need a new soil.

> Historians in future years will have to say there lived a great people—a black people— who bore their burdens of oppression in the heat of many days and who, through tenacity and creative commitment, injected new meaning into the veins of American life.[23]

Martin Luther King answered his rhetorical question, "chaos or community," by dreaming of founding a new community. The unjust treatment he accorded George Washington, ignoring Washington's moral anguish about slavery and denying Washington's liberation of his slaves in his will, may be attributed to King's own ambition to rival Washington as a founder. But King failed where Washington succeeded. It remains for us to figure out why.

Martin Luther King Jr.'s Failure

Let me repeat my observation that there are few if any questions about race and culture that we entertain in 2020 which had not been considered, in some manner, by King in 1967. Nor would many deny that black communities deteriorated culturally in the three decades after his death, when his influence hardly diminished. Nothing illustrates this better than the emergence of "hate speech" proscriptions that exempt black folk. It was once common in the homes of American blacks whom I knew to admonish youths to avoid terms like "nigger" in referring to one another. Such precepts continued into the 1960s. But since then they have disappeared almost altogether. I submit that they have disappeared because of the successful invocation of the false notion of a black culture and the correlative exculpation of blacks for all sorts of "bad behavior" on the grounds of their "victim" status. King's opting to shape community among blacks rather than to shape a community on American principles is the immediate moral cause of this enormous transformation in our society. One could add that this has also affected the economic status of large parts of the black community that have accepted King's presuppositions about liberty and security. Not blacks alone but also many whites have fallen prey to King's misguided principles.

For many, it was easy to transition from thinking of blacks as different and inferior to thinking of blacks as unassimilably different. This move released mental and moral energy which otherwise could have been used to build community. For guilty consciences anxious to escape responsibility, but at a loss as to what course to pursue, the idea that one could embrace "diversity" or "multiculturalism" (or the idea of a separate black community which merited respect as distinct) provided a natural outlet. Then it was no longer necessary to ask whether America had succeeded in fulfilling its principles on its own terms.

Of course, the nettlesome question of economic and social inequality remained—at least the inequality that could not be reduced to cultural difference. Since it is impossible to measure the connection between economic progress and respect for cultural difference, it follows that diminishing inequalities constitute no evidence at all of a need for special treatment for American blacks. In fact, thinking this way is actually paradoxical. Let me explain.

It is commonly supposed that special programs for blacks are justified by their "history" and not their present circumstances. That means one cannot demand either personal or cultural accommodations to American society to show the effects of the special programs. So the question of "progress" is impossible to measure. All that is left is the standard of "representation" as a totem to express King's goals. This is why we often hear of "underrepresented minorities" in the workplace, in schools, and in government offices, appointed and elective. What is actually meant, however, remains vague. As long as a single minority individual anywhere might be said to be less advantageously situated than he or she might wish, it will be said that minorities are underrepresented. And it will be impossible to criticize minority culture—especially black culture—or to talk about what will bring genuine economic improvement to black communities. The paradox, then, is that presumptions about what is needed for black progress are the very things that stymie black progress.

Nothing the nation does, including "massive government expenditures," can ever genuinely satisfy the demands that King made for a new American community without its American roots. But what *is* possible for the United States today is to discover a way to reconnect ideas of American community with both expectations of as well as obligations to American blacks. But this cannot be accomplished without refuting and overturning the cultural exceptionalism built by King and others. The most recent evidence of that cultural exceptionalism is on display in the "1619 Project," which has gained wide currency and is on prominent display in a glossy *New York Times Magazine* display.[24] The upshot of the project is the argument that the contributions of enslaved Africans are mainly responsible for American prosperity.

Let's begin by asking the obvious question: Is it true that American blacks in 2022 (or 1967 for that matter) reflect in their characters, habits, attitudes, and prospects the full weight of three hundred years of suffering by American blacks? Take an individual black, born in this generation. In what way does he or she bear the weight of three hundred years of black experience? Are his or her natural endowments irrelevant? Their family circumstances? Their friends? The accidents that befell them in the course of their lives? What about the three hundred and sixty years of broader American experience and the much longer European experience stretching back to prehistory? When calculating the impact of the past on just one person, what sense does it make to focus on the experience of slavery? He wears no stripes on his back! My point is that it is an entire fiction that black people today still feel the pains of the past.

I will make this more personal. Family lore has it that my great-grandfather freely emigrated from the West Indies to the United States shortly before the onset of the War for the Union in 1861. He had been enticed by an offer of economic opportunity— i.e., he was recruited to be a foreman on a large farm in the South. By that time, of course, it had become increasingly difficult to smuggle slaves into the country in violation of the law, but evasions remained possible. When, therefore, Great-Grandfather Sidiphus arrived in the United States and discovered that he was just another slave, one of those evasions was revealed.

The point of this story is not that of fraud and betrayal—both of which were very real. Nor is it to invoke the oppression of slavery, though that was very real. It is rather to raise the very poignant question of whether Sidiphus's initiative in seeking out opportunities of economic advance for himself and his later family was justified by the results. At first glance, it may not appear so. But when one reflects that his enslavement was not long-lived, that the country to which he looked as a land of opportunity soon liberated its slaves, and that he did eventually build a family, a large family that experienced the disadvantages of living as a despised minority among people who sought to foreclose opportunities to prosper, but finally, also produced offspring who advanced to the highest levels of achievement and responsible office in the country, one must ask whether Sidiphus indeed made a mistake. It turned out that the economic opportunity he sought did indeed redound to the benefit of his posterity—and others besides.

Moreover, that fact seems to have a direct relationship to the design and effect of American institutions and beliefs. This means, in sum, that our picture of the past must reflect multiple pathways and outcomes and not merely simplistic blacks and whites. And that great fact has been missed by far too many thought leaders in the late twentieth and early twenty-first centuries.

Race has long been a problem in the United States in ways adequately explained in various technical writings, including some of my own. It has not, however, been proven that race is an integral part of American culture. It is a logical error to confuse what is pervasive with what is integral. And it is a moral error to derive necessary conclusions from accidental determinants. The conclusion that racism is intrinsic or integral to American principle constitutes such a moral error. On the basis of this moral error, Martin Luther King Jr., and others besides, have created a fiction of black culture and community that serves a single purpose—namely, to extract American blacks from the warp and woof of an American culture regarded as fatally flawed.

The reality in the United States has been and remains plural communities fused (and continuing to fuse) into a single American culture. There exist plural black communities, no less than plural white communities—despite the reality that black communities in the main have not been constituted by family migrations as white communities typically have been. The relatively successful effort to flatten the plural black communities into a single conception of *the* black community represents a significant political accomplishment, which has done little to alter the social landscape. On that social landscape, accordingly, one still witnesses the leading dynamic of American culture—assimilation—occurring under the lengthening shadow of a changing political reality. That changing political reality means we might reasonably wonder how long the American dynamic will persevere, as the supporting political fretwork continues to evolve to accommodate the goals of King's "revolution." Must it ever after be regarded as settled that political representation consists in identity group participation? Or will it again become possible to imagine political representation as the representation of individuals. Assimilation has occurred heretofore on the basis of the latter dynamic—individual representation—which operated to attenuate group loyalties. The current trajectory of group representation, however, heightens the political significance of group loyalties.

I have written above of the disappearance of certain social practices in the black families that I knew. Others speak and have routinely written (dating at least from the Moynihan Report[25]) of the disappearance of supportive social institutions and practices in black communities plagued by crime, illegitimacy, and other dysfunctions. All evidence suggests a social migration toward the new political standard of participation in society, a standard that distinguishes groups and group rights and that measures social obligation strictly in relation to group identity. More and more, then, I am judged not as an individual but as a "black" person. This is a disintegration of that larger patriotism which is founded in the *individual's* rights. The lesser patriotism—the group identity—undermines the larger patriotism.

My argument about undermining American patriotism would not make sense if it were true that American principles fail to secure any reasonable prospect of pervasive liberty, and provide no foundation for genuine community and prosperity. I think they do, but I also think that we have not given them a chance to be tested adequately on this question of race. For King, and nearly all who followed him, have preferred the lesser patriotism of black identity rather than the larger patriotism of individual identity rooted in American principles. Not since the beginning of the civil rights movement have we tried to test those principles. Ironic, isn't it?

The civil rights movement may inadvertently have spawned the most serious obstacle to the progress of American blacks in our time. This is the paradox I mentioned earlier. Black leaders have turned to group identity rather than individual identity and American principles of assimilation. The result has been cultural stagnation for some black communities. Just as Americans discovered in the Revolution of 1776 that they could not see the end of their journey unless they committed themselves to the point where they could not turn back, both black and white Americans must commit themselves to the project of *American* identity before they can experience the results of that project.

Therefore, the task to renew the appeal of American community and the legitimacy of assimilation—including standards of decent behavior—falls not to American blacks or whites *per se* but to every American. For King's failed response to the great crisis draws the chaos nearer with each revolution of our political solar system.

The way forward is not too difficult to discern. We should learn from the course followed by King rather than follow it. King discarded a history of accomplishment for a paean of victimization. He neglected even his own middle-class biography to weave a story of deprivation into the lineage of every black. Sadly, King committed black people to subjugation to cultural identity in purchase of political cachet.

Elsewhere I've written that George Washington's success may be attributed to the fact that he preferred justice to patriotism.[26] Certainly it is true, one may insist, that King preached justice above patriotism. But why, then, may he not be regarded as equally successful? The answer comes in two parts. First, what one preaches does not always reveal one's purpose. Second, and more pertinent, even if one grants, as I do, that King preached justice, everything must hinge on the question of presumptions about the requirements of justice. Getting them wrong will cause even a noble intent to miscarry.

Exploring that important question will return us to the question of the economic prospects for American blacks (or the question of race and economics in general), and in doing so, we can follow no finer examples than those of Frederick Douglass (who closed the nineteenth century) and Booker T. Washington (who opened the twentieth) on that precise question.

Growing and Prospering While Suffering

The real test of an economic system lies in its capacity to resist the distorting effects of partial and discriminating interventions. While the logic of trade is unvarying—and color-blind—the imposition of political or cultural restraint can direct it away from its natural currents. Nothing illustrates this better than the pattern of Jim Crow legislation at the end of the nineteenth century that sought to enforce segregation in public transportation. The reason such laws were required in Louisiana, Tennessee, Georgia, and elsewhere was precisely because the market operating in the absence of restraint would not sustain segregation. The emergence of Jim Crow, therefore, constitutes *prima facie* evidence of economic conditions otherwise favorable to effective participation in the market by American blacks.

That is the story told so effectively by Frederick Douglass and Ida Wells-Barnett in 1893 in the essays collected in *The Reason Why*, which challenges the Columbian Exposition's exclusion of American blacks in the story of American industrial and cultural progress. Wells-Barnett, indeed, declared that the neglected story "would best illustrate [America's] moral grandeur."[27]

> The exhibit of the progress made by a race in 25 years of freedom as against 250 years of slavery, would have been the greatest tribute to the greatness and progressiveness of American institutions which could have been shown the world.[28]

What is remarkable about this claim is the context in which it is made, a context that Douglass and Wells-Barnett emphatically make plain: In a scant twenty-five years since 1865 (the war's end), the population of blacks in the United States had virtually doubled (four million to eight million). Moreover, that natural increase had been accompanied by extensive accomplishments in educational, agricultural, industrial, and cultural development. Census reports demonstrate in considerable detail a portrait of solid participation in the economy. They do so, however, against the backdrop of the "outrages upon the Negro in this country."[29]

Nor were they sparing in detailing those outrages, which included drastic restrictions of the franchise, coordinated exclusions from political office, deprivation of material resources, and most significantly, widespread campaigns of violence and brutalization characterized by thousands of lynchings throughout the country. In other words, the transition in only a quarter of a century from the status of a mere "commodity"—nearly imbrued chattel—to that of demonstrated humanity transpired in the ferocious heat of a furnace of rejection, a heat so intense that Douglass could maintain that "what the colored people gained by the war they have partly lost by the peace."[30]

To say that they did not wear rose-colored glasses would be an understatement. Retelling the story from 1619 to 1893, they comprehended every reversal and disappointment.

Nevertheless, Douglass was able to aver:

As to the increased resistance met with of late, let's use a little philosophy. It is best to account in a hopeful way for this reaction and even to read it as a favorable symptom. It is a proof that the Negro is not standing still. He is not dead, but alive and active. He is not drifting with the current, but manfully resisting it and fighting his way to better conditions than those of the past, and better than those which popular opinion prescribes for him. He is not contented with his surroundings but wholly dares to break away from the path and hew out a way of safety and happiness for himself in defiance of all opposing forces...

The enemies of the Negro see that he is making progress and they naturally wish to stop him and keep him in just what they consider his proper place...

But the Negro has said a decided no to all this, and is now by industry, economy, and education wisely raising himself to conditions of civilization and comparative well being beyond anything formerly thought possible for him...

What the Negro has to do then, is to cultivate a courageous and cheerful spirit, use philosophy and exercise patience. He must embrace every avenue open to him for the acquisition of wealth. He must educate his children and build up a character for industry, economy, intelligence and virtue. Next to victory is the glory and happiness of manfully contending for it...

Our situation demands faith in ourselves, faith in the power of truth; faith in work and faith in the influence of manly character.[31]

The counsel of resistance in the face of adversity was made not in a vacuous appeal to hopefulness but in reliance upon "vine and fig" investment—hard and patient labor. That counsel, in turn, shows confidence in the power of economic self-reliance to reverse political and cultural disadvantages. The prudence of this counsel could be measured in a fair test of economic self-reliance. Booker T. Washington took up that challenge.

When Do We Reach QED?

In 1893, Washington delivered a series of speeches articulating the foundations of his project at Tuskegee Institute. In these addresses he explained that the purpose of his institute was to demonstrate that "the Negro race" should be recognized as a contributor to the nation's well-being instead of "a burden, a menace to your civilization and commercial life."[32]

Washington made his arguments most comprehensively in his 1899 Memorial Address on Abraham Lincoln, which took its place alongside the similar and earlier famous address by Douglass at the dedication of the Freedmen's Memorial to Lincoln. In his own address, Washington was careful to establish Lincoln as a bridge figure who can link American whites and American blacks in a common cause.[33] That cause would transcend emancipation and open a window onto the life of "unfettered freedom" for black and white alike.

> A freedom from dependence on others' labor to the independent or self-labor; freedom to transform unused and dwarfed hands into skilled and productive hands; to change labor from drudgery into that which is dignified and glorified; to change local commerce into trade with the world; to change the Negro from an ignorant man into an intelligent man; to change sympathies that were local and narrow into love and good-will for all mankind; freedom to change stagnation into growth, weakness into power; yea, to us all, your race and mine, Lincoln has been a great emancipator.[34]

This is Washington's way of transforming Jerome Ferris's painting "Lincoln and the Contrabands" (the spirit captured in Douglass's celebration of Lincoln) into a portrait of "Lincoln and the Citizens," where the dilemmas of difference are erased through the fruits of industry. It is important to observe that Washington's counsel of self-reliance (hardly surprising in a man who, as a boy, walked 500 miles in order to obtain a higher education at Hampton Institute) conveys not exhortation to black separatism but confidence in black agency. The nexus between self-sufficiency and eventual assimilation, resting on the efficacy of the free market, presupposes that real change requires mutual respect and independence of parties rather than dependence of one party on another.

This was forcefully brought home to me in 2018 when I led forty-five schoolteachers on a tour of civil rights sites and monuments throughout the South. As we visited Selma, Alabama, we paused at Bethel AME Church, where the protesters who crossed the Edmund Pettus Bridge gathered to prepare themselves for their famous march in 1965. As we sat in the sanctuary and I was addressing the assembly on the context and endeavors of that great event, I looked up and around at the inside of that church and broke off mid-sentence. After a pause I said, "This splendid architecture was erected in the first decade of the twentieth century, in the very teeth of repressive rage—think of the lynchings all over the nation at this time." I then asked, "Who built this building?"

We all knew. It was the black churchgoers. They had constructed an edifice of impressive beauty and solidity. Then I asked another question.

"Is it not impossible to imagine the people who could do this as somehow disabled, limited, unable to provide for themselves even in the midst of great suffering?"

The obvious answer was that it is impossible. We resolved from that moment no longer to bear the image of a people who were awaiting rescue as the characteristic image of the American black.

Between the opening and the end of the twentieth century, however, there was resistance to the approach argued by Douglass and Washington. Sociologist and writer W. E. B. Du Bois, for example, advocated political and legal rather than market initiatives. Du Bois became increasingly disenchanted with market-based exertions in the face of lynchings and race riots that seemed to put black economic independence out of reach. The burgeoning black capital and professional classes were narrowly constrained when not simply burned out or killed. And that was often taken as an expression of the nature of capitalism rather than what it really was—namely, extra-legal, legal, and non-economic repression.

By the middle of the twentieth century, the Douglass-Washington current reached its consummation in the 1950 release of a half-dollar coin bearing the images of George Washington Carver and Booker T. Washington. That symbolized the appeal of the argument for growth through economic presence. By the same time, however, not only had the arguments of Franklin D. Roosevelt—captured in the United Nations Declaration of Human Rights—gained complete purchase, but growing anti-capitalist sentiment among black leaders began to surge, eventually to crest in the creation of the national holiday for Martin Luther King Jr. Between these two events—the release of the Carver-Washington half-dollar and the establishment of the King holiday—something was lost in American black cultures: continued confidence in the efficacy of self-reliance.

Washington's most powerful and comprehensive speech ("The Educational and Industrial Emancipation of the Negro" in February 1903) apparently lost traction during those years. In that speech, Washington, like Douglass before, provided a comprehensive narrative of the American experience, in which he delineated with great clarity the meaning of freedom. In that speech, he powerfully weaves together the importance of independence and agency with the underlying foundation of Christian principle.

> Those are most truly free today who have passed through great discipline. Those persons in the United States who are most truly free in body, mind, morals, are those who have passed through the most severe training—those who have exercised the most patience and, at the same time, the most dogged persistence and determination.
>
> To deal more practically and directly with the affairs of my own race, I believe that both the teachings of history as well as the results of everyday observation should convince us that we shall make our most enduring progress by laying the foundation carefully, patiently in the ownership of the soil, the exercise of habits of economy, the saving of money, the securing of the most complete education of hand and head, and the cultivation of Christian virtue...
>
> I repeat here what I have often said in the south. The Negro seeks no special privileges. All that he asks is opportunity—that the same law which is made by the white man and applied to the one race be applied with equal certainty and exactness to the other.[35]

Washington was no less specific and demanding in what he sought of the dominant race: "No race can degrade another without degrading itself. No race can assist in lifting another without itself being broadened and made more Christ-like."[36]

Washington made clear that even in the face of enormous suffering, growth remains possible, as long as there is respect for individual agency. When Washington answered the question of what is to be done for the Negro, his reply was, "Let him alone." This is what he meant when he said that "freedom is enough." For the black man is no less suited to provide for himself than any other human being. Despite the cultural setbacks I have described in this chapter, the reality is that demonstrable progress is evident in the accomplishments and advances to date of the black middle class. What remains perplexing is the continuing tendency in public discourse to discount that progress and speak instead of black victimhood. In other words, history has proved what Douglass and Washington set out to demonstrate, but current conversation persistently fails to attend to that history.

This is not the place to explore in depth today's cultural preference for the counterfactual over the actual relationship between race and economics. But I can say at least this much—that we no longer assume that man's good has already been provided by his own form and constitution. We have presumed instead that what becomes of a man or woman depends upon what society will do for him or her. As a consequence, the natural and necessary instruments of peace and prosperity are systematically disregarded in favor of constructivist attempts to remake humanity by governmental means. We saw that tendency in Roosevelt and his successors. We know, too, that it lies at the heart of a secular approach to the question of humanity. Oddly, and even paradoxically, we suffer from a disposition to rely upon human self-sufficiency to create human meaning, while disregarding the evidence that the individual human is already invested with the powers needed to earn a repose "under his own vine and fig tree."

5

WHOSE FOURTH OF JULY?

Black Patriotism and Racial Inequality in America

Glenn C. Loury

Introduction

I am a black American intellectual living in an age of persistent racial inequality in my country. As a black man, I feel compelled to represent the interests of "my people." (But that reference is not unambiguous!) As an intellectual, I feel that I must seek out the truth and speak such truths as I am given to know. As an American, at this critical moment of "racial reckoning," I feel that imperative all the more urgently. But, I ask, what are my responsibilities? Do they conflict with one another? My conclusion is this: My responsibilities as a black man, as an American, and as an intellectual are not in conflict.

Moreover, I think a case can be made for unabashed black patriotism, for a forthright embrace of American nationalism by

This chapter is adapted from a lecture delivered at the University of Colorado Boulder on February 8, 2021, the text of which was published on *Quillette* under the title "Unspeakable Truths about Racial Inequality in America"; and a lecture entitled "Whose Fourth of July? Blacks and the American Project," hosted by Arizona State University's School of Civic and Economic Thought and Leadership (SCETL) on February 1, 2021, the text of which was published in *City Journal* under the title "The Case for Black Patriotism."

black people. Accordingly, I doubt whether the currently fashionable standoffishness characteristic of much elite thinking about blacks' relationship to the American project—as exemplified, for instance, by the *New York Times*'s 1619 Project—serves the interests, rightly understood, of black Americans. The "America ain't all it's cracked up to be" posture is, in my view, a sophomoric indulgence for blacks at this late date. In fact, our birthright citizenship in what is arguably history's greatest republic is an inheritance of immense value. So my answer for black Americans to Frederick Douglass's famous question of 1852, posed anew in the title of this essay, is: "Ours!"

I defend this as best I can in what follows. After elaborating on the dilemma at hand, I illustrate the insufficiencies of the dominant narrative, highlighting in particular the threat "cancel culture" poses to a rational discourse about racial inequality that our country now so desperately requires. I do this by enunciating out loud what have increasingly become some unspeakable truths—so brace yourselves! I then build a positive case for black patriotism that is rooted in an understanding of the nature of the American project. I propose this sort of patriotism as a model for how an intellectual who truly loves "his people" should respond to racial inequality.

The Challenge Posed to the Black Intellectual

I begin with a provocation: Consider this story from my hometown newspaper, the *Chicago Sun-Times*, that ran on May 31, 2016. (Things have only gotten worse since.) I ask you to bear with me here because these details matter. We must look them squarely in the face:

> Six people were killed, including a 15-year-old girl, and at least 63 others were wounded in shootings across Chicago over Memorial Day weekend.

The total number of people shot during the weekend this year surpassed the 2015 holiday, when 55 people were shot, 12 fatally, over Memorial Day weekend.

The most recent homicide happened late Monday in the Washington Park neighborhood on the South Side.

Officers responding to a call of shots fired about 11 p.m. found James Taylor lying on the ground near his vehicle in the 5100 block of South Calumet, according to Chicago Police and the Cook County medical examiner's office. Taylor, who lived in the 6500 block of South Ellis, had been shot in the chest and was pronounced dead at the scene, authorities said.

Witnesses at the scene were not cooperating with detectives.

About the same time, a man was shot to death in the West Rogers Park neighborhood on the North Side.

Officers responding to a call of shots fired about 11 p.m. found 39-year-old Johan Jean lying in a gangway in the 6400 block of North Rockwell, authorities said.

Jean, who lived in the 100 block of North Ashland in Evanston, was shot in the neck and taken to Presence Saint Francis Hospital in Evanston, where he was later pronounced dead, authorities said. Police said he was 25 years old.

A source said the shooting stemmed from a dispute between two women. One of them has a child with the man and the other was his girlfriend. Both women were armed, and the man was eventually shot during the argument. No weapons were recovered from the scene.

About 5:20 p.m. Saturday, a man was shot to death in the Fuller Park neighborhood on the South Side.

Garvin Whitmore, 27, was sitting in the driver seat of a vehicle with a passenger, 26-year-old Ashley Harrison, in the 200 block of West Root, when someone walked up to the vehicle and shot him in the head, according to police and the medical examiner's office.

Whitmore, of the 5800 block of West 63rd Place, was pronounced dead at the scene at 5:29 p.m., authorities said.[1]

All of the victims who died were black people. Sixty-three shot, six dead, one weekend, one city. Here's the thing: Reports such as this could be multiplied dozens of times, effortlessly. If a black intellectual truly believes that "Black Lives Matter," then what is he supposed to say in response to such nauseating reports—that "there is nothing to see here"? I think not.

Violence on such a scale involving blacks as both perpetrators and victims poses a dilemma to someone like myself. On the one hand, as the Harvard legal scholar Randall Kennedy has observed, we elites need to represent the decent law-abiding majority of African Americans cowering fearfully inside their homes in the face of such violence. We must do so not just to enhance our group's reputation, as in the "politics of respectability," but mainly as a precondition for our own dignity and self-respect.[2]

On the other hand, we elites must also counter the demonization of young black men which the larger American culture has for some time now been feverishly engaged in. Even as we condemn murderers, we cannot help but view with sympathy the plight of many poor youngsters who, though not incorrigible, have nevertheless committed crimes. We must wrestle with complex historical and contemporary causes internal and external to the black experience that help to account for this pathology. (There's no way around it—this is pathology. The behavior in question here is not okay. That one can adduce social-psychological explanations does not resolve all moral questions.)

Where is the self-respecting black intellectual to take his stand? Must he simply act as a mouthpiece for movement propaganda aiming to counteract "white supremacy"? Has he anything to say to his own people about how some of us are living? Is there space in American public discourses for nuanced, subtle, sophisticated moral engagement with these questions? Or are they mere fodder for what amount to tendentious, cynical, and overtly politically partisan arguments on behalf of something called "racial equity"? And what about those so-called "white intellectuals"? Do they have to remain mute? Alternatively, must they limit themselves to incanting antiracist slogans?

I don't know all the answers here, but I know that those victims in Chicago had names. I know they had families. I know they did not deserve their fate. I know that black intellectuals must bear witness to what is actually taking place in our midst; must wrestle with complex historical and contemporary causes both within and outside the black community that bear on these tragedies; must tell truths about what is happening instead of hiding from the truth with platitudes, euphemisms, and lies.

I know that, despite whatever causal factors may be at play, we black intellectuals must insist that each youngster is capable of choosing a moral way of life. I know that, for the sake of the dignity and self-respect of my people as well as for the future of my country, we American intellectuals of all colors must never lose sight of what a moral way of life consists of. And yet I fear we are in imminent danger of doing precisely that. I will explain why this is the case by way of several unspeakable truths.

On Racial Disparity

My first unspeakable truth is this: Downplaying behavioral disparities by race is actually a bluff. Socially mediated behavioral issues lie at the root of today's racial inequality problem. They are real and must be faced squarely if we are to grasp why racial disparities persist. This is a painful necessity. Activists on the Left of American politics claim that "white supremacy," "implicit bias," and old-fashioned "antiblack racism" are sufficient to account for black disadvantage. But this is a bluff that relies on "cancel culture" to be sustained. Those making such arguments are, in effect, daring you to disagree with them. They are threatening to "cancel" you if you do not accept their account: You must be a "racist," one who thinks something is intrinsically wrong with black people, if you do not attribute pathological behavior among them to systemic injustice. You must think blacks are inferior, for how else could one explain the disparities? Thus, you will be convicted of the offense of "blaming the victim."

I claim this is a dare, a debater's trick. At the end of the day, what are those folks saying when they declare that "mass incarceration" is "racism"—that the high number of blacks in jails is a self-evident sign of racial antipathy? To respond, "No. It's mainly a sign of anti-social behavior by criminals who happen to be black," one risks being dismissed as a moral reprobate. This is so even if the speaker is black. Just ask Justice Clarence Thomas: No one is immune from cancellation.

But we should all want to stay in touch with reality. Common sense and much evidence suggest that, on the whole, people are not being arrested, convicted, and sentenced because of their race. Those in prison are mainly those who have broken the law—who have hurt others, stolen things, or otherwise violated the basic behavioral norms which make civil society possible. Seeing prisons as a racist conspiracy to confine black people is an absurd proposition. No serious person could really believe it. Indeed, it is self-evident that those taking lives on the streets of St. Louis, Baltimore, Philadelphia, and Chicago are, to a man, behaving despicably. Moreover, those bearing the cost of such pathology are almost exclusively other blacks. An ideology that ascribes this violent behavior to racism is laughable. Of course, this is an unspeakable truth—but no writer or social critic, of whatever race, should be canceled for voicing it.

Or consider the educational achievement gap. Antiracism advocates, in effect, are daring you to notice that some groups send their children to elite colleges and universities in outsized numbers compared to other groups due to the fact that their academic preparation is magnitudes higher, better, and finer. They are daring you to declare such excellence to be an admirable achievement. Intellectual mastery is achieved only through effort; no one is born already possessing it. So why are some youngsters acquiring these skills and others not? That is a very deep and interesting question, one which I am quite prepared to entertain. But the simple retort, "racism," is laughable—as if such disparities have nothing to do with behavior, with cultural patterns, with what peer groups value, with how people spend their time, or with what they identify as being critical to their own self-respect. I maintain that anyone who actually believes such nonsense is a fool.

According to the politically correct script, Asians are sardonically called a "model minority." Well, as a matter of fact, a pretty compelling case can be made that "culture" is critical to their success. If you are unconvinced, read Jennifer Lee and Min Zhou's book *The Asian American Achievement Paradox*.[3] They have interviewed Asian families in Southern California, trying to learn how their children are being accepted into Dartmouth, Columbia, and Cornell at such high rates. They find that these families exhibit cultural patterns, embrace values, adopt practices, engage in behavior, and follow disciplines that orient them in such a way as to facilitate the achievements of their children. It defies common sense, as well as the evidence, to assert that they do not. Conversely, it is absurd to assert that the paucity of African Americans performing near the top of the intellectual spectrum—I am talking here about academic excellence, and about the low relative numbers of blacks who exhibit it—has nothing to do with the behavior of black people and is due to institutional forces alone. No serious person could believe this.

Nor does anybody actually believe that 70 percent of African American babies being born to a woman without a husband is (1) a good thing or (2) due to antiblack racism. People say this, but they don't believe it. They are bluffing—daring you to observe that the twenty-first-century failures of African Americans to take full advantage of the opportunities created by the twentieth century's revolution of civil rights are palpable and damning. These failures are being denied at every turn, and these denials are sustained by a threat to "cancel" dissenters for being "racists." This position is simply not tenable. The end of Jim Crow segregation and the advent of the era of equal rights was transformative for blacks. And now—a half-century down the line—we still have significant disparities. I agree that this is a shameful blight on American society. But the plain fact of the matter is that some considerable responsibility for this sorry state of affairs lies with black people ourselves. Dare we Americans acknowledge this?

Leftist critics tout the racial wealth gap. They act as if pointing to the absence of wealth in the African American community is, *ipso facto*, an indictment of the system—even as black Caribbean and African immigrants are starting businesses, penetrating the professions, presenting themselves at Ivy League institutions in outsize numbers, and so forth.[4] In doing so, they behave like other immigrant groups in our nation's past. Yes, they are immigrants, not natives. And yes, immigration can be positively selective. Still, something is dreadfully wrong when adverse patterns of behavior readily visible in the native-born black American population cannot adequately be discussed—to the point that anybody daring to mention them risks being canceled as a racist. This bluff can't be sustained indefinitely. Despite the outcome of the 2020 election, I believe we are already beginning to see the collapse of this house of cards.

On the Meaninglessness of "Structural Racism"

The invocation of "structural racism" in political argument is both a bluff and a bludgeon. It is a bluff in the sense that it offers an "explanation" that is not an explanation at all and effectively dares the listener to come back. For example, if someone says, "There are too many blacks in prison in the United States, and that's due to structural racism," what you're being dared to say is, "No. Many blacks are criminals, and that's why there are so many in prison. It's their fault, not the system's fault." And it is a bludgeon in the sense that use of the phrase is mainly a rhetorical move. Users don't even pretend to offer evidence-based arguments beyond citing the fact of the racial disparity itself. The "structural racism" argument seldom goes into cause and effect. Rather, it asserts shadowy causes that are never fully specified, let alone demonstrated. We are all just supposed to know that it's the fault of something called "structural racism," abetted by an environment of "white privilege," furthered by an ideology of "white supremacy" that purportedly characterizes our society. Any racial disparity, then, can be totally explained by the imputation of "structural racism."

History, I would argue, is rather more complicated than such stories would suggest. Racial disparities have multiple interwoven and interacting causes, encompassing culture, politics, economics, historical accident, environmental influence, and yes, even the nefarious doings of particular actors who may or may not be "racists," as well as systems of law and policy that disadvantage some groups without having been so intended. I want to know what people are talking about when they say "structural racism." In effect, use of the term expresses a disposition and a sentiment. It calls me to solidarity. It asks for my fealty, for my affirmation of a system of belief, without actually explaining the historical phenomenon. It's a very mischievous way of talking, especially in a university, although I can certainly understand why it might work well on Twitter.

Let me give an example. During the New Orleans floods, low-lying areas were the first to get wiped out. Blacks were over-represented among those who were dispossessed by the floods because they are poorer, and housing is more affordable in low-lying areas. But it would be a stretch to say that the flood itself was a racist event. One might choose to tell a racial narrative about it. One might emphasize, for example, that blacks are poorer because of a history of racism. But what would this accomplish? If I really wanted to remedy the racially disparate effects of the flood, I would address myself to poverty—even to white poverty, should it fall within my purview. I do not see the necessary connection between the existence of extreme inequality, which is real enough, and the existence of systemic racism. I prefer to go on a case-by-case basis. If one wishes to impress upon me that the effects of the New Orleans flood reflect systemic racism, I am not going to argue with him about the use of those words. But that doesn't give me a clue what to do about it.

On the Racialization of Police Violence

Another unspeakable truth: We must put the police killings of black Americans into perspective. There are about 1,200 fatal shootings of people by the police in the United States each year, according to the carefully documented database kept by the *Washington Post* which attempts to enumerate every single instance of a fatal police shooting.[5] Roughly 300 of those killed are African Americans, about one-fourth, while blacks are about 13 percent of the population. That's an overrepresentation, though still far less than a majority of the people who are killed. (That's right, more whites than blacks are killed by police in the country every year. You wouldn't know that from the activists' rhetoric.)

Now, 1,200 may be too many. I am prepared to entertain that idea. I would be happy to discuss the training and recruitment of police, their rules of engagement with citizens, and the accountability that they should face in the event they overstep their authority. These are all legitimate questions. And there is a racial disparity—although, as I have noted, there is also a disparity in blacks' rate of participation in criminal activity. I am making no claims here, one way or the other, about the existence of discrimination against blacks in the police use of force. This is a debate on which evidence could be brought to bear. There may well be some racial discrimination in police use of force, especially nonlethal force.

But in terms of police killings, we are talking about 300 black victims per year. Not all of these are unarmed innocents. Some are engaged in violent conflict with police officers that leads to them being killed. Some are instances like George Floyd—unquestionably problematic in the extreme—that deserve the scrutiny of concerned persons. Still, we need to bear in mind that this is a country of more than 300 million people with scores of concentrated urban areas where police regularly interact with citizens. Tens of thousands of arrests occur daily in the United States. So, these events—which are extremely regrettable and often do not reflect well on the police—are, nevertheless, quite rare.

To put it in perspective, there are about 17,000 homicides in the United States every year, *nearly half of which involve black perpetrators*. The vast majority of those have other blacks as victims. For every black killed by the police, more than twenty-five other black people meet their end because of homicides committed by other blacks.[6] This is not to ignore the significance of holding police accountable for how they exercise their power vis-à-vis citizens. It is merely to notice how very easy it is to overstate the significance and the extent of this phenomenon, precisely as the Black Lives Matter activists have done.

Thus, the narrative that something called "white supremacy" and "systemic racism" has put a metaphorical "knee on the neck" of black America is simply false. The idea that as a black person I dare not step from my door for fear that the police would round me up, gun me down, or bludgeon me to death because of my race is simply ridiculous. That is like not going outdoors for fear of being struck by lightning. This tendentious posture toward all incidents where violent conflict emerges between police and an African American, such that each is interpreted as the latter-day instantiation of the lynching of Emmett Till, is simply preposterous. Fear of being "canceled" is the only thing that keeps many white people outside of the alt-Right from saying so out loud. "White silence" about racism is not "violence," nor is it tacit agreement. But in the era of cancel culture, it should worry us nonetheless.

I also want to stress the dangers of seeing police killings primarily through a racial lens. These events are regrettable regardless of the race of the people involved. Invoking race—emphasizing that the officer is white, and the victim is black—tacitly presumes that the reason the officer acted as he did was because the dead young man was black, and we do not necessarily know that. Moreover, once we get into the habit of racializing these events, we may not be able to contain that racialization merely to instances of white police officers killing black citizens. We may find ourselves soon enough in a world where we racialize instances of black criminals killing unarmed white victims—a world no thoughtful person should welcome, since there are a great many such instances. Framing them in racial terms is counterproductive in ways too obvious to detail.

When criminals harm people, they should be dealt with accordingly. They do not represent others of their race when they act badly. White victims of crimes committed by blacks ought not to see themselves mainly in racial terms if someone steals their automobile, beats them up, takes their wallet, breaks into their home, or abuses them. But people are playing with fire when they gratuitously bring a racial sensibility to police-citizen interaction. That will not be the end of the story.

On the Threat of White Backlash

Yet another unspeakable truth: There is a dark side to the "white fragility" blame game. I suspect that what we are hearing from the progressives in the academy and the media is but one side of the "whiteness" card. I wonder if the ideology dominated by the terms "white guilt," "white apologia," and "white privilege" cannot exist except also to give birth to a "white pride" backlash, even if the latter is seldom expressed overtly—since it is politically incorrect to do so.

Confronted by someone who is constantly bludgeoning me about the evils of colonialism, urging me to tear down the statues of "dead white men," insisting that I apologize for what my white forebears did to the "peoples of color" in years past, and demanding that I settle my historical indebtedness via reparations, I well might begin to ask myself, were I one of these "white oppressors": On exactly what foundations does human civilization in the twenty-first century stand? I might begin to enumerate the great works of philosophy, mathematics, and science that ushered in the "Age of Enlightenment," that allowed modern medicine to exist, that gave rise to the core of human knowledge about the origins of the species and the universe. I might begin to tick off the great artistic achievements of European culture: the architectural innovations, the paintings, the symphonies. And then, were I in a particularly agitated mood, I might even ask these "people of color," who think that they can simply bully me into a state of guilt-ridden self-loathing: "Where is 'your' civilization?"

Everything I just said exemplifies "racist" and "white suprema-cist" rhetoric. I wish to stipulate that I would never actually say something like that myself, nor am I attempting to justify that position. I am simply noticing that, if I were a white person, this reasoning might tempt me—and I suspect it is tempting a great many white people. We can wag our fingers at them all we want, but they are a part of the racism-monger's package. How can we make "whiteness" into a site of unrelenting moral indict-ment without also occasioning it to become the basis of pride, of identity, and ultimately, of self-affirmation?

One risks cancellation for saying this, but the right idea is that of Gandhi and Martin Luther King Jr., which today is being propounded by folks like Thomas Chatterton Williams: that we must transcend our racial particularism and stress the universality of our humanity. That is, the right idea is to march on—if only fitfully and by degrees—toward the goal of "race-blindness," toward a world where no person's worth is seen to be contingent upon racial inheritance. This is the only way to effectively address a legacy of historical racism without running into a reactionary chauvinism. Promoting anti-whiteness (and Black Lives Matter often seems to flirt with this) may cause one to reap what one sows in a backlash of pro-whiteness. Here we have yet another unspeakable truth which, as a responsible black intellectual, I have a duty to report.

On the Unspeakable Infantilization of "Black Fragility"

I would add that there is an assumption of "black fragility," or at least of black lack of resilience, lurking behind these antiracism arguments. Blacks are being treated like infants whom one dares not to touch. One dares not say the wrong word in front of us, ask any question that might offend us, or demand anything from us, for fear that we will be adversely impacted. The presumption is that black people cannot be disagreed with, criticized, called to account, or asked for anything. Much is said about what America owes us—reparations for slavery, for example. But no one asks black people, "What do you owe America?" How about duty? How about honor?

When you take agency away from people, you remove the possibility of holding them to account, of making judgments about their behavior according to fixed standards. If a youngster who happens to be black has no choice whether or not to join a gang, pick up a gun, and become a criminal, since society has failed him by not providing adequate housing, health care, income support, or job opportunities, then it becomes impossible to effectively discriminate between the black youngsters who do and do not pick up guns and become members of a gang in those conditions. It also becomes impossible to maintain within African American society a judgment of our fellows' behavior and to affirm expectations of right-living. After all, every one of us is the victim of antiblack racism. The end result of all this is that we are leveled down morally by a presumed lack of control over our lives and lack of accountability for what we do.

What is more, there is a deep irony in first declaring white America to be systemically racist, then mounting a campaign to demand that whites recognize their own racism and deliver blacks from its consequences. I want to say to such advocates: "If, indeed, you are right that your oppressors are racists, why would you expect them to respond to your moral appeal? You are putting yourself on the mercy of the court while simultaneously decrying the court as unrelentingly biased." The logic of such advocacy escapes me. I can only conclude that this is not really about effecting a political outcome. This is about performance, about emotional display. It succeeds in soliciting a positive response from white people who don't want to be called racist or don't want to be on the wrong side of history—and, we might add, from corporations that want good branding. Meanwhile, those who condemn our white supremacist society and its indifference to black humanity ignore the very fact of their own power. They continue to make an appeal the effectiveness of which is negated by the very premises of their argument.

On Wokeness in the University

A particularly troubling fact about all these "unspeakable truths" is that they are now unspeakable even within, and perhaps *especially* within, the university. It ought to be the place of the university to think through difficult matters. Fundamentally, was what happened to George Floyd in Minneapolis a racial incident in continuous historical connection with other incidents of lynching and physical abuse of black people by the authorities? I declare here and now that that's an arguable question. I am not trying to decide it; I am merely pointing out that reasonable people could take different positions on that question. To what extent is the overrepresentation of African Americans in the criminal justice system a consequence of the failures of the development of African American personality in a large swath of the low-income population because of structures of social organization characteristic of the community? To what extent are the incidents of police violence involving black men embedded within a structure of police-citizen interaction freighted with the overrepresentation of African Americans among violent criminal offenders? Or to what extent are the mechanisms of advocacy, fundraising, activism, and organization fostering backlash as they interact with the political institutions in the United States? Dare we even tolerate inquiry of such a kind?

The university should be trying to facilitate rational deliberation about these questions. But in today's climate, it is much easier to wave a banner or jump on a bandwagon. So the university champions diversity and inclusion. It redoubles its efforts to increase black faculty. It enhances its affirmative action program. It interrogates the curriculum to see whether it comports with this or that fad and fancy prescribing the "appropriate" way of talking about race. But I say to universities: If you really want to take a stand on racial inequality, take a stand on behalf of an analytical and rational examination of questions that people ordinarily approach from emotion. The university should be a safe space for political incorrectness, for trafficking in ideas that make one uncomfortable. Why set up an enclave outside of the influences of day-to-day commercial activity, a citadel where open inquiry and balanced reflection can take place, then freight it with endless moral virtue signaling?

The last thing I will say regarding the university is that hiring black (or any other attributive character) faculty is not an effective response to racial inequality in America. It may or may not be a good thing; we can debate that. But if you think you are remedying racial inequality in America when you start head-counting in one of the most elite venues of the society, you are wildly mistaken. What you are actually responding to is the self-interested advocacy of particular groups of people (who happen to be minorities) on behalf of their own professional interest. You're not addressing the question of racial inequality which is reflected in the lives of the millions of black and brown people who are at the bottom of society, who are trapped in enclaves devoid of opportunity, who have to attend failing schools, who fear for their physical safety when they step outside, who are hungry, who don't have good housing, who lack good health care in a pandemic. Counting the color of the faculty members at an elite university is a luxury, a sophistic indulgence. It's not a deep issue of social justice.

Racial Equality and the American Project

Having assessed the inadequacies of the current discourse around race, it is now time to consider how we might achieve "true equality" for black Americans. It is first crucial to address competing narratives about the American project, for the narrative that we blacks settle on is fundamentally important. Is this, basically, a good country that affords boundless opportunity to all who are fortunate enough to enjoy the privileges and bear the responsibilities of American citizenship? Or is this, basically, a venal, immoral, and rapacious bandit-society of plundering white supremacists, founded in genocide and slavery and propelled by capitalist greed and unrepentant racism? Of course, there is some warrant in the historical record for both sentiments, but the weight of the evidence overwhelmingly favors the former. I wish to argue that the founding of the United States of America was a world-historic event by means of which Enlightenment ideals about the rights of individual persons and the legitimacy of state power were instantiated for the first time in real institutions. To this extent, what happened in 1776 was vastly more significant for world history than what happened in 1619.

The United States of America fought fascism in the Pacific and Europe in the mid-twentieth century, and thereby helped to save the world. Our democracy, flawed as it most surely is, nevertheless became a beacon to billions of people throughout what came to be known as "the free world." We stood down, under the threat of nuclear annihilation, the horror which was the Union of Soviet Socialist Republics. Moreover, here in America, we have witnessed since the end of the Civil War the greatest transformation in the status of an enserfed people (which was what emancipation of the slaves effected in the creation of what came to be called the American Negro) that is to be found anywhere in world history.

Some forty million strong, we have become by far the richest and most powerful population of African descent on the planet. The issue, then, is a question of narrative. Are we going to look through the dark lens of the United States as a racist, genocidal, white supremacist, illegitimate force? Or are we to see our nation for what it has become over the course of the last three centuries—that is, the greatest force for human liberty on the planet? This conflict of narratives is worth fighting about—with Black Lives Matter activists, with Colin Kaepernick and his cohorts, with the editorial staff of the *New York Times*, and with those officials who exercise power in the presidential administration of Joseph R. Biden.

The narrative we choose will influence our assessment of certain key periods in American history. There is, of course, the Civil War, which left 600,000 dead in a country of 30 million. The incredible trauma of this event was felt for decades. Now, people will say that the war wasn't fought to end slavery—it was fought to preserve the union. Lincoln, they say, would have been happy to see the union preserved even if slavery had persisted.[7] I expect that this is correct, although he surely abhorred slavery. But the fact is that the consequence of that war, together with the Thirteenth, Fourteenth, and Fifteenth Amendments to the U.S. Constitution enacted just afterward, was to make chattel—the African slaves and their descendants—into citizens. And in the fullness of time, they became *equal* citizens. Should it have taken a hundred years? No. Should they have been enslaved in the first place? No, they ought not to have been. But we must not forget that slavery had been a commonplace human experience since antiquity. Emancipation—the freeing of slaves *en masse* as the result of a movement for abolition—*that* was a new idea. It was a Western idea, the fruit of Enlightenment, that was brought to fruition over a century and a half ago in our own United States of America with the liberation of millions of people. Such an achievement surely would not have been possible without the philosophical insights and moral commitments cultivated in the seventeenth and eighteenth centuries in the West—ideas about the essential dignity of human persons, and about what can legitimate a government's exercise of power over its people. Something new was created in America at the end of the eighteenth century. Slavery was a holocaust out of which emerged something that advanced the morality and the dignity of humankind—namely, emancipation. The abolition of slavery and the incorporation of Africa-descended people into the body politic of the United States of America was an unprecedented and world-historic achievement.

Consider also the astonishing transformation of status for black Americans in the twentieth century. To those who pooh-pooh the American Dream as irrelevant to blacks (or worse), I wish to say the following: "Have you bothered to notice what has happened here in the United States in the last century?" In the mid-twentieth century, the modal occupation for African American men was farm laborer, and the typical occupation of African American women was domestic servant. The median family income of blacks was significantly lower than that of whites. The status of African American education, of African American voting rights and citizenship, and of African American access to the professions was abysmal. This was the case within my own lifetime.[8]

But look at what has happened in the last seventy-five years for African Americans. A huge middle class has developed. There are black billionaires. The influence of black people on American culture is stunning and has global resonance. Black Americans are the richest and most powerful people in large numbers of African descent on the planet. To put it into perspective, there are 200 million Nigerians, and the gross national product of Nigeria is just about $1 trillion per year. America's GNP is over $20 trillion a year, and we 40 million African Americans have claim to roughly 8 to 10 percent of it. Thus, we have access to five times the income of a typical Nigerian. What is more, the very fact that the cultural barons and elites of America—those who run the *New York Times* and the *Washington Post*, who give out Pulitzer Prizes and National Book Awards, who make the grants at the MacArthur Foundation, who run the human resource departments of corporate America—have bought into the woke racial sensibility hook, line, and sinker gives the lie to such pessimism that the American Dream doesn't apply to blacks. It most certainly and emphatically does apply, and it is coming to fruition daily. To dismiss this reality is to tell our children a lie.

Of course, highlighting the progress we have witnessed does not in itself answer the question at hand: How do we overcome the obstacles that still remain to racial equality in America? I am reminded, amid the contemporary turmoil, of the period after the Emancipation, more than 150 years ago. There was a brief moment of pro-freedmen sentiment during Reconstruction, in the immediate aftermath of the Civil War, but it was eclipsed by the long, dark night of Jim Crow. Blacks were set back. Yet in the wake of this setback emerged some of the greatest achievements of African American history. The freedmen who had been liberated from slavery in 1863 were almost universally illiterate. Within a half-century, their increased literacy rate rivaled anything that has been seen, in terms of a mass population acquiring the capacity to read.[9] That was really very significant, for it helped bring them into the modern world.

We now look at the black family and lament the high rate of births to unmarried mothers and so forth. But that is a modern, post-1960 phenomenon. In fact, the health of the African American social fiber coming out of slavery was remarkable. The evidence for this is well-documented. Businesses were built. People acquired land and skills. People educated their children. They constantly faced opposition at every step along the way—"No blacks need apply," "White only," this and that and the other—but nevertheless they built a foundation from which the civil rights movement would eventually launch in the mid-twentieth century. And that movement definitively changed the politics of the country.[10] As my friend Robert Woodson is fond of saying, "When whites were at their worst, we blacks were at our best." Such potentiality seems now to have been forgotten as we throw ourselves on the mercy of the court. "There's nothing we can do," we say. "We're prostrate here. Our kids are not doing as well, our communities are troubled, and we demand that you save us."

This is the very same population about which a noble history of extraordinary accomplishment under unimaginably adverse conditions can be told. "Pull yourself up by the bootstraps" is a kind of cliché, and people will laugh and roll their eyes when you say it. But there is wisdom to be gleaned here. Take responsibility for your life, because no one is coming to save you. It's nobody else's job to raise your children. It's nobody else's job to pick the trash up from in front of your home. No, it's not fair. But the expectation of fairness is another kind of delusion. People think there is some benevolent being in the sky who will make sure everything works out fairly, but it is not so. Life is full of tragedy, atrocity, and barbarity. This is not right, but it is the way of the world.

We are, of course, warranted in claiming certain rights as citizens of the United States. The right to be treated without discrimination and to be afforded the privileges and immunities of citizenship—that is an endowment protected by civil rights law (and necessarily so). Nevertheless, our jails are overflowing with brown men and women who have been found guilty under criminal law. This is only in small part a reflection of overt discriminatory treatment. It is in main part a reflection of huge disparities in the behavior of individuals in terms of criminal offending. There are complex historical reasons for those disparities, and the depredations of economic discrimination against generations past should be cited as one of them. But what are you actually going to *do* about the disparity? Well, you can tinker with the law. You can make drug offending a misdemeanor instead of a felony. You can try to improve the behavior of police. But at the end of the day, if you have too many kids running around firing guns at each other in gang disputes, you are unequal in that respect. Likewise for the racial disparities in the proficiency of reading and mathematics of adolescent Americans. You want to do something about that? We can have a debate about types of schooling, budgets, and whatnot, but ultimately, no one can educate your children for you. The responsibility belongs to the community.

It is not only futile but dangerous to rely on others to shoulder our communal responsibilities. For if we rely on others to come to our rescue, we are putting ourselves into an unequal, asymmetric relationship in which there is a patron and a client. The patron is the moral agent, because he has the capacity to respond to or refuse our demand. And the patron is the possessor of power, because he has the power to determine whether or not we have a better outcome. When we as black people allow ourselves to be patronized, then, we are stripped of both moral agency and power. This, it ought to be clear, is antithetical to the goal of racial equality.

Here, then, is my final unspeakable truth, which I utter now in defiance of "cancel culture": If we blacks want to walk with dignity—if we want to be truly equal—then we must realize that white people cannot give us equality. We actually have to seize equal status. I feel obliged to report that equality of dignity, equality of standing, equality of honor, equality of security in one's position in society, equality of being able to command the respect of others—this is not something that can be simply handed over. Rather, it is something that we have to wrest with our bare hands from a cruel and indifferent world with hard work, inspired by the example of our enslaved and newly freed ancestors. We have to make ourselves equal. No one can do it for us.

Conclusion

Black Americans face profound, existential challenges. Fortunately, we have the benefit of doing so while residing in a free, prosperous, decent, and open democratic society. There is nothing contradictory or oxymoronic about declaring oneself, at one and the same time, a black freedom fighter and an American patriot. Moreover, black Americans face an unparalleled opportunity: the opportunity to save the prospect of freedom in the United States. For it may be fairly stated that this incredible nation may not otherwise survive.

Those who want to take Abraham Lincoln's name off school buildings do not really understand the foundations of their own security and prosperity. Likewise, they fail to recognize the most effective way to advance their best interests in the twenty-first century. We need the country to solve the problem of racial inequality. Why gratuitously invoke an antinationalist stance on behalf of a project which requires national collaboration in order to bear fruit?

The root of the issue is whether we should, in some important sense, *love* this republic of which we are birthright citizens. I am not talking about blind fealty. I am asking if we should embrace the project as ours rather than defining ourselves in opposition to it. I believe if we look critically at the American project, understanding what it actually represents in the development of human civilization over the last five hundred years, we will recognize that the constitutional republic which is the United States of America constitutes a context within which our aspirations for freedom and equality can be most effectively realized. Therefore, it deserves to be endorsed, supported, embraced, loved, fought for, and died for (heaven forbid it should come to that). This is true for African Americans every bit as much as everybody else.

To conclude, let me call your attention once again to that escaped slave and great abolitionist, Frederick Douglass, who in 1852 asked America whether he had a share in the nation's inheritance. Douglass was cautiously hopeful about the prospect that America might be faithful to its founding principles and grant liberty and equality to his people. But he had to plead with his audience to consider the gravity of the circumstance; he had to indict his country for not standing up to its own ideals. That was in the 1850s. Here we are now in the year 2022. The question that Frederick Douglass posed, which was still an open one at the time, has been answered by history: The Fourth of July belongs to all of us. The question confronting black Americans in 2022, then, is not whether we are included within the body politic of the United States; we most emphatically are. The great challenge before us is to decide what we will make of this enormous civic inheritance.

6

CREATING AN OPPORTUNITY SOCIETY AND UPWARD MOBILITY FOR THE BLACK COMMUNITY AND PEOPLE OF ALL RACES

Ian V. Rowe

Introduction

There is no singular state of black America. Like any other assemblage of individuals artificially grouped together, each African American person may be a native-born American, Jamaican immigrant American, Sudanese refugee American, wealthy American, impoverished American, female American, male American, homeless American, mansioned American, married American, single American, religious American, atheist American, gay American, straight American, married parent American, single parent American, college-educated American, former American president, current American vice president, American Supreme Court justice, urban American, suburban American, or any of a myriad of characteristics that can shape his or her status as an American.

Beyond the aforementioned attributes, the state of each of these black individuals with hyphenated American identities is further differentiated by the range of personal decisions made daily on matters large and small. Do I exercise versus sit in front of the TV, or read a book versus doomscroll for hours, or eat more healthily versus dine at McDonald's, or play with my kids versus work until past their bedtime, or obey the law versus commit a crime, or walk versus drive, etc.? The daily choices are endless. The point is that the status of any random black American (like any human being) depends largely on a wide range of individual factors like mindset, behaviors, and skills that cumulatively far outpace the impact of the lone dimension of race.

Yet when it comes to discussing matters of race, too often black people are denied the dignity of being responsible for the individual choices we make that are the most direct causes toward whatever effects we may experience in our own individual lives. This tendency to treat individual black people as just stand-ins for a larger group identity—i.e., "black America"—is particularly true today as the United States is undergoing a national reckoning on race.

Since the death of George Floyd in 2020, caused by a police officer now convicted for his murder, America has been immersed in a long-awaited "national conversation about race." Protests in the streets declaring ACAB (All Cops Are Bastards), demands for defunding and demilitarizing the police, calls for criminal justice reform—all have become part of a new rallying cry for racial justice. The debate is the extent to which innocent black people are being hunted by white police officers who are part of a systemically racist system and who unlawfully use deadly force as a form of state-sponsored terrorism against black Americans, regardless of the circumstances of the specific incidents that fuel much of the attention.

Beyond policing, the "national conversation" is forcing virtually every institution in the United States to examine its policies, practices, and procedures regarding race. From education to health care to housing, and even to bird naming[1] and rock climbing,[2] everywhere it seems is a search for racism that is not solely interpersonal, but carries with it one of the omnipresent adjectives of *structural, endemic, systemic, embedded, enshrined,* or *institutional.* This "blame-the-system" ideology is driven by the assumption that forms of structural discrimination based on race, class, gender, and other identity markers combine to form a fortress of intersectionality, too tall for (especially black) individuals to prosper across generations. America's ingrained past, present, and future racism, sexism, classism, and every other type of -ism together rob young (especially black) people of the ability to be *masters of their own fate,* and render them powerless as adults to become agents of their own uplift.

In a blame-the-system worldview, a network of oppressive structures just happens *to* entrenched, *marginalized* (especially black) populations that have no recourse but to submit. Black people are essentially treated as if they are mere hapless participants, victims of racist systems that exert an insurmountable, discriminatory force that is beyond the control of those with darker skin color to overcome.

Thus, rather than a focus on ensuring equal opportunity for individual black Americans or extolling the virtues of hard work, the focus is increasingly on forcing institutions to achieve racial "equity" at the group level, usually between black and white Americans.

This form of "equity" is usually defined as the absence of disparities in either: (a) the difference between black and white proportional or absolute achievement, or (b) the difference in the percent of black people represented in an institution versus the percent of black people in the population. Either way, achieving "racial equity" sets a ceiling on black achievement, which is a reprehensible objective. This quest for "racial equity" is forcing society to look at racial disparities in an array of categories—such as lower black performance levels relative to whites in educational outcomes, incarceration rates, poverty levels, upward mobility, etc.—and to demand a causal explanation as to why these disparities exist and persist.

For example, the Federal Reserve recently released the report "Disparities in Wealth by Race and Ethnicity in the 2019 Survey of Consumer Finances," which announced the following:

> In the 2019 survey, White families have the highest level of both median and mean family wealth: $188,200 and $983,400, respectively (Figure 1). Black and Hispanic families have considerably less wealth than White families. Black families' median and mean wealth is less than 15 percent that of White families, at $24,100 and $142,500, respectively.[3]

Figure 6.1 displays median (top panel) and mean (bottom panel) wealth by race and ethnicity, expressed in thousands of 2019 dollars.

For some, this disparity in racial wealth—white family median wealth is more than $160,000 greater than black family median wealth—is proof positive of past and present racial discrimination, especially when viewed solely through the prism of race. For purveyors of this argument, it just follows that the only strategy to close the racial wealth gap then must be massive government redistribution programs or reparations in which black people are cumulatively given trillions of dollars to compensate for what they consider generational theft. This is in contrast to more developmental strategies that invest in strengthening stable families, expanding educational opportunities and school choice, and incentivizing work over government dependency, which are the more tried-and-true strategies that people of all races have used to generate wealth.

Figure 6.1 White Families Have More Wealth than Black, Hispanic, and Other or Multiple Race Families in the 2019 SCF[4]

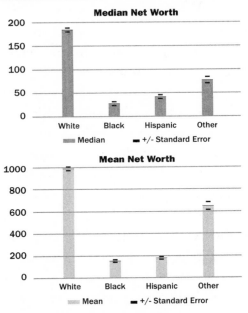

Source: Federal Reserve Board, 2019 Survey of Consumer Finances.

Indeed, Tressie McMillan Cottom, a sociologist and writer, wrote a *Washington Post* op-ed entitled "No, College Isn't the Answer. Reparations Are" that represents a worldview that places government action at the center of black renewal. In it, Cottom argues that "when you start talking about poverty and race, inevitably most folks fall back on the usual tropes: blacks should care more about school, go to college, increase their graduation rates, choose the right majors." The problem with this approach, she argues, is that "degrees cannot fix the cumulative effect of structural racism. In fact, over five decades of social science research show that education *reproduces* inequality."[5]

Ironically, I will show later in this essay how the consideration of just two additional factors—marital status and a college degree—completely reverses the $160,000 wealth gap, but in favor of blacks over whites. Unfortunately, in the current debate, multivariate analysis that considers multiple factors to understand the underlying causes driving racial disparities is overlooked in favor of much more simplistic explanations. In the famous words of Ibram X. Kendi, author of *How to Be an Antiracist,* "As an antiracist, when I see racial disparities, I see racism."[6]

The question for researchers is whether this kind of monocausal thinking leads to effective solutions for black people. If systemic racism is truly the sole or primary cause of racial disparities, then a logical conclusion of that mindset is that every solution tends to be systematically or institutionally focused on race as well. In this light, what is it that individual black people can do to lead a self-determined life? Are there any factors within our control that can empower us to reach our individual potential? To help address this question, in this essay, I explore three areas to consider in determining how best to empower more individual black people to live lives of their own choosing:

1. First and foremost, the family is a cornerstone of black freedom and prosperity and should be protected and promoted as such. The first section of this essay is adapted from a June 2021 study I released with Brad Wilcox and Wendy Wang, entitled "Less Poverty, Less Prison, More College: What Two Parents Mean for Black and White Children." We find a striking pattern that counters the narrative that systemic racism is determinative, and insurmountable for black people who might otherwise succeed. Our findings show that black children from intact, two-parent families *do better* than white children from single-parent families when it comes to poverty, prison, and college graduation. In sum, family structure matters. It reaffirms what most

sensible people from academia to the policy world have acknowledged about the importance of strong and stable families for kids. Indeed, in 2015, scholars from Brookings and Princeton reported on the enduring scientific consensus: "Most scholars now agree that children raised by two biological parents in a stable marriage do better than children in other family forms across a wide range of outcomes."[7]

2. Furthermore, since there is a clear link between stable family structure and intergenerational wealth building, the family should be at the center of the discussion about closing the racial wealth gap. The second section is adapted from May 2021 testimony I provided to the United States Congress Joint Economic Committee at a hearing focused on "Examining the Racial Wealth Gap in the United States." While the first section highlights the importance of family structure to reducing poverty, lessening incarceration rates, and improving college graduations in the black community, this section develops in greater detail the importance of strong families and marriage to generating wealth across generations.

3. Finally, these discussions about marriage and family are gaining in importance, because American blacks cannot (and need not) rely indefinitely on the legal and political privileges that have smoothed their path to success in the past. In the decade that launched with 2020, we will likely see a Supreme Court decision that ends race-based affirmative action in higher education and beyond at the same time that black people have demonstrated it is no longer necessary to perpetuate racial preferences for upwardly mobile steps such as college admission. As our country is engaged in a national reckoning that has increased focus on the role that race plays in public education, this section highlights the irony that there is a real possibility that race

may soon be eliminated as a factor in school admissions, at least in higher education.

Less Poverty, Less Prison, More College: What Two Parents Mean for Black and White Children[8]

Research recently conducted by myself, Wendy Wang, and W. Bradford Wilcox reveals three facts that bear significantly on the state of black America: First, children are significantly more likely to avoid poverty and prison, and to graduate from college, if they are raised in an intact two-parent family. Second, from poverty to college graduation to incarceration, black children and young adults from two-parent families are more likely to be flourishing than their white peers from single-parent families. Third, on average, black young adults from families headed by their mother and father are more likely to be flourishing educationally than black young adults from non-intact homes.

Princeton University sociology professor Sara McClanahan summarized the social scientific consensus about the importance of family structure for children with her colleague Gary Sandefur in the following passage from their magisterial 1994 book, *Growing Up with a Single Parent: What Hurts, What Helps*: "Children who grow up in a household with only one biological parent are worse off, on average, than children who grow up in a household with both of their biological parents, regardless of the parents' race or educational background."[9]

In recent years, many other scholars have come to similar conclusions, from Paul Amato at Penn State to Isabel Sawhill at the Brookings Institution to Melanie Wasserman at UCLA.[10] The consensus view has been that children are more likely to flourish in an intact, two-parent family, compared to children in single-parent families or stepfamilies.

But this consensus view is now being challenged by a new generation of scholarship and scholars. For instance, in December 2019, sociologist Christina Cross at Harvard University published an op-ed in the *New York Times*, entitled "The Myth of the Two-Parent Home," which contended that "living apart from a biological parent does not carry the same cost for black youths as for their white peers."[11] In the *Times* and in another June 2021 op-ed in the *Harvard Gazette*, she draws on her work indicating that black children are less affected by family structure on a number of educational outcomes to make the argument that family structure is less consequential for black children.[12] In recent years, other family scholars have also called into question the idea that children do better in stable two-parent families.[13]

One practical implication of this revisionist line of research is that children may not benefit from having their father in the household. Another implication is that the value of the two-parent family may be markedly different across racial lines, with black children less likely to benefit from such a family. Accordingly, it is necessary to investigate two questions:

1. Are black children more likely to flourish in an intact, two-parent home compared to black children raised by single parents or in stepfamilies? The following research focuses on these three subgroups because they are the largest family groups for American children today, including African American children. And it seeks to answer this question by looking at three important outcomes: child poverty, college graduation, and incarceration.

2. Is the association between family structure and child outcomes markedly different by race? The following compares white and black children in intact, two-parent families to their peers in non-intact families—single-parent families, stepfamilies, and other families. The aim is to determine

if the association is different for black children compared to white children on the three outcomes noted above.

Family Structure and Black Child Outcomes

Today, 37 percent of black children are living in a home headed by their own two biological parents, 48 percent are living in a home headed by a single parent, and 4 percent are living in a stepfamily with one biological parent and one non-biological parent, according to the March 2020 Current Population Survey (CPS).[14] This research explores how these three family structures are associated with child poverty, college graduation, and incarceration, drawing on data from the American Community Survey (ACS) 2015–2019 Five Year Estimates[15] and the National Longitudinal Survey of Youth (1997 cohort). Specifically, NLSY97 follows the lives of a national representative sample of American youth born between 1980 and 1984. The survey started in 1997 when the youth were ages 12 to 17. Figure 6.2 shows the wave that was surveyed in 2013/2014, when the cohort was at least 28 years old.

Figure 6.2 indicates that black children in homes headed by single parents are about 3.5 times more likely to be living in poverty compared to black children living with two parents in a first marriage, our measure of intact families in the ACS.[16] Those in likely stepfamilies are approximately 2.5 times more likely to be poor.[17] Moreover, after controlling for maternal education, age, children's age, and gender, we find that the odds of being poor for black children in non-intact families are 3.7 times higher than for black children in intact, married families.[18] Clearly, black children in stable, married families are better off financially.

Figure 6.3 shows that college graduation is markedly more common among black young adults raised by their two biological parents, our measure of intact families in the NLSY97.[19] Specifically,

Figure 6.2   Child Poverty Rate, by Child's Race and Family Living
Arrangements

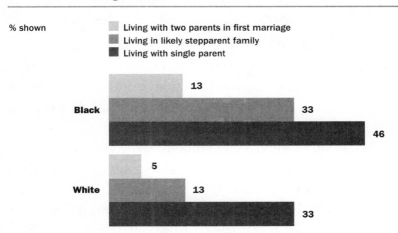

% shown   Living with two parents in first marriage
Living in likely stepparent family
Living with single parent

Note: Based on children under age 18. ACS identifies "social" parental relationship and not necessarily biological parents. Children with widowed parents are excluded from analyses.
Source: American Community Survey Five-Year Estimates, 2015–2019.

Figure 6.3   College and Prison for Black Young Adults, by Family Structure

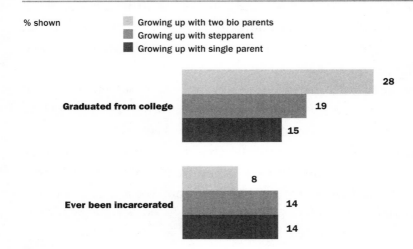

% shown   Growing up with two bio parents
Growing up with stepparent
Growing up with single parent

Note: Based on young adults' outcomes by age 28. Other type of family structures are not shown because of small sample sizes.
Source: National Longitudinal Survey of Youth 1997 (NLSY97).

data from the NLSY97 indicate that young adults from intact families are almost twice as likely to graduate from college than their peers who grew up with single parents, and approximately 1.5 times more likely to have a college degree compared to peers in stepfamilies. After controlling for maternal education, as well as young adults' gender, age, and AFQT scores, we find the odds of black young adults getting a college degree are almost 70 percent higher if they were raised by their own two parents. Clearly, on average, black young adults from families headed by their mother and father are more likely to be flourishing educationally than black young adults from non-intact homes.[20]

There is also a clear connection between family structure and incarceration for black young adults. Black young adults who grew up in a single-parent home are about 1.8 times more likely to have spent time in prison or jail by their late twenties, compared to their peers from a home headed by two biological parents. Those from stepfamilies are also more likely to have been incarcerated. In a multivariate context with the same controls noted above, young black adults in non-intact homes have about two times the odds of ever having been incarcerated compared to their peers in intact homes.

Because patterns in college completion and incarceration vary by gender, it is beneficial to explore the link between family structure and these two outcomes separately for young black men and women. Figure 6.4 indicates that young black men from an intact, two-parent family are much more likely to graduate from college than their peers raised by single parents and stepfamilies, and their incarceration rate is also much lower (14 percent, vs. 24 percent for single parents and 26 percent for stepfamilies). A similar pattern applies to young black women as well. More than one-third of young black women (36 percent) from intact families have had a college degree by their late twenties; the share among

Figure 6.4   College and Prison for Young Black Men and Women, by Family Structure

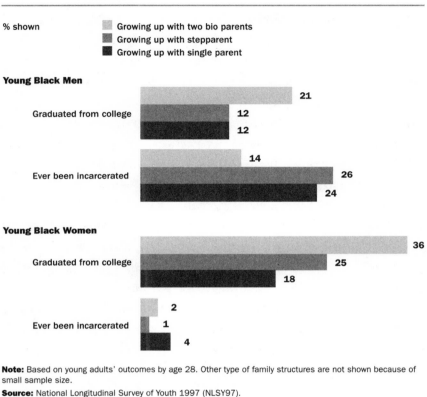

% shown   Growing up with two bio parents
Growing up with stepparent
Growing up with single parent

Young Black Men

Graduated from college — 21 / 12 / 12

Ever been incarcerated — 14 / 26 / 24

Young Black Women

Graduated from college — 36 / 25 / 18

Ever been incarcerated — 2 / 1 / 4

Note: Based on young adults' outcomes by age 28. Other type of family structures are not shown because of small sample size.
Source: National Longitudinal Survey of Youth 1997 (NLSY97).

black women raised by single parents is 18 percent, and the share among stepfamilies is 25 percent.

Black-White Comparison

Clearly, there are differences in poverty, college graduation, and incarceration by family structure among African Americans. But are these differences similar to or different from the ones for whites? Note that 67 percent of white children today are in homes headed by their biological parents, 21 percent of white children are in homes headed by a single parent, and 6 percent are living with a biological parent and stepparent, according to the March 2020 Current Population Survey.

The first noteworthy finding in comparing patterns across race, gender, and family structure is that black children from intact families do uniformly better than white children from single-parent households. From poverty to college graduation to incarceration, black children and young adults from two-parent families are more likely to be flourishing than their white peers from single-parent families. For instance, 36 percent of young black women from intact families have graduated from college compared to just 28 percent of young white women from single-parent families. Likewise, 14 percent of young black men from intact families have been incarcerated, compared to 18 percent of young white men from single-parent families. Moreover, 13 percent of black children in intact families are poor compared to 33 percent of white children in single-parent families.

At the same time, it is important to note that Figures 6.4 and 6.5 show that whites are more advantaged within each family structure category. For instance, only 28 percent of black young adults from intact families have graduated from college compared to 47 percent of white young adults from intact families. This is a large difference and is but one example of the fact that a stable two-parent family is not a panacea when it comes to addressing racial inequalities in America. The nation's legacy of racial discrimination, unequal access to a quality education, concentrated poverty, and ongoing experiences with racial prejudice are among the structural factors that help explain the racial differences in outcomes between blacks and whites who have the same family structure.

The third noteworthy finding here, as shown in Table 6.1, is that the family structure association for black and white children is similar when it comes to poverty and prison. Net of controls,

Figure 6.5   College and Prison for White Young Adults, by Family Structure

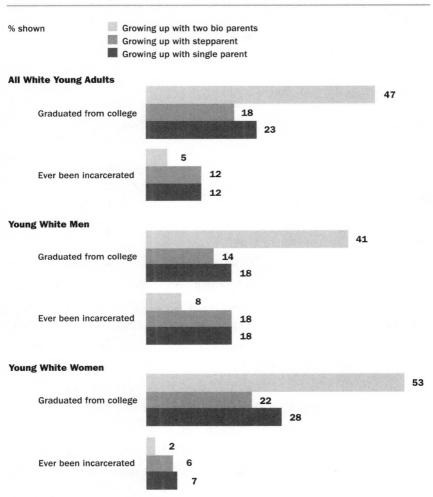

% shown
- Growing up with two bio parents
- Growing up with stepparent
- Growing up with single parent

All White Young Adults

Graduated from college
- 47
- 18
- 23

Ever been incarcerated
- 5
- 12
- 12

Young White Men

Graduated from college
- 41
- 14
- 18

Ever been incarcerated
- 8
- 18
- 18

Young White Women

Graduated from college
- 53
- 22
- 28

Ever been incarcerated
- 2
- 6
- 7

Note: Based on young adults' outcomes by age 28. Other type of family structures are not shown because of small sample size.
Source: National Longitudinal Survey of Youth 1997 (NLSY97).

being in non-intact homes more than triples both black and white children's odds of being in poverty. As young adults, those growing up from non-intact families are twice as likely to have been incarcerated compared to those from intact families, regardless

Table 6.1   Odds Ratios for Children/Young Adults of Non-intact Families vs. Intact Families

	White	Black
Child Poverty	3.8	3.7
College Graduation	.4	.6
Incarceration	2.4	2.1

Note: Logistic regression models were run separately for whites and blacks. Results for child poverty control for maternal education, maternal age, child gender, and child age, based on ACS 2015–2019. Results for college graduation and incarceration control for maternal education, respondent's age, gender, and AFQT, based on NLSY97.

of race. For both black and white children, growing up in a home with one's two parents seems to reduce one's risk of poverty and prison in about the same way.

But consistent with Cross's research, the link between family structure and college completion is clearly weaker for blacks than for whites. Net of controls, growing up in a non-intact family reduces the odds of college graduation by 60 percent for white young adults, but only by 40 percent for black young adults. Nevertheless, both black and white young adults from non-intact families are still at a disadvantage relative to their peers who grew up with both parents. In other words, it is also clear that black young adults from intact families are markedly more likely to graduate from college than their black peers in non-intact families—and white peers from non-intact families.

Summary of Findings

Using new census data and the National Longitudinal Survey of Youth, my co-authors and I found that black and white children from intact homes are significantly more likely to be flourishing economically, educationally, and socially on the three outcomes examined here: child poverty, education, and incarceration.

At the same time, consistent with Cross's research, we do find that the association between family structure and one major education outcome, college graduation, is weaker for black children than white children. Nevertheless, young black adults are significantly more likely to graduate from college if they grew up in an intact family.

Our results also indicate that a stable, two-parent family is no panacea for African American children. Black children in stable, two-parent families are more likely to experience poverty and incarceration, and are less likely to graduate from college, compared to their white peers from stable, two-parent families. Racial inequality casts a shadow even on black children in intact families.

To be clear, this descriptive brief does not make claims about causality. A number of factors not measured in the preceding research may confound the associations between family structure and child outcomes documented here. Young adults' family structure growing up is obviously endogenous to their family income, for instance, given that married parents tend to have a higher income than single parents. Here, progressives tend to minimize the ways that family income is a consequence of family structure (two parents can more easily earn a decent income than one parent) even as conservatives tend to minimize the ways that a stable marriage is a consequence of a decent income (relationships are stronger when they are undergirded by a steady income).

What we can conclude is this: Consistent with a longstanding social scientific consensus[21] about family structure, children are significantly more likely to avoid poverty and prison, and to graduate from college, if they are raised in an intact two-parent family. This association remains true for both black and white children. In the vast majority of cases, these homes are headed by their own married mother and father.[22]

In sum, it is no "myth" to point out that boys and girls are more likely to flourish today in America if they are raised in a stable, two-parent home. It is simply the truth that white and black children usually do better when raised by their own mother and father, compared to single-parent families and stepfamilies. Our results, then, also suggest that the fraying fabric of American family life, where more kids grow up apart from one of their two parents—usually their own father—is an "equal opportunity tsunami," posing obstacles to the healthy development of children from all backgrounds.

Family Formation and the Racial Wealth Gap[23]

I am a proud product of the New York City public school system, which I attended from kindergarten through twelfth grade, and a graduate of Brooklyn Tech High School, Cornell University College of Engineering, and Harvard Business School. In addition to my work at the American Enterprise Institute, I am the founder and CEO of Vertex Partnership Academies, a new network of character-based, International Baccalaureate high schools, set to open our first campus in the Bronx in 2022.

Many of our parents faced racial discrimination and other challenges in their own lives. They feared that their children might as well. But these parents chose our schools because they wanted their children to develop the necessary skills and habits to become agents of their own uplift and build a better life, even in the face of structural barriers. In District 8, only 2 percent of the nearly 2,000 public school students beginning high school in the South Bronx in 2015 graduated ready for college four years later.[24] A shocking 98 percent of the students either dropped out of high school before completing their senior year—or if they did manage to graduate, were still required to take remedial, catch-up classes in community college due to low math and reading scores on state exams. By contrast, at our all-boys school at 151st Street and Grand Concourse in the South Bronx, in 2018–19, the last year state tests were administered, nearly 70 percent of our students passed the state math exam.[25]

I share this data point because, while we as a country are having crucial conversations about race, it is easy to forget that the racial disparities we are seeking to close originate early in life—long before they show up as statistical gaps in financial wealth, home ownership, or educational achievement. If only 2 percent of the mostly black and brown kids in the Bronx are graduating from high school and are capable of doing even basic reading and math, why would we reasonably expect these same kids to flourish in higher education and the workplace as adults: starting businesses, getting married, having children within marriage, or experiencing any of the other landmarks along the path into the middle class and beyond?

If we truly care about upward mobility, we should be wary of the goal to achieve "racial equity." Consider that in 2019, only one third of all eighth grade students scored "Proficient" on the National Assessment of Progress in reading.[26] Each year since the Nation's Report Card was first administered in 1992, fewer than half of the nation's white students in the fourth, eighth, and twelfth grades scored NAEP proficient in reading.[27] The sad irony is that closing the black-white achievement gap, and thus achieving racial equity, would only grow black student outcomes from sub-mediocrity to full mediocrity.

As we consider strategies to create an opportunity society and upward mobility for people of all races, I submit the two-pronged philosophy we practiced in our schools: Start early with the end in mind; and study the success of those who have achieved excellence, not just equity.

A range of studies have identified "toxic levels of wealth inequality," especially between black and white Americans. According to the Federal Reserve's 2019 Survey of Consumer Finances, the wealth gap between black and white Americans at the median—the middle household in each community—was $164,100. The median black household was worth only $24,100; the median white household, $188,200—seven times more than the median black household.[28] For some, this gap is vibrant proof of a permanent and insurmountable legacy of racial discrimination.

As a result, today's public discourse is dominated by the disempowering narrative that, unless institutional barriers are removed, black Americans will remain trapped in a perpetual cycle of economic victimhood. The Institute for Policy Studies notes, "Changes in individual behavior will not close the racial wealth divide, only structural systemic policy change can do that."[29] In "What We Get Wrong about Closing the Racial Wealth Gap," William Darity Jr. et al. assert, "There are no actions that black Americans can take unilaterally that will have much of an effect on reducing the racial wealth gap."[30] *New York Times* reporter Nikole Hannah-Jones argues: "None of the actions we are told black people must take if they want to 'lift themselves' out of poverty and gain financial stability—not marrying, not getting educated, not saving more, not owning a home—can mitigate 400 years of racialized plundering."[31]

Imagine you are a twelve-year-old black boy living in the South Bronx, with aspirations of working hard to achieve the American Dream. Yet you are repeatedly told there is nothing you can do individually to achieve that goal. Imagine further that this message comes from adults who claim to advocate on your behalf, and yet they tell you it is pointless to even try. Simply because you are black, they inform you, you have no individual ability to close the racial wealth divide.

As someone who has run public charter schools in low-income communities in the Bronx, I know how debilitating such a narrative can be for a student's hopes and aspirations. Rather than helping that young man develop personal agency and an understanding of the behaviors most likely to propel him into success, this message will only teach what psychologists term "learned helplessness."

Not only does this message of hopelessness depress human motivation, it is also demonstrably wrong. It also ignores the tremendous public investment that has been made in the war on poverty, particularly child poverty. According to my AEI colleague Angela Rachidi, U.S. spending on poor children has increased seventeen-fold since the 1960s, and in recent years, the government has spent more on children per capita than many other developed countries when considering three major categories of spending: cash support and tax breaks for families, primary and secondary education, and health. As Figure 6.6 indicates, by 2018, federal spending on means-tested programs reached more than $300 billion per annum, and generally shifted to in-kind

Figure 6.6   Federal Expenditures on Children and Poverty[32]

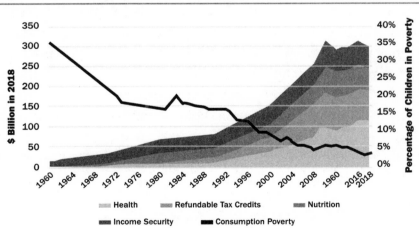

Note: Expenditure data include estimates of federal expenditures in ten-year intervals from 1960 to 2000 and annually from 2008 to 2018 according to source methodology. Consumption poverty data are available for 1960, 1972, 1973, 1980, 1981, and annually for 1983 according to source's methodology.

Source: Expenditure data come from *Kids' Share Report: Analyzing Federal Expenditures on Children*, Urban Institute, 2010, 2011, 2013–19, https://www.urban.org/policy-centers/cross-center-initiatives/kids-contex/projects/kids-share-analyzing-federal.

support such as food benefits, refundable tax credits, and health care coverage. Consumption-based poverty measures place the child poverty rate at less than 5 percent today, because of these massive government transfer programs.[33]

Yet the racial wealth gap persists for certain communities. This is why we have to study success for those black and other communities that are thriving. There are structural barriers that have to be addressed and individual choices that should be promoted. For example, there *are* decisions within the control of black kids—and children of all races—that increase their likelihood to improve their economic outcomes within a single generation and thus their ability to transfer wealth across generations.

For example, while strengthening family stability would not single-handedly close the racial wealth gap, it is a controllable factor that heavily influences economic outcomes. The same 2019 Survey of Consumer Finances that shows the average black family has one seventh the wealth of the average white family also shows the reverse when family structure is considered. Indeed, black households headed by two married parents have slightly higher wealth than the median net worth of the typical white, single-parent household (Figure 6.7).

And when education is considered, on an absolute basis, the median net worth of black households with two college-educated

Figure 6.7   Median Net Worth of Two-Parent Black Households vs. Single-Parent White Households with Children

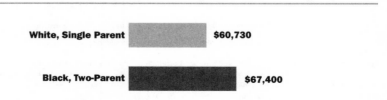

White, Single Parent $60,730

Black, Two-Parent $67,400

Note: Households headed by a "widowed" parent were excluded from analyses.
Source: Author's calculations from Board of Governors of the Federal Reserve System, "Survey of Consumer Finances (SCF)," 2019, https://www.federalreserve.gov/econres/scfindex.htm.

parents is nearly $220,000, more than three times that of the typical white, single-parent household. See Figure 6.8. While the racial wealth gap is $164,000 in favor of whites over blacks when race is considered alone, when family structure and education are incorporated, it is $158,870, *completely reversed in favor of blacks over whites.*

Moreover, the 2017 report "The Millennial Success Sequence" finds that a stunning 91 percent of black people avoided poverty when they reached their prime young adult years (ages 28–34) if they followed the "success sequence"—that is, they earned at least a high school degree, worked full-time so they learned the dignity and discipline of work, and married before having any children, in that order.[34] In his study "Where Is the Land of Opportunity? The Geography of Intergenerational Mobility in the United States," Raj Chetty studied the intergenerational mobility of more than 40 million children and their parents. He found that *hyper-local* factors—most notably measures of father presence and marriage rates in a given location—drive upward (or downward) mobility and thus the intergenerational transfer of wealth.[35]

There is no silver bullet intervention that will magically close gaps in racial outcomes, especially when those gaps have causal factors that begin very early in life. But if we know there

Figure 6.8 Median Net Worth of Two-Parent College-Educated Black Households vs. Single-Parent White Households with Children

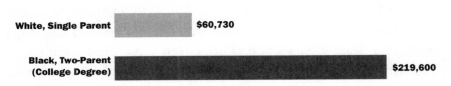

Note: Households headed by a "widowed" parent were excluded from analyses.
Source: Author's calculations from Board of Governors of the Federal Reserve System, "Survey of Consumer Finances (SCF)," 2019, https://www.federalreserve.gov/econres/scfindex.htm.

are factors beyond race, such as education, family stability, and so many others, that can make a difference in the lives of kids, then our approach to upward mobility should be to promote *empowering* behaviors instead of defeatist messages.

That is why policy interventions such as widespread school choice are so important. Ensuring every parent, regardless of race, income level, or zip code, has the power to choose a great public school for his or her child will do a lot more to close the racial wealth gap than reifying race in policy and rhetoric at every opportunity. As a leader of public charter schools, I want to see recognition that charter schools are public schools, and that more options should be given to students and families. Such race-neutral interventions that level the playing field, provide a solid education, and encourage wealth-building behaviors would shape a strong policy portfolio.

Beyond pulling policy levers, we have a moral imperative to encourage young people of all races to adopt a new cultural norm around education, work, and responsible parenthood. This is particularly true given the new normal of nonmarital child-bearing across race. My research focuses on nonmarital births to women aged 24 and under. In 2019, for the tenth consecutive year, at least 70 percent of births to all women in that age group were outside of marriage, according to CDC Final Birth Data. By race, the nonmarital birth rate for black women 24 and under was 91 percent, and it was 61 percent for white women aged 24 and under.[36]

In addition, nearly 40 percent of unmarried women aged 24 and under who gave birth in 2019 were already mothers, giving birth to at least their second child. Given these multiple births, unmarried women aged 24 and under who gave birth in 2019 alone were raising an estimated 850,000–1,000,000 children, according to the CDC Wonder database.[37]

This pattern of out-of-wedlock childbearing is often established at a young age. According to the CDC Wonder database, in 2019, almost two thirds (64 percent) of first out-of-wedlock births were to women 24 and under. Like kids of teen mothers, these children are at much greater risk of experiencing child poverty, poor education, lack of upward mobility, traumatic stress, and many other adverse childhood experiences that impede their ability to generate wealth later in life. If we want to reduce such risks and mitigate the economic distress that usually ensues for both parent and child, we must educate adolescents about the likely outcomes associated with different behaviors and encourage them to think critically about the timing of family formation.

This is why there is growing consensus around the need for public information campaigns targeted to young people that would promote the creation of healthy, stable families, which can take many forms but are most often created through education, work, marriage, then children, in that order. Both the AEI/ Brookings Working Group on Poverty and Opportunity[38] and Harvard University's Closing the Opportunity Gap initiative[39] strongly recommend a large-scale marketing campaign that uses social and mass media and engages local institutions like the church, schools, civic organizations, and neighborhood influencers to change and normalize a new set of behavioral expectations around family formation.

In addition to public information campaigns, young people of all races must learn the concept of "earned success," the notion that money generated through hard work is much more rewarding than money simply given to us. Schools can encourage entrepreneurship by building awareness of the new forms of venture capital dedicated to changing the face of entrepreneurship. An excellent example of the new initiatives is Harlem Capital Partners, an early-stage venture capital firm on a mission to invest in 1,000 minority and female founders over the next twenty years. Another is Netflix, which announced in August 2020 that they would allocate an estimated $100 million of their cash holdings toward "financial institutions and organizations that directly support Black communities in the U.S." As Netflix says, "Bringing more capital to these communities can make a meaningful difference for the people and businesses in them, helping more families buy their first home or save for college, and more small businesses get started or grow."[40]

In sum, educators, philanthropists, policymakers, and business leaders should support these types of initiatives and evidence-based curricula that help young people build agency by descriptively (versus prescriptively) teaching the "success sequence" in schools, encourage wealth creation by improving access to venture capital, and organize social and mass media campaigns to normalize a new set of behavioral expectations around family formation. Without these steps, sending additional money to low-income young adults will do little to meaningfully alter their chances to achieve the American Dream in the long run.

Race-Based Affirmative Action Will Likely Soon Be Replaced by Class-Based Affirmative Action

When my parents, Vincent and Eula Rowe, emigrated to this country from Jamaica, West Indies, in the 1960s, they were very cognizant of America's history of racial oppression. My parents knew that racism was very real and had literally been enshrined into U.S. law. But they also knew the country was changing. Despite the inherent contradictions between its founding ideals and the history of slavery and Jim Crow segregation, America had made steady progress dismantling laws that imposed a racial hierarchy. The Civil Rights Act of 1964 and the Voting Rights Act of 1965 had just been signed.

They moved to Brooklyn with me and my brother during

a very tumultuous time in race relations. Yet my parents knew that opportunities for black and all Americans were growing and were making it more possible for formerly persecuted people to surmount the obstacle of racism they experienced and that still persisted throughout American society. My dad always used to say that you have to be prepared for opportunities when they come your way. My parents weren't wealthy, so they put me in public school and I got a great K–12 education in Brooklyn and Queens, which gave me the foundation for all that I have been able to achieve throughout my career.

And so I have dedicated much of my life to ensuring kids of all races have access to a high-quality, tuition-free, public education, regardless of race, family structure, class, or zip code. As my dad counseled, my goal is to ensure they are prepared for the enormous opportunities that are coming their way.

And now I am also proud to say that in 2022, I am launching Vertex Partnership Academies, which seeks to be the first-of-its-kind network of character-based, International Baccalaureate public charter high schools, dedicated to equality of opportunity, individual dignity, and our common humanity. Vertex Student Scholars will be immersed in a culture of democratic discourse guided by the four cardinal virtues of Courage, Justice, Temperance, and Wisdom. With the first campus scheduled to open in the Bronx in September 2022, Vertex will empower each student scholar to choose either: (1) the International Baccalaureate *Diploma Program* that prepares them to enroll and thrive in premier colleges and universities in the country or abroad; or (2) the International Baccalaureate *Career Program* that prepares them to graduate with a professional credential and directly enter the labor market with skills in a particular industry.

I provide this background because it is essential that we continue to build institutions that can prepare black students for opportunity. This is even more relevant as a movement grows to eliminate race and ethnicity as factors in college admissions. Race-based affirmative action in higher education was first established in 1978 with the *Regents of the University of California v. Bakke*, 438 U.S. 265 decision. That decision upheld a university's right to allow race to be one of several factors in university admissions but found the use of specific racial quotas unconstitutional.

Twenty-five years later, in 2003, the Supreme Court upheld the University of Michigan Law School's decision to deny admission to Barbara Grutter, a white Michigan student, who had applied with academic credentials sufficiently worthy to earn her admission. However, Ms. Grutter was denied entry, partially due to the law school's open practice of providing admissions preference to certain minority groups to ensure a critical mass of students could be achieved. In a 5–4 opinion, the Court held that the Equal Protection Clause in the Constitution did "not prohibit the law school's narrowly tailored use of race in admissions decisions to further a compelling interest in obtaining the educational benefits that flow from a diverse student body." Even though she had ruled in the affirmative, Justice Sandra O'Connor noted that it had been twenty-five years since the famous Bakke case. In her majority opinion, O'Connor wrote that "race-conscious admissions policies must be limited in time," adding that the "Court expects that 25 years from now, the use of racial preferences will no longer be necessary to further the interest approved today."[41]

It is noteworthy that O'Connor's prediction would set 2028 as the year in which race-based affirmative action would come to an end. But that timeline might be accelerated. Students for Fair Admissions is a nonprofit membership group of more than 20,000 students, parents, and others who believe that racial classifications and preferences in college admissions are unfair, unnecessary, and unconstitutional. Their mission is to support and participate in litigation that will restore the original principles of our nation's civil rights movement: "A student's race and ethnicity should not be factors that either harm or help that student to gain admission to a competitive university."[42]

Students for Fair Admissions is pursuing a case against Harvard University alleging racial discrimination against Asian applicants in undergraduate admissions. According to the *Northwestern Law Review*, the case "is one of the most notable recent equal protection challenges to be advanced almost exclusively on the basis of statistical evidence...[and] could well end affirmative action in higher education and beyond if it winds up at the Supreme Court."[43] Figure 6.9 contains information that Harvard University was forced to reveal about its admissions process by race.

Figure 6.9 Harvard's Preferences for Underrepresented Minorities[44]

Harvard's admissions data revealed astonishing racial disparities in admission rates among similarly qualified applicants. SFFA's expert testified that applicants with the same "academic index" (a metric created by Harvard based on test scores and GPA) had widely different admission rates by race.

Admit Rates by Race/Ethnicity and Academic Decile					
Academic Decile	White	Asian American	African American	Hispanic	All Applicants
10	15.3%	12.7%	56.1%	31.3%	14.6%
9	10.8%	7.6%	54.6%	26.2%	10.4%
8	7.5%	5.1%	44.5%	22.9%	8.2%
7	4.8%	4.0%	41.1%	17.3%	6.6%
6	4.2%	2.5%	29.7%	13.7%	5.6%
5	2.6%	1.9%	22.4%	9.1%	4.4%
4	1.8%	0.9%	12.8%	5.5%	3.3%
3	0.6%	0.6%	5.2%	2.0%	1.7%
2	0.4%	0.2%	1.0%	0.3%	0.5%
1	0.0%	0.0%	0.0%	0.0%	0.0%

App. 179–80; J.A.6008–09. For example, an Asian American in the fourth-lowest decile has virtually no chance of being admitted to Harvard (0.9%); but an African American in that decile has a higher chance of admission (12.8%) than an Asian American in the *top* decile (12.7%).

As the table above shows, if you are a black student in the top two academic deciles, you have a more than one in two chance of being admitted to Harvard University, and your likelihood of entry is more than four times that of white and Asian students. And this phenomenon is not just Harvard. You would likely find that kind of opportunity for black kids at virtually every institution of higher education. Students for Fair Admissions has a very strong case that Harvard is violating Title VI of the Civil Rights Act of 1964, which prohibits discrimination on the basis of race, color, or national origin by any program or activity receiving federal funds. Fundamentally, the charge is that Harvard is preferencing African American and Hispanic students and in effect penalizing Asian American student applicants through its weighting of race in its selection process.

Ironically, if Students for Fair Admissions does win this case, then racial preferences would disappear in college admissions. But would that change outcomes for the type of black students gaining entry? Would a large segment of these black students still be able to earn admission even without racial preferences? The answer is likely yes. According to *MarketWatch*:

> The black students that elite colleges do admit increasingly come from either mixed-race backgrounds or immigrant families from Africa or the Caribbean... Only between 9% and 13% of black American 18- and 19-year-olds are immigrants or come from immigrant families. But one long-term study cited by author Paul Tough shows that at "highly selective private colleges,... students from black immigrant families plus students with one black and nonblack parent [rose] from about 40 percent of black students in the 1980s... to about 60 percent in the late 1990s."[45]

This phenomenon is examined in the study "Exploring the Divergent Academic Outcomes of U.S.-Origin and Immigrant-Origin Black Undergraduates," which explains that

> immigrant-generational differences among Black students stem from their differing cultural perspectives on education. John Ogbu and colleagues (Ogbu, 1991, 2003; Ogbu & Simons, 1998) have offered the *Cultural-Ecological Theory of School Performance* to explain performance differences between immigrant-origin and U.S.-origin Blacks. According to John Ogbu, the achievement differences between these two groups stem from the different cultural adaptations of voluntary immigrants versus involuntary immigrants (or involuntary minorities). Voluntary minority immigrants attribute the discriminatory treatment they receive in their host societies to their status as "guests in a foreign land" and believe that the barriers they face are temporary challenges they can overcome through hard work, greater acculturation, and academic attainment (Ogbu, 1991; Ogbu & Simons, 1998). Ogbu argues that these perspectives lead voluntary immigrants to place greater value on educational success, as a collective, relative to involuntary minorities who entered their host societies through conquest, colonization, and enslavement (Ogbu, 1991; Ogbu & Simons, 1998). Involuntary minorities tend to view discriminatory treatment as permanent and institutionalized. According to Ogbu, these groups often do not believe that education will enable them to overcome systemic oppression and attain economic success or societal status and, accordingly, invest less time and resources in an effort to achieve academic success.[46]

So there is a community of black students demonstrating that racism is not a life sentence of despair. Where some might apply the daunting adjectives of *systemic, institutional,* and *structural* in front of the word *racism,* these young people would apply the overcoming adjective of *surmountable.*

One fascinating development is that the likely discontinuation of race-based affirmative action may usher in class-based affirmative action. Indeed, in his book *The Remedy: Class, Race and Affirmative Action,* Richard Kahlenberg argues that it is time to replace race with class preferences and highlights that "while it is true that a disproportionate number of ethnic and racial minorities are also members of the lowest socioeconomic class, the main barriers they face are due to poverty rather than race." In his analysis, Kahlenberg "examines how the rationale for affirmative action has moved inexorably away from its original commitment to remedy past discrimination and instead has become a means to achieve racial diversity, even if that means giving preference to upper-middle-class blacks over poor whites."[47]

The black community is entering a phase in which two phenomena are occurring at the same time: (1) There is a growing likelihood that a Supreme Court decision is imminent that eliminates race-based affirmative action; and (2) there is overwhelming evidence that black students, particularly from African and Caribbean nations who place high value on academic success, as well as those native-born black people that are raised in stable, two-parent households, disproportionately enter elite universities. The takeaway demonstrates that racial preferences in education and elsewhere may soon not exist and, as a testament to this nation's progress in empowering young black people to reach their potential, may no longer even be necessary. Rather than relying on those preferential programs by race, the black community is far better off to focus on development strategies such as strengthening marriage and two-parent families, revitalizing faith communities, demanding parental choice in education, and stimulating more entrepreneurship and new business creation.

Conclusion

In 2014, Raj Chetty and his Opportunity Insights team at Harvard produced a landmark study, "Where Is the Land of Opportunity? The Geography of Intergenerational Mobility in the United States." In it, Chetty et al. studied the intergenerational mobility of more than 40 million children and their parents. They found that *hyper-local* factors—most notably measures of father presence and marriage rates in a given location—drive upward (or downward) mobility and thus the intergenerational transfer of wealth. Specifically, they found that "the strongest predictors of upward mobility are measures of family structure such as the fraction of single parents in the area."[48]

In a separate 2018 study, "Race and Economic Opportunity in the United States: An Intergenerational Perspective," Chetty and his colleagues set out to determine the most powerful neighborhood factors behind the gap in economic mobility for poor black and white boys. The biggest factor? The "fraction of low-income black fathers present" in a neighborhood. In other words, poor black boys in neighborhoods with high numbers of black fathers were significantly more likely to realize the American Dream.[49]

The *New York Times* reported on the same research with a story headlined "Extensive Data Shows Punishing Reach of Racism for Black Boys." Rather than focusing on the factors that led to success, the article led with this: "Black boys raised in America, even in the wealthiest families and living in some of the most well-to-do neighborhoods, still earn less in adulthood than white boys with similar backgrounds."[50] In a letter to the editor responding to the *New York Times* story, a reader, Paul Bauer, asked, "What can be done by a single citizen to improve the lives of the disadvantaged black boys?" Noelle Hurd, assistant professor of psychology at the University of Virginia, responded:

Ultimately, the problem is a societal one and not an individual one, so solutions will have to be at the systemic level—like changing public policies and practices and policies within schools and law enforcement agencies. It is a mistake to think that there is any one thing a person can do at the individual level to sidestep the consequences of living in a racist society.[51]

If there is a state of black America, its condition will be determined by whether the approach taken by millions of individual black Americans to achieve upward mobility is viewed through the hopeless lens of "living in a racist society," which leads one to believe that only structural solutions are the answer, or through the lens of what would be possible if factors such as access to high-quality education and stable families, found most frequently in married, two-parent households, became more of the norm for millions of black children.

The challenge for black and other leaders is how to most effectively critique America's history as a short-lived example of state-sanctioned oppression while also celebrating how its enduring principles have provided the world an indispensable model for how a formerly enslaved people can now regularly produce some of the country's most influential leaders in virtually every facet of American life.

In our national conversation regarding race, we must be able to explore the nuance that both structural barriers and individually driven factors such as family structure play a part in determining child outcomes. Most importantly, what do we teach the next generation about their ability to develop the personal agency to overcome those barriers? How would you thrive in a world in which racial preferences were no longer offered in college admissions? If you are twelve years old, do you have the power to solve housing segregation?

Perhaps the next generation of students should learn that a staggering 97 percent of millennials who obtained at least a high school degree, worked full-time, and married before having children are not poor. Rather than pummel young people with reminders of the barriers over which they have no control, maybe it would be good to share the power over decisions that they do have to determine their own destiny. For example, in June 2018, scholars Ron Mincy, Wendy Wang, and Brad Wilcox presented their new research on "Black Men Making It in America: The Engines of Economic Success for Black Men in America"[52] in a panel at the American Enterprise Institute. Their study, published by AEI and the Institute for Family Studies, looked at the patterns of success of black men in America, examining the roles of military service, education, work, and marriage in their lives. As the then-CEO of the Public Prep Network, I joined a panel following the presentation to discuss the study and provide my perspective on the factors that lead to success for black men in America—education, work, marriage, faith, military service, and a sense of personal agency—as referred to in the study.[53] As I said during the panel, "These are the ingredients of success for all Americans, regardless of race, male or female. And I think that's just a very powerful and hopefully unifying message for how we can move forward." Below I quote their three major findings:

- **Black men's economic standing.** More than one-in-two black men (57%) have made it into the middle class or higher as adults today, up from 38% in 1960, according to a new analysis of Census data. And the share of black men who are poor has fallen from 41% in 1960 to 18% in 2016. So, a substantial share of black men in America are realizing the American Dream—at least financially—and a clear majority are not poor.

- **The institutional engines of black men's success.** As expected, higher education and full-time work look like engines of success for black men in America. But three other institutions that tend to get less attention in our current discussions of race—the U.S. military, the black church, and marriage—also appear to play significant roles in black men's success. For instance, black men who served in the military are more likely than those who did not to be in the middle class when they reach mid-life (54% vs. 45%), according to our new analysis of the National Longitudinal Survey of Youth (NLSY79). Black men who frequently attended church services at a young age are also more likely to reach the middle class or higher when they are in their fifties: 53% of those men who attended church as young men made it, compared to 43% who did not. Finally, about 70% of married black men are in the middle class, compared with only 20% of never-married black men and 44% of divorced black men.

- **The importance of individual agency.** Black men who score above average in their sense of agency—measured by reports that they feel like they are determining the course of their own lives versus feeling like they do not have control over the direction of their lives—as young men or teenagers in the late 1970s are more likely to be prosperous later in life. Specifically, 52% of black men who had a higher sense of agency as young men made it into at least the middle class when they reached age 50, compared to 44% of their peers who did not have that sense of agency.[54]

As outlined earlier, I partnered with Brad Wilcox and Wendy Wang to produce a 2021 study: "Less Poverty, Less Prison, More College: What Two Parents Mean for Black and White Children." Figure 6.10 summarizes some of the key findings.

These two studies are emblematic of widely accepted research that shows that single parenthood among young adults is one of the top predictors of child poverty, school suspensions, incarceration, and educational disadvantage.[55] Unmarried young mothers are far more likely to experience high levels of partnership instability and family complexity, each of which is associated with poorer child well-being and intergenerational transmission of *disadvantage.*

Research like this has kept some influential thinkers and journalists on the Left defending the scientific consensus about marriage, fatherhood, and family. "I think that my half of the political spectrum—the left half—too often dismisses the importance of family structure," noted *New York Times* columnist David Leonhardt, responding to another of Chetty's studies. "Partly out of a worthy desire to celebrate the heroism of single parents,

Figure 6.10 Black Children from Intact, Two-Parent Families Do Better than White Children from Single-Parent Families[56]

Black children do better than white children when it comes to poverty, prison and college when they are raised in an intact, two-parent home and white children are raised in a single-parent family.

36% of young Black women from intact, two-parent families have graduated from college compared to just **28%** of young white women from single-parent families.

14% of young Black men from intact, two-parent families have been incarcerated, compared to **18%** of young white men from single-parent families.

Source: The Institute for Family Studies, 2021.

progressives too often downplay family structure. Social science is usually messy, with correlation and causation difficult to separate. But the evidence, when viewed objectively, points strongly to the value of two-parent households."[57]

It must be said that a stable, two-parent home does not guarantee success for a child. Nor does being raised in a low-income, single-parent household make failure a certainty. But overwhelming data and common sense suggest that family stability matters significantly in virtually every facet of a child's future life. Consider President Obama's 2013 speech on violence after yet another fatal shooting of a teenager in Chicago: "There's no more important ingredient for success, nothing that would be more important for us reducing violence than strong, stable families—which means we should do more to promote marriage and encourage fatherhood."[58]

If we really want to help young black people break the intergenerational cycle of poverty, we need a serious effort to reframe the decisions governing passage into young adulthood. In light of this, educators, venture capitalists, and philanthropists should work together to develop and pilot evidence-based curricula that help young people build agency by teaching the success sequence in schools, create greater access to private capital to encourage entrepreneurship and wealth creation, and organize social and mass media campaigns to normalize a new set of behavioral expectations around family formation.

Understanding these patterns of success for both black men and women is why in 2020 I was proud to help found 1776 Unites, a project of the Woodson Center. Led by primarily black activists, educators, and scholars, 1776 Unites acknowledges that

> racial discrimination exists—and works towards diminishing
> it. But we dissent from contemporary groupthink and rhetoric

about race, class, and American history that defames our national heritage, divides our people, and instills helplessness among those who already hold within themselves the grit and resilience to better their lot in life.[59]

1776 Unites has developed free K–12 lesson plans based on the ten "Woodson Principles" of Competence, Integrity, Transparency, Resilience, Witness, Innovation, Inspiration, Agency, Access, and Grace. The curriculum offers lessons on black excellence in the face of unimaginable adversity, such as the nearly 5,000 Rosenwald schools built during the Jim Crow era that exclusively educated more than 700,000 black children throughout fourteen Southern states. These lessons have now been downloaded more than 15,000 times by educators in all fifty states, and are being used in private, charter, district, and parochial schools, after schools, home schools, prison ministries, and wherever character formation is happening for children.

In summary, the state of individual black Americans is strong because increasingly individual black Americans have greater control over their destiny. Yes, there are structural barriers like the absence of school choice. And yes, race-based affirmative action may soon be eliminated. But patterns of success exist within the black community, with the anchor being as President Obama described on Father's Day in 2008: "Of all the rocks upon which we build our lives, we are reminded today that family is the most important." There is no singular silver bullet that will guarantee success for black Americans, but there is much to be hopeful for.

7

POVERTY IN THE AFRICAN AMERICAN COMMUNITY

A Twenty-First-Century Approach to Measuring Economic Progress

Precious D. Hall and Daphne Cooper

Introduction

This chapter seeks to explore the economic inequality and poverty that remain persistent in the African American community in the twenty-first century. It explores persistent poverty using a model of institutional policies that have served to keep African Americans as a permanent underclass, thus withholding from them any measure of true equality—which we foundationally understand as both racial and economic justice. This study relies on the premise that public policies, programs, and institutional practices have impacted the African American community, and we will challenge the long-standing, misdirected paradigm that has been used by the government to attempt to alleviate poverty. We posit that although legislation passed under major reforms such as the New Deal and the Great Society programs made an attempt to eliminate poverty, it suffered from the fatal flaws of trying to blame or fix the individual on a micro level instead of blaming the structural failures within the government system itself on a meso level.

This work will discuss the faces of oppression—exploitation, marginalization, powerlessness, cultural imperialism, and violence, as defined by Iris Marion Young[1]—and how they are reflected in models of poverty that we argue are ill-fitted for accurate measurements of poverty within the African American community. Ultimately, we will challenge the structural inadequacies of U.S. governmental policies and reconceptualize poverty by proposing a paradigm shift in public policy and the measurements used to develop public policies. We suggest that the old paradigm must be challenged and changed and that we must look at the political, economic, and social structures that have failed African Americans, who continue to have higher poverty rates than white Americans and who face continuous barriers to employment, quality health care, educational attainment, and affordable housing. We promote the Making a Difference (MAD) Model, which combines the Structural, Geographic, Cumulative/Cyclical, and Cultural Theories of poverty into one model that suggests alternative measures for economic and racial progress in the twenty-first century.

Ultimately, we posit that the MAD Model must serve as a framework and guide for policymakers to implement new public policies that would better address the poor and underprivileged in the United States. The MAD Model would be useful to policymakers, allowing them to improve the quality of life among those individuals and families that remain persistently poor through the increased allocation and equitable distribution of resources and funding.

Economic Power and Wealth

The state of black America is still in shambles! Yes, the poverty rates for African Americans and Hispanics did reach an all-time historic low in 2019.[2] However, inequality persists. In the United States, 26 percent of black Americans under the age of eighteen live in households that experience food insecurity,[3] 36 percent of black Americans stated that they have no retirement savings or pension whatsoever,[4] and 21.2 percent of black Americans still live in poverty.[5] And all of this was reported before the coronavirus pandemic hit our country, further crushing those already at the margins of society. The wealth gap before the pandemic was atrocious; now, for many, rising out of poverty has turned into something not just beyond their grasp but completely out of reach. While mainstream America caught the coronavirus, "black America caught hell," as black, Latino, and indigenous people got sick and died at higher rates.[6] The disproportionate impact on these communities of color revealed a disturbing reality: Racial fault lines are real in America and systematic racial oppression continues, especially when we look at economic power and wealth.

The Center for American Progress's "Systemic Inequality" 2018 report confirms that wealth is unequally distributed by race in the United States. The report explains that

> African American families have a fraction of the wealth of white families, leaving them more economically insecure and with far fewer opportunities for economic mobility...Even after considering positive factors such as increased education levels, African Americans have less wealth than whites. Less wealth translates into fewer opportunities for upward mobility and is compounded by lower income levels and fewer chances to build wealth or pass accumulated wealth down to future generations.[7]

Today, we still must ask: Have social policies helped or hindered the social conditions of African Americans? This report relies on the premise that public policies, programs, and institutional practices have impacted the African American community and will challenge the long-standing misdirected paradigm that was used by President Lyndon B. Johnson to eliminate poverty with his Great Society legislation. We posit that although the legislation of the Great Society made an honest attempt to eliminate poverty, it suffered from the same fatal flaws of trying to blame or fix the individuals on a micro level instead of blaming the structural failures within the government system itself on a meso level.

According to the World Bank, a basic definition of poverty is "the lack of what is necessary for material well-being—especially food, but also housing, land, and other assets. In other words, poverty is the lack of multiple resources that leads to hunger and physical deprivation." These material deprivations have psychological effects as well.[8] Those in poverty, particularly African Americans, live in a state in which their social welfare is at risk, as living in poverty often also includes suffering from poor health, inadequate health care, and either inappropriate or unaffordable housing. The economic suffering of people of color is not new and we maintain that there is a direct relationship between the government's social policies and the social conditions of African Americans. Most African Americans have been struggling economically since their forebears received their freedom from slavery in America. Historically, a condition of poverty has been institutionally created and reinforced since the ratification of the Thirteenth Amendment. The condition of poverty today is a result of cumulative disadvantage, and cumulative "disadvantages do not cascade by accident."[9]

Persistent poverty affects people who experience deprivation over many years and whose average incomes are below the poverty line for an extended period of time; those who are encountering hardship at a certain stage in the life cycle; and "those discriminated against because of their social position at the local, regional or national level."[10] Individuals who live in persistent poverty experience several forms of disadvantage, and public policy often serves only to trap them in poverty and close opportunities to escape.[11] This work will discuss how failed federal policies and programs have caused African Americans to remain a permanent underclass. This has helped to create a culture in which African Americans have learned to adapt to lifestyles that allow them to function in impoverished conditions due to the institutional barriers and attitudes that have persisted over centuries and decades.

Differences in Poverty Rates

African Americans in the United States are much more likely to live and/or remain in poverty than most other population groups. According to the Henry J. Kaiser Family Foundation's State Health Facts, 9 percent of whites, 21.2 percent of African Americans, 17.2 percent of Hispanics, 9.7 percent of Asians, and 24.2 percent of Native Americans were living in poverty in 2019 in the United States.[12] History has shown that "substantial progress for racial minorities," including African Americans, has taken place in the last forty years, but the "life chances"—the economic opportunities that would lift or keep one out of poverty—of "the average black or Latino child are still very different from those of his average white or Asian classmate."[13]

Daniel R. Meyer and Geoffrey Wallace, in "Poverty Levels and Trends in Comparative Perspective," argue that there are "substantial differences in poverty rates" for certain groups that have persisted since 1968.[14] A 2006 study looked at individuals and families that have the highest risk of poverty. Meyer and Wallace explain that individuals in female-headed families have the highest poverty rates at nearly 32 percent and that poverty is closely linked with the education levels of the primary member of the family unit. The highest poverty rates that have been above 20 percent include African Americans and people living in families whose heads of household do not have a job, a high school diploma, or a college degree. In addition, those with low earnings or no earnings were "at very high risk of poverty, because in the United States programs to supplement low earnings are generally not generous enough to bring them above the poverty level."[15] These characteristics reveal "the critical importance of the labor market" and the fact that African Americans have higher poverty rates because "race is still strongly connected to opportunity and outcome in the United States."[16] This connection is not and could not be fixed with a simple change in law. According to Mary Corcoran, "African Americans are many times more likely to be long-term poor than are whites, and they are much less likely to be upwardly mobile, either within or across generations."[17] Research continues to show that there is a dramatic difference in poverty rates across different racial categories. (See Figure 7.1.)

Levels and Faces of Oppression

Ann Chih Lin and David R. Harris argue that race is central to any attempt to assess poverty because in the United States, our economy, our cultural frameworks and repertoires, and our government policies have been shaped by a history of racial relations and racially inflected decision-making. As a result, our institutions, practices, and beliefs can foster racial disadvantage without any deliberate effort to discriminate.[18]

However true this may be, it is still vital, as Devah Pager notes, "to consider the significance of discrimination in the context of persistent poverty among members of racial or ethnic minority groups."[19]

It is true that within systems of oppression individual persons sometimes intentionally harm others; this is natural, as

Figure 7.1   U.S. Poverty Rates: 1974–2019[20]

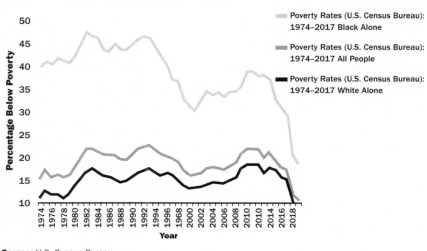

Source: U.S. Census Bureau.

oppression does not occur on a single level. Inequality can be maintained and reproduced at the individual, institutional, and cultural levels. According to Maurianne Adams and Ximena Zúñiga, the individual or micro level of oppression "refers to persons in themselves and in relationship with others," while the institutional or meso level "refers to social institutions such as schooling, banking, and finance, and criminal justice institutions that enforce the law and political institutions that create the law." Finally, the cultural/societal or macro level refers to "the broad, abstract understandings that pervade a social system." These are the "prevailing norms and values that govern communication style, gender roles, family structure, expectations of physical and mental capacities, relationships to time and place, aesthetic standards, and more."[21] The present work focuses on the institutional failures of social and economic policies that place culturally imperialistic norms upon African Americans. We posit that most legislation aimed at alleviating poverty has grown out of "the legacy of accumulated and persistent inequality" that enables institutions to "perpetuate themselves and often outlive their original intentions."[22]

All forms of oppression, including economic oppression, are reflected in society in multidimensional ways. Iris Marion Young describes the five faces of oppression: exploitation, marginalization, powerlessness, cultural imperialism, and violence.[23] From an abstract point of view, Young says, "all oppressed people face a common condition": "some inhibition of their ability to develop and exercise their capacities and express their needs, thoughts, and feelings."[24] Although this occurs in the abstract, not all oppression of groups looks the same. In this sense, oppression is a general term for injustice. For Young, oppression is a structural concept which can occur even from those who may mean well.[25] We assert that although there have been laws and policies aimed at helping African Americans, the misuse and abuse of the "bootstrap mentality" has contributed to the persistent poverty within the African American community.

The concept of one lifting himself up by his own bootstraps sounds heroic in theory, but in American history, although people of color are often reminded of how many white European Americans have used their own bootstraps to obtain economic stability and success, this is a myth. The myth of the bootstrap mentality was even discussed by such leaders as Martin Luther King Jr. toward the latter part of his life. Dr. King, in an interview given to NBC News eleven months prior to his murder, expounded upon the myth of the bootstrap mentality. King reminded the country that America freed the slaves through the Emancipation Proclamation in 1863 "but gave the slaves no land, or nothing in reality...to get started on."[26] He also explained that at the same time America refused to give the Negroes any land, it gave away millions of acres of lands in the West and Midwest to white

Europeans, which gave them an "economic base" and head start. This economic base included land, land grant colleges built with government money, county agents that provided expertise in farming, low interest rates provided to farmers, and subsidies from the government not to farm. This economic floor granted to white Europeans was not granted to black Africans (now Americans), and so "emancipation for the Negro was really freedom to hunger; it was freedom to the winds and rains of heaven. It was freedom without food to eat or land to cultivate, and therefore it was freedom and famine at the same time."[27] The emancipation that was provided to freed slaves turned them to nature without providing any real subsistence; yet the very same people provided with economic subsistence continue to say that blacks ought to pull themselves up and out of poverty, when they themselves were given more than a helping hand by government institutions.

The reality for Dr. King, which still stands today, is that "when white Americans tell the Negro to lift himself by his own bootstraps, they don't look over the legacy of slavery and segregation."[28] In 1963, King maintained that it is not only incorrect, but "a cruel jest to say to a bootless man that he ought to lift himself by his own bootstraps, and many Negroes...have been left bootless...as a result of a society that deliberately made his color a stigma and something worthless and degrading."[29] In the United States, we continue to see these disparities persist, especially when we look at the plight of black farmers in recent years and during the 2020 coronavirus pandemic. It is no secret that millions of people have suffered and continue to suffer economically due to the detrimental effects of the pandemic. However, one group that has been overlooked are black farmers, who make up about 1.3 percent of farmers in the United States.[30] Not only have black farmers been excluded from all United States Department of Agriculture (USDA) subsidies, but any aid received by black farmers during the pandemic was on average eight times less than their white counterparts received.[31] Years from now, when we see the rates of black farmers continue to decline, will we discuss how white farmers received more of a helping hand from the government when times were rough, or will we discuss how white farmers persisted through this tough time with sheer grit and determination? In the twenty-first century, the myth of the bootstrap mentality is one that continues to be rooted in oppression.

Exploitation: A Steady Process

Regarding the first face of oppression—exploitation—Young maintains that "oppression occurs through a steady process of the transfer of the results of the labor of one social group to benefit another."[32] This form of exploitation has been used against African Americans dating back to the country's long institution of slavery, in which the literal labor of black slaves from Africa was used exclusively for the material wealth of whites. In 1967, King explained that "the Negro was a slave in this country for 244 years...This led to the 'thingification' of the Negro."[33] Through the exploitation of slavery, the personhood of black Africans was removed, preventing them from being looked upon with the same status and worth as other human beings. Historically, in this country, "no other ethnic group has been a slave on American soil" and "the color [of the black person] became a stigma" that pervaded American society.[34] Young acknowledges that the "injustices of exploitation cannot be eliminated by the redistribution of goods, for as long as institutionalized practices and structural relations remain unaltered, the process of transfer will re-create an unequal distribution of benefits." To remedy this exploitation requires the "reorganization of institutions and practices of decision making."[35] It is the bootstrap mentality that erroneously believes that what is needed is not institutional restructuring, but personal attitude adjustments.

Marginalization: Living Just Outside the Circle

Historically, exploitation has been more explicit, but today oppression "increasingly...occurs in the form of marginalization." Marginalization involves casting individuals out of mainstream society because the system of labor either cannot or will not use them.[36] In the past, we have seen the rise of marginalization during the Jim Crow era after the institution of slavery was constitutionally banned. Yet the practice of marginalization was couched in terms of freedom of choice and mere preference on all sides by the Supreme Court in the *Plessy v. Ferguson* decision. Young recognizes the danger of marginalization: It means that "a whole category of people is expelled from useful participation in social life and thus potentially subjected to severe material deprivation and even extermination."[37] In a society where others have plenty, the material deprivation is especially unjust. However, having access to material goods alone does not compensate for the oppressive nature of marginalization, as marginalization can remain in the form of "uselessness, boredom, and lack of self-respect."[38]

Powerlessness: A Lack of Opportunity

In addition to exploitation and marginalization, powerlessness is another face of oppression often swept outside of public debate and discussion. According to Young, powerlessness denotes "a position...that allows persons little opportunity to develop and exercise skills"; they have "little or no work autonomy" and a limited ability to "exercise...creativity or judgment in their work." The powerless lack "authority, status, and sense of self."[39] Along with exploitation and marginalization, powerlessness refers to "relations of power and oppression that occur by virtue of the social division of labor" and to "structural and institutional relations" that limit the material possibilities for individuals, which includes both "resources they have access to and the concrete opportunities they have or do not have to develop and exercise their capacities."[40]

Cultural Imperialism: The Narrative of the Dominant Experience

At the foundation of the structural and institutional concepts of exploitation, marginalization, and powerlessness lies cultural imperialism. Cultural imperialism refers to the imposition of dominant opinions or sentiments upon dissentient or sub-groups within a larger society. It further often leads to stereotyping subgroups and marking them as "other."[41] This form of imperialism involves "the universalization of the dominant group's experience and culture, and its establishment as the norm." The dominant groups subsequently "project their own experiences as a representative of humanity as such."[42] Cultural imperialism is furthered through the myth of the bootstrap mentality, which is an illogical assumption that African Americans were in a position of poverty and inequality because they wanted to be or because they did not work hard enough, while our white counterparts have been beneficiaries of decades of government benefits (in the form of congressional acts giving away land in the West and Midwest, the construction of government-funded land-grant colleges, low-interest rates to establish farms, and federal farming subsidies). Essentially, continuing in the vein of cultural imperialism as laid out by Young, we see a dominant narrative about poverty being placed upon African Americans that is not historically reflective of the African American experience. As King explained, African Americans want to be people, not subject to stigmatization or deprivation, which has been prevalent in government treatment and policies.[43]

Cultural imperialism becomes even more evident in the discussions around African Americans who are recipients of government welfare. According to Jo Anne Schneider:

> The many reforms of the 1960s shifted public assistance from a program that excluded people of color to a system epitomized by the stereotypical African American welfare mom... To conservatives, welfare continues to be a problem because African Americans lack the appropriate "cultural values" to get themselves out of poverty.

In contrast, "for many social activists and liberal academics, high welfare rates and the middle-class (read white) backlash against welfare are the direct result of racism."[44]

Violence: The Overt and Subtle Reality

The final face of oppression, violence, recognizes the systematic violence that members of some groups face. These groups live with the fear of "random, unprovoked attacks on their persons or property, which have no motive but to damage, humiliate, or destroy the person."[45] It is not merely the act of violence itself that is oppressive, but its existence as a systematic social and sometimes institutional practice. Violence does not require "direct victimization," but makes its presence felt in the daily knowledge that one is liable to the violation of his freedom and dignity solely on the basis of group identity.[46] This violence is often tolerated and normalized within society. Violence can take the form of legalized, physical assaults on one's person and property, as demonstrated in the many forms of political repression inflicted upon African Americans from slavery through the civil rights movement, or it can take the subtler form of harmful and detrimental stereotypes.

Charles Jones, quoting R. Goldstein, defines repression (speaking here in the context of political repression) as "government action which grossly discriminates against persons or organizations viewed as presenting a fundamental challenge to existing power relationships or key governmental policies, because of their perceived political beliefs."[47] History has given us several examples of overt repression and subtle repression. In an overt sense, we have seen what the government did to marginalized organizations fighting for change, such as the Black Panther Party.[48] Yet in a subtler sense, we have seen and continue to see the harmful and detrimental stereotypes painting African Americans as angry, lazy, uneducated, yet shrewd enough to be able to exploit the government for subsistence without having to work—remember the Welfare Queen discussed by Ronald Reagan?[49] These instances demonstrate how violence as a face of oppression manifests itself institutionally in multiple ways, even when individuals and organizations seek to address issues of oppression within their own communities through institutional change.

These faces of oppression demonstrate how poverty can be not only institutionalized, but used as a measure to subvert attempts to remedy poverty by the very same institutions that have created and contributed to the oppression in the first place. The failure to recognize the impact of institutions while erroneously promoting a false "bootstrap mentality" is what makes it difficult for any program to truly remedy poverty and bring about both racial and economic justice. Now, we will take a look at the Great Society's attempts to alleviate poverty and its ultimate failure.

The Great Society

The War on Poverty refers to the programs and policies created under Lyndon B. Johnson's Great Society to eliminate and/or lessen poverty in the United States. "For the first time," Linda Faye Williams explains, "the United States government was given the power to intervene directly to ensure recognition of the constitutional rights of all its citizens in every state."[50] Most importantly, the War on Poverty was the U.S. government's systematic approach to eliminate or minimize poverty. The legislation targeted African Americans for inclusion on the agenda, which represented a turning point in U.S. social policy.

The War on Poverty was ambitious in its effort, but it was not a panacea, since it was wrapped up in political motivations and did not always seriously address difficult questions of social reform and civil rights in the United States. The administrations of President John F. Kennedy and his successor, Lyndon B. Johnson, became the primary organizers to offer a governmental response to the poverty crisis in the mid-twentieth century. Both had to deal with the concern that poverty would threaten America's progress, and both administrations pushed for economic growth that would create full employment and social reform that would enable the poor to access what President Johnson called "the good life."[51] Johnson in particular wanted presidential power so that he could "give things to people—all sorts of things to all sorts of people, especially the poor and the blacks."[52]

Unlike previous programs that failed to address the status of African Americans in any fundamental way, the Great Society legislation benefited African Americans. Franklin Delano Roosevelt and John F. Kennedy had shown little eagerness to sacrifice their domestic and economic programs on the stage of civil rights. Kennedy achieved only limited success for poor people through his cautious efforts to counter poverty, which were mostly constrained to implementing safe policies.[53] But Johnson recognized that blacks and Latinos suffered from the lack of access to quality health programs, decent housing, and jobs. He initiated legislation to rectify these inequities by transforming the nation's social policy. He declared an unconditional War on

Poverty to create a new institutional base for antipoverty policies and civil rights efforts, of which many African Americans were the beneficiaries through the effects of economic opportunities. Johnson's goal was to help individuals, families, and communities to help themselves.

According to Daniel Halloran, the War on Poverty constituted "a new conceptual approach to the problem of poverty." It was "an attempt to uncover and strike at the roots of poverty and destroy its causes instead of treating its symptoms." The War on Poverty was "not concerned with helping the poor to be more comfortable in their poverty...but rather, with helping the poor to arise from poverty."[54] Halloran says that the War on Poverty "was not a product of a long, fruitful period of congressional debate." Rather, its programs were "rushed through Congress on the tide of emotionalism following President Kennedy's death." The War on Poverty "did not constitute so much a well-structured administrative plan as a disjointed series of programs clustered around a dynamic new concept that society should attack the causes of poverty instead of merely treating its symptoms."[55]

Although the War on Poverty did not eradicate poverty in the United States, it had a profound effect on many people's lives and it significantly shaped the social and economic commitments of the federal government toward African Americans. Some might even argue that the Great Society was on par with the Civil Rights Act of 1964, which for many was one of the most important legislative actions furthering equal opportunity and attempting to eradicate discrimination against people of color.[56] However, the Great Society, for all its noble efforts, failed to acknowledge the broader historical claims of American blacks, which we ultimately believe was a failure steeped in institutionalized cultural imperialism.

Models of Persistent Poverty

There are four theories of poverty that are relevant to this study: Structural Poverty Theory, Geographic Theory, Cumulative/Cyclical Theory, and the Culture of Poverty Theory. We posit that while no one theory will explain all instances of persistent poverty, we can use a combination of several theories to address the issues of poverty, thus promoting an interactive model to lay the foundation for appropriately measuring economic poverty in the twenty-first century. Our model, the Making a Difference (MAD) Model, is a theoretical framework that blends the Structural, Geographic, and Cumulative/Cyclical Theories. The Culture of Poverty Theory addresses or explains the persistent poverty among African Americans from the white narrative; therefore, we reject many aspects of the Culture of Poverty Theory, along with certain aspects of the other theories, and prescribe the MAD Model to explain persistent poverty among African Americans in the United States.

Structural Theory

We selected the Structural Theory because it weakens the misplaced, misdirected mainstream theories that focus solely on individual attributes as the cause of poverty. The Structural Theory does not look at the individual as the cause of poverty; it looks at poverty as the result of structural failings at the economic, political, and social levels. This theory suggests that United States poverty is largely the result of structural failings which consist of

> (1) the inability of the U.S. labor market to provide enough decent-paying jobs for all families to avoid poverty or near-poverty; (2) the ineffectiveness of American public policy in reducing levels of poverty via the social safety net; and (3) the fact that the majority

of Americans will experience poverty during their adult lifetimes, which suggest the systematic nature of U.S. poverty.[57]

This theory maintains that "there simply are not enough well-paying jobs to support all of those (and their families) who are looking for work."[58] Research has shown that "during the past twenty-five years the American economy has increasingly produced a larger number of low-paying jobs, jobs that are part-time, and jobs that are lacking in benefits."[59]

Poverty in the United States is "a failure of the economic structure to provide sufficient opportunities for all who are participating in that system." As a result, "millions of families find themselves struggling below or precariously close to the poverty line."[60] The Structural Theory also demonstrates "failure at the political and policy level," specifically within "social and economic programs directed to economically vulnerable populations [that] are minimal in their ability to raise families out of poverty." For the past twenty-five years, Americans have witnessed "an overall retrenchment and reduction in the social safety net. These reductions have included both a scaling back of the amount of benefits being transferred and a tightening of program eligibility."[61]

According to Robert Mark Rank, failure has nothing to do with the individual; it is failure at the structural level. Policymakers "lose sight of the fact that governments can and do exert a sizable impact on the extent of poverty within their jurisdictions."[62] The Structural Theory has been included as a part of our model because it explains how systematic barriers prohibit the poor from access to and accomplishment within key social institutions, which has nothing to do with failure of the individual. Once policymakers understand and accept this, they will be able to use antipoverty programs to "get more jobs, improve schooling for the poor, equalize income distributions, remove discrimination bias from housing, banking, education, and employment, and assure equal political participation by poor persons."[63] Policymakers have redirected society's ills upon easy targets (the least powerful citizens), rather than recognizing the real issues or showing any concern for the poor. Persistent poverty in the United States will continue to exist through structural barriers linked to selection criteria that will directly or indirectly exclude groups of people based on inappropriate standards, such as discrimination and institutionalized racism, thus rendering many individuals economically powerless.

Geographic Theory

The Geographic Theory demonstrates that place influences racial differences in poverty. According to Michael Stoll:

> Place is the locus of economic activity and amenities that give value to areas. Places are more valuable economically and socially when there is greater density of economic activity (businesses, jobs), and valuable amenities and public goods (good schools and neighbors, parks, low crime, museums).[64]

Stoll says that having an "attachment to places with these valuable assets is expected to reduce one's risk of poverty...By contrast, living far from these amenities is thought to increase one's risk of being poor."[65] In the words of Ted K. Bradshaw, the Geographic Theory of poverty suggests that "social advantages and disadvantages concentrate in separate areas."[66] Poverty is caused by geographical disparities such as "rural poverty, ghetto poverty, urban disinvestment, Southern poverty, third-world poverty, and other framings of the problem [which] represent a spatial characterization of poverty." This theory explains that "people, institutions, and cultures in certain areas" are marginalized and thus "lack the objective resources needed to generate well-being and income, and that they lack the power to claim redistribution."[67] The Geographic Theory was selected because it illustrates that there is a considerable amount of social and economic inequality within neighborhoods, which perpetuates racial segregation, isolation, and the concentration of disadvantaged African Americans.[68] It explains that racial groups, in particular whites and blacks, are residentially segregated. According to Stoll, the persistence of poverty in central cities "reinforces the notion that place might matter" in addressing poverty.[69]

Stoll continues, "Many racially segregated neighborhoods are disadvantaged and suffer disproportionately from problems such as high concentrations of poverty, joblessness, hopelessness, and the political indifference of elites (Massey and Denton 1993)."[70] Research shows that "segregated neighborhoods impose enormous costs on minority residents, such as the unavailability of good schools, worse health outcomes, negative role models, a lack of economic opportunities, and social isolation (Massey and Denton 1993; Wilson 1987)." The weakness of this theory is that more research is needed to address the issue of race, place, and poverty.[71]

According to Wendy Shaw, "space is not a backdrop for capitalism"; it is "restructured by it and contributes to the system's survival. The geography of poverty is a spatial expression of the capitalist system."[72] According Bradshaw, Goldsmith and Blakely argue in their book *Separate Societies* (1992) that

> the joint processes of the movement of households and jobs away from poor areas in central cities and rural regions creates a "separation of work, residence, and economic, social and political life"...these processes...are multiplied by racism and political indifference of the localities in which they flourish.[73]

Bradshaw also references W. J. Wilson's book *The Truly Disadvantaged* (1987), which "holds that the people from ghetto areas with the highest levels of education, the greatest skills, widest world view, and the most extensive opportunities were the ones who migrated out of central city locations to other places."[74] This exodus of black middle-class workers and manufacturing jobs from inner-city neighborhoods left behind swells of jobless, poor, segregated, and socially isolated people.

Cumulative and Cyclical Theory

The Cumulative and Cyclical Theory of Poverty was selected to build upon the components of the aforementioned theories and to link economic factors at the individual level with the structural factors operating at the geographical level. The Cyclical Theory of Poverty demonstrates how multiple problems accumulate by presenting the individual and her community as caught in a spiral of social ills. Once these social ills dominate, "they close other opportunities and create a cumulative set of problems that make any effective response nearly impossible."[75] According to Bradshaw, "This theory has its origins in economics in the work of [Gunnar] Myrdal...who developed a theory of 'interlocking, circular, interdependence within a process of cumulative causation' that helps explain economic underdevelopment and development."[76] Myrdal's work reveals that "personal and community well being are closely linked in a cascade of negative consequences" and that "the interdependence of factors creating poverty accelerates once a cycle of decline is started."[77] We selected this theory because it explains the spirals of poverty by showing how "problems for individuals (earnings, housing, health, education, self confidence) are interdependent and strongly linked to community deficiencies (loss of business and jobs, inadequate schools, inability to provide social services) etc."[78]

The limitation of the Cyclical Theory of Poverty is its complexity, which reflects a real problem: The linkages and interdependence between various causes of poverty "are hard to break because each is reinforced by other parts of the spiraling system."[79] Community-level crisis leads to individual crisis and vice versa, and each accumulates, causing spirals of poverty and increasing powerlessness among certain groups.

Culture of Poverty Theory

The Culture of Poverty Theory is a social theory explaining the cycle of poverty. It suggests that poverty is caused by a subculture that "adopts values that are non-productive and are contrary to norms of success."[80] Oscar Lewis was the first to popularize the concept of the "culture of poverty." He described it as a way of life, a combination of certain traits passed on through generations, that stems from a group's adaptation to poverty and "being at the bottom" in an industrialized, capitalist society. The culture of poverty is "both an adaptation and a reaction of the poor to their marginal position in a class-stratified, highly individuated, capitalistic society."[81] The culture of poverty also assumes that persistent poverty involves a psychological aspect that is firmly rooted in the individual and family structure.[82] The weakness of the Culture of Poverty Theory is that it tends to present negative connotations and characterizations about the poor that are highly stereotypical. These stereotypes are perpetuated through the cultural imperialist face of oppression that universalizes the narrative of the dominant group.

The Moynihan Report (1965) was a study that borrowed aspects of the Culture of Poverty Theory to explain African American poverty in the 1960s. This controversial report promoted the idea that most of the poverty within the black community was due to a history of slavery and subsequent unemployment and underemployment that prompted a necessary adaptation of one's lifestyle as a coping mechanism for poverty. The weakness of the report, like the weakness of the theory it draws from, is that it ultimately places the blame for poverty on the victim, thus removing the social duty of the government to alleviate poverty. Once poverty is viewed as the fault of the poor and not of government policy, their culture, not social injustice, is believed to cause and perpetuate poverty. Thus the attention is turned back on the individual rather than the structures that constrict him.

The Moynihan Report and the Culture of Poverty Theory paved a way for policymakers to perform their social duties and guided policies in a certain direction. A former Democratic representative has noted that ideas about the cultural roots of poverty have played an important role in "shaping how lawmakers choose to address poverty issues."[83] Patricia Cohen explains that the 1960s were a decade in which poverty in the United States was blamed on the victim and the discussion about a culture of poverty flourished.[84] According to Bradshaw, "The underlying argument of conservatives...is that government welfare perpetuated poverty by permitting a cycle of 'welfare dependency' where poor families develop and pass on to others the skills needed to work the system rather than to gain paying employment."[85] Some scholars believed that a culture of poverty exists while others denied it. According to Oscar Lewis, there were always contradictions when evaluating the poor that stemmed from the power struggle of competing groups and their ascribing poverty to a culture of poverty, or an adaptation to certain common problems or traits among families with the lowest income levels and the least education.[86] Cohen notes that "Moynihan's analysis never lost its appeal to conservative thinkers" and that Moynihan's "arguments ultimately succeeded when President Bill Clinton signed a bill in 1996 'ending welfare as we know it.'"[87]

Now, once again, after decades of silence, scholars are speaking openly about the culture of poverty, "conceding that culture and persistent poverty are enmeshed."[88]

Scholars suggest that a culture of poverty exists among African Americans because of their lack of a work ethic, inappropriate family values, ethic of dependency, and/or personal inadequacies, suggesting that all these deficiencies are passed from one generation to the next. These scholars fail to look into some of the root causes of poverty, such as: an industrial capitalist society with its inherent inequalities in wage labor and production for profit; a high rate of unemployment; underemployment for unskilled labor; low wages; and a failure to provide social, political, and economic organization for the low-income population. The economic exploitation of African Americans for centuries has given way to literal and metaphorical violence that subjects African Americans to stereotypes that are untrue, and that further perpetuates their marginalization. Contrary to societal portrayals, research indicates that the poor do not differ from the better-off parts of society in their values, and that there are various sources of possible inequalities, not only from the cash income from wages but from assets, private income, and employment benefits. Nevertheless, Culture of Poverty Theory proponents argue that because the poor adapt their lifestyle to deal with poverty, a culture of poverty becomes institutionalized and is very difficult to escape.

The MAD Model

Each of the models of poverty discussed above—Structural, Geographical, Cumulative/Cyclical, and Culture of Poverty—has valid points, but none of them singularly reflects in totality how and why African Americans have remained in poverty. To that extent, we prescribe what is called the Making a Difference (MAD) Model to accurately measure and define poverty in the twenty-first century. The MAD Model takes an interactive approach that considers all the faces of oppression (exploitation, marginalization, powerlessness, cultural imperialism, and violence) and measures their combined effects on poverty within the African American community. The effect of each of the causes of poverty dealt with by a particular model can change depending on factors in a separate model, which is why an interactive approach is needed.

Our prescribed MAD Model uses such an interactive approach to demonstrate how and why African Americans have remained in poverty. Each theory—Structural, Geographic, Cumulative/Cyclical, and Cultural—is interconnected, with only one theory blaming the individual victim for being poor. The Structural, Geographic, and Cumulative/Cyclical theories define poverty as a systemic failure at the political, economic, or social level which has caused African Americans to remain poor. The government did not stabilize nor pour resources into the African American communities despite knowing that they were faced with many barriers and had limited opportunities and resources to achieve income and well-being. The federal government played an active and deliberate role in concentrating poverty in racially segregated neighborhoods located far from amenities, shopping, and services. Public housing and residential segregation have caused African Americans to remain socially and economically deprived within neighborhoods.

The MAD Model explains that once a cycle of decline has started within a specific community, it perpetuates a spiral of poverty through the loss of businesses and jobs (Structural), substandard housing (Geographic), and inadequate public schools and inefficient social services (Geographic and Cumulative), which leads the community and its members into a crisis where they learn to adapt and cope with poverty (Culture). The Culture of Poverty Theory explains the cycle of poverty in the United States from the white perspective, blaming the poor and their "culture" for the problems they experience. The MAD Model explains that the political, economic, and social structures of government are flawed and that this is the primary reason why African Americans have remained poor and underprivileged in the United States.

The purpose of the MAD Model is to draw attention to the root causes of persistent poverty and thus prompt a paradigm shift in U.S. public policy. We believe that the MAD Model provides the federal government with prescriptions to look at problems differently, focusing on the structures of government instead of the individual. The MAD Model must serve as a framework or guide for policymakers to implement new public policies that would better address the poor and underprivileged in the United States. The MAD Model would be useful to policymakers, allowing them to improve the quality of life among those individuals and families that remain persistently poor by allocating more resources and funding and distributing them equitably across structural and geographical lines to lessen the cumulative cultural effects of poverty.

Stephanie Riegg Cellini et al., drawing from Greg Duncan's *Years of Poverty, Years of Plenty*, point to the need for models of poverty such as the MAD Model:

> A complete explanation of why people are poor would require many interrelated theories—theories of family composition, earnings, asset accumulation, transfer programs, and the macro-economy to name a few. Further complicating the task, a complete poverty theory would need to be based upon the family, while most theories are based upon individuals.[89]

Many agree that the official measure of poverty in the United States is flawed. Measuring poverty using the MAD Model will give policymakers a different perspective and a chance to create policies that will actually lessen or alleviate poverty in the United States. In order to do this, policymakers will need to rely on multiple measures and study their interactive effects upon one another. Taking a serious approach to the cycle of wealth inequality, for example, policymakers must address the history of employment discrimination, housing/mortgage discrimination, health disparities, and substandard public education in impoverished areas.[90] According to Hanks, Solomon, and Weller:

> Persistent labor market discrimination and segregation also force blacks into fewer and less advantageous employment opportunities than their white counterparts...Even when African Americans pursue higher education, purchase a home, or secure a good job, they still lag behind their white counterparts in terms of wealth. Moreover, the disparities between white and black Americans can nearly always be traced back to policies that either implicitly or explicitly discriminate against black Americans.[91]

Research demonstrates that racism "has produced segregated neighborhoods with fewer hospitals, higher rates of chronic illnesses, and unequal access to health care," which continues to be a contributing factor to poverty.[92] Using the MAD Model will help policymakers take direct action to make intentional, systematic changes to "an American system built on suppression, oppression, and the concentration of power and wealth."[93]

When it comes to twenty-first-century measurements of wealth or the lack thereof, we promote using the following variables: labor market/employment, access to quality health care, educational attainment, and affordable housing. We chose the labor market as one of the variables because it takes into account "the inability of the U.S. labor market to provide enough decent-paying jobs for all families to avoid poverty or near-poverty."[94] The labor market is critical when considering why African Americans have higher poverty rates, because, as we have seen, "race is still strongly connected to opportunity and outcome in the United States."[95] Additionally, access to quality education, health care, and housing were chosen to help further explain how systematic barriers prohibit the poor from access to and accomplishment within key social institutions, which also demonstrates the structural failings and ineffectiveness of American public policy.

We need twenty-first-century solutions for twenty-first-century problems. These measures and their interactions would more accurately capture the struggles of poverty and should be used in any research on economic trends in the twenty-first century.

Recommendations

Poverty exists; poverty is real; poverty can be remedied through an institutional paradigm shift. This paradigm shift requires the government to focus not just on institutional policies, but on the societal and institutional attitudes that blame the powerless individuals for their positions instead of looking at the historical and current exploitation, imperialism, marginalization, and violence that have contributed to widespread levels of poverty within specific communities. In addition, it is up to the government to understand that with regard to developing stronger policies to aid the black community, nothing is being asked of them other than what has been and continues to be given to white Europeans.

"Institutions are complex entities," to change which demands multiple inputs and resources across many groupings within and outside the particular institutions.[96] People of color, especially black descendants of Africa, want genuine freedom; we all want equality and to be treated as people. But what that equality looks like and how it will come about needs to reflect the accurate history of institutions and institutional attitudes and their role not only in the lives of black descendants of Africa, but in the lives of Europeans as well.

Going forward, the shift that must occur is one in which we truly seek to make a difference by studying the interactive effects of the labor market, property ownership, access to health care, and educational attainment. We must assess these factors for the role they play in the economic exploitation, marginalization, imperialism, powerlessness, and violence in the lives of African Americans and how they are enabled and produced at multiple levels of government. This is the only way that we will be able to make genuine progress toward both racial and economic justice. The first step to remedying the problem is to recognize not only the problem but its root causes as well. To this extent, our call to action requires that in the twenty-first century we move away from singular explanations for poverty within the African American community, and that we consistently and unapologetically point out the compounding effects of failed institutional policies and measurements that have perpetuated culturally imperialistic narratives.

Conclusion

The persistent poverty that exists among African Americans in the twenty-first century in the United States is the unanticipated consequence of public policy that was intended to alleviate or lessen poverty but has, in fact, caused it to worsen. Federal policies have had an impact on African Americans; some policies have prevented, changed, or eradicated undesirable social conditions, while others have caused African Americans to remain deprived and disadvantaged. When Lyndon Johnson pushed forward his Great Society legislation, we do not believe that he did so with the intention of not succeeding. We do not believe that he was a cruel and heartless man who operated in word and not deed. Rather, we believe that he and other policymakers that participated in the process were unable to recognize that poverty has as much to do with institutional attitudes as it does with the institutional policies themselves. It was inevitable that the War on Poverty programs would fall short of remedying the persistent poverty of African Americans.

The Great Society was flawed, and the policies put forward since the Great Society continue to be flawed. In the administrations after Johnson, there was Nixon's Southern Strategy, which included the notion of black capitalism, while simultaneously ignoring black Americans' lack of capital and failing to provide them any; Reagan's creation of Enterprise Zones; tax credits developed under the Clinton Administration; and new incentives to invest in forgotten and underserved communities presented by the forty-fifth president.[97] All these administrations have put policies in place that ultimately benefit the owners of capital and not those living at or below the poverty level. Until we reach the point of understanding the compounding institutional factors that create and maintain poverty, we will continue to see economic injustice and by extension racial injustice.

When looking at the economic progress of some African Americans today, it would be easy to think that economic justice has been achieved. More African Americans today are educated and have obtained midlevel and executive careers than ever before, and African Americans have achieved the greatest levels of wealth that have ever been seen in the United States. However, we must be careful not to look at the exceptions and turn them into the rule. We must understand that although there are more "success" stories in the twenty-first century, there still remains the fact that unemployment for African Americans remains higher than for white Europeans, that the poverty rates of African Americans remain almost three times as high as those of white Europeans, and that African Americans' accumulation of household wealth continues to significantly lag behind that of white Europeans. This is even truer today, as McKinsey & Company has speculated an economic recovery time of more than five years for certain sectors from the coronavirus pandemic that has negatively impacted Hispanic and African American communities most of all in the initial stages of the recovery.[98] White Americans have recovered more than half of their job losses, whereas only a third of African Americans have recovered. And even within the African American community, recovery among mothers has been slower than among fathers.[99] The reality we are facing is that while some have faced a pandemic recession, others are still facing a depression.[100]

On the whole, public policies have had a negative effect on African Americans, contributing significantly to a persistent state of poverty—and for those not in poverty, a serious wealth gap—and causing them to face unemployment, underemployment, and inadequate access to health care, housing, and education. These are continuous reminders that economic justice has not yet been realized even after so many have fought and died for it. It is time for an updated approach that can truly Make a Difference in the lives of those who have faced insurmountable obstacles in this country and who, although they have managed to survive and thrive, have all the while been castigated and placated without any true measure of economic or racial justice.

8

MARRIAGE, FAMILY, ABORTION, AND POVERTY IN BLACK AMERICA

Star Parker with Robert Borens

The title *The State of Black America* immediately conjures up a sense that a discussion of problems is about to follow. And legitimately so. We do not depart from the observations of others that, on average, American blacks suffer social and economic problems disproportionately. Central to these problems is the persistence of poverty rates higher than the national average and higher, on average, than poverty rates for other ethnic groups.

Understanding why disproportionate poverty rates persist in many black communities is crucial if we are to grasp whether and how, through public policy or through other means, persistent poverty might be addressed. It is common today to attribute problems in black communities to racism. But to what extent can persistent black poverty be attributed to ongoing racial discrimination? And if racism is not, in fact, the sole or primary cause, where else might we look for an explanation?

The civil rights movement in the 1960s was supposed to be the watershed moment when the issue of racism in America would finally be solved. Following this, one might have expected that problems in black communities—problems pertaining to education,

housing, health care, poverty, crime, and wealth accumulation—
would be alleviated.

But here we are in 2022, more than half a century after the
Civil Rights Act of 1964 became law, and this is what the Census
Bureau tells us about poverty rates. (See Figures 8.1. and 8.2.)

The percentage of American blacks in poverty, over a half
century after the signing of the Civil Rights Act in 1964, is still
far out of proportion to the national average and to the number
of American blacks as a percentage of the population. In 2019,
blacks constituted 13.2 percent of the population, but 23.8 percent
of those in poverty.[1] The percentage of those in poverty who were
blacks was 1.8 times greater than the percentage of blacks in the
general population.

We may attempt to explain these realities by arguing that persistent racial discrimination is causing persistent black poverty,
which will force us to conclude that the measures for combatting
racism enacted in the 1964 Civil Rights Act were ill-conceived
and/or inadequate. Alternatively, we may conclude that the disproportionate persistence of poverty in black America derives
from causes over and above racism. In what follows, we present
data to build a credible case for the latter position.

Table 8.1 is from the Census Bureau's report "Income and
Poverty in the United States: 2019."

For the general population, we see a dramatic difference in
incidence of poverty between people in households with and
without a married couple, with people in single-female households
registering a poverty rate more than five times higher than that
of married households.

Table 8.2 shows what this picture looks like broken down
by race.

The data, looking specifically at white Americans and American blacks, show the same picture as the aggregate data for the
whole population. The incidence of poverty correlates to the
structure of household. The greater likelihood a household is

Figure 8.1 Poverty Rate by Race and Hispanic Origin: 1959–2019[2]

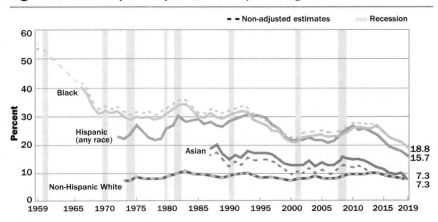

Note: The data for 2017 and beyond reflect the implementation of an updated processing system. The data for 2013 and beyond reflect the implementation of redesigned income questions. Data for Blacks is not available from 1960 to 1965. Historical estimates for Asians, Blacks and non-Hispanic Whites are adjusted to account for the significant impact of these survey redesigns. The adjusted series accounts for the impact of these recent improvements over the entire data series. This adjustment is not made in our official publications and table packages because it requires the assumption that the impact of the data improvements would have been identical in all years, an assumption that is less likely to be accurate in years further away from these methodology changes.

Source: U.S. Census Bureau, Current Population Survey, 1960 to 2020 Annual Social and Economic Supplement (CPS ASEC).

Figure 8.2 Ratio of Proportion in Poverty Relative to Total Population by Race and Hispanic Origin: 1959–2019[3]

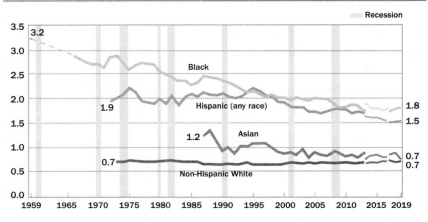

Note: People as of March the following year. Data for Blacks is not available for 1960 to 1965. The data for 2017 and beyond reflect the implementation of an updated processing system. The data for 2013 and beyond reflect the implementation of redesigned income questions.

Source: U.S. Census Bureau, Current Population Survey, 1960 to 2020 Annual Social and Economic Supplement (CPS ASEC).

Table 8.1   People in Poverty by Type of Family: 2019[4]

Persons in primary families in the U.S. (1000s)	263,696
Number below poverty	22,431
Percent below poverty	8.5
Persons in married-couple families	198,495
Number below poverty	9,036
Percent below poverty	4.6
Persons in families with female householder, no spouse present	46,255
Number below poverty	11,262
Percent below poverty	24.3
Persons in families with male householder, no spouse present	18,946
Number below poverty	2,133
Percent below poverty	11.3

Source: Semega et al., "Income and Poverty in the United States: 2019," 58, Table B-2.

Table 8.2   People in Poverty by Race and Type of Family: 2019[5]

WHITE ALONE	
Persons in primary families (1000s)	200,954
Number below poverty	14,295
Percent below poverty	7.1
Persons in families with female householder, no spouse present	27,848
Percent of total persons in families	13.9
Number below poverty	6,007
Percent below poverty	21.6
BLACK ALONE	
Persons in primary families (1000s)	34,033
Number below poverty	5,777
Percent below poverty	17.0
Persons in families with female householder, no spouse present	13,939
Percent of total persons in families	41.0
Number below poverty	4,118
Percent below poverty	29.5

Source: Semega et al., "Income and Poverty in the United States: 2019," 61, 63, Table B-5.

headed by a single female indicates a dramatically increased incidence of poverty.

The correlation between family structure and the incidence of poverty appears to hold true for both white Americans and

American blacks. The difference is that among blacks there is a dramatically higher incidence of families headed by a single female. Among whites, individuals in single female headed households represent 13.9 percent of all individuals in families; among blacks, they represent 41 percent. Furthermore, per the Statista Research Department, in 2019 the percentage of black families headed by a married couple living below the poverty line was 6.4 percent, *1.4 percent below the national average for all families.*[6]

Data from the National Center for Education Statistics, as shown in Figure 8.3, indicate the percentage of children under age 18 living in poverty by race/ethnicity and family structure.

Figure 8.3 Percentage of Children under Age 18 in Families Living in Poverty, by Child's Race/Ethnicity and Family Structure: 2019[7]

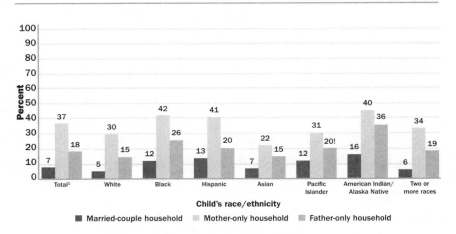

! Interpret data with caution. The coefficient of variation (CV) for this estimate is between 30 and 50 percent.

[1]Includes respondents who wrote in some other race that was not included as an option on the questionnaire.

Note: A "mother-only household" has a female householder, with no spouse present (i.e., the householder is unmarried or their spouse is not in the household), while a "father-only household" has a male householder, with no spouse present. Includes all children who live either with their parent(s) or with a householder to whom they are related by birth, marriage, or adoption (except a child who is the spouse of the householder). Children are classified by their parents' marital status or, if no parents are present in the household, by the marital status of the householder who is related to the children. The householder is the person (or one of the people) who owns or rents (maintains) the housing unit. For additional information about poverty status, see https://www.census.gov/topics/income-poverty/poverty/guidance/poverty-measures.html. Race categories exclude persons of Hispanic ethnicity. Although rounded numbers are displayed, the figures are based on unrounded data.

Source: U.S. Department of Commerce, Census Bureau, American Community Survey (ACS), 2019. See *Digest of Education Statistics 2020*, table 102.60.

The connection between family structure and poverty appears to be fundamental, transcending racial and ethnic differences. This leads us to hypothesize that a higher incidence of households not headed by married couples may be an overlooked determinant of the higher incidence of poverty among American blacks.

If we accept family structure as *a* key determinant in the incidence of poverty, we must then ask why American blacks have such a disproportionately lower incidence of households headed by married couples. This question leads us to consider the incidences of abortion and out-of-wedlock births, which are related to the issue of family structure.

Abortion

The breakdown of the incidence of abortion in 2018 by race, according to the CDC Abortion Surveillance Report published in 2020, is shown in Table 8.3.

Roughly one third of all abortions in the United States are among non-Hispanic black women, with the result that this group has the highest abortion rate (number of abortions per 1,000 women) as well as the highest abortion ratio (number of abortions per 1,000 live births). Non-Hispanic black women have an abortion rate 3.4 times higher than that of non-Hispanic

Table 8.3   Reported Abortions, by Known Race/Ethnicity: 2018[8]

White	38.7%
Black	33.6%
Hispanic	20%
Other	7.7%

Source: Katherine Kortsmit et al., "Abortion Surveillance—United States, 2018," Centers for Disease Control and Prevention, *MMWR Surveillance Summaries* 69, no. 7 (November 2020): 19, Table 5, https://www.cdc.gov/mmwr/volumes/69/ss/pdfs/ss6907a1-H.pdf.

Table 8.4   Reported Abortions, by Known Marital Status: 2018[9]

Married women	14.8%
Unmarried women	85.2%

Source: Kortsmit et al., "Abortion Surveillance—United States, 2018," 20, Table 6.

white women and an abortion ratio 3.0 times higher than that of non-Hispanic white women.[10]

The breakdown of abortion by marital status, per the CDC, is shown in Table 8.4.

Again, the factor of marriage enters the picture, with the number of abortions among unmarried women amounting to more than five times the number of abortions among married women.

Out-of-Wedlock Births

According to a report issued by the National Center for Health Statistics, unmarried births in 2019 break down as shown in Table 8.5.

Table 8.5   Births to Unmarried Women, by Race and Hispanic Origin of Mother: 2019[11]

Race/Ethnicity	Births to Unmarried Women	Total Births	%
White	540,981	1,915,912	28
Black	383,774	548,075	70
Hispanic	461,730	886,467	52
Other (American Indian/Alaska Native; Asian; Native Hawaiian/Other Pacific Islander)	52,482	276,989	19
All races and origins	1,498,113	3,747,540	40

Source: Joyce A. Martin et al., "Births: Final Data for 2019," *National Vital Statistics Reports* 70, no. 2 (March 2021): https://www.cdc.gov/nchs/data/nvsr/nvsr70/nvsr70-02-508.pdf, 27, Table 9; 13, Table 1.

Figure 8.4   The Decoupling of Marriage and Childbearing[12]

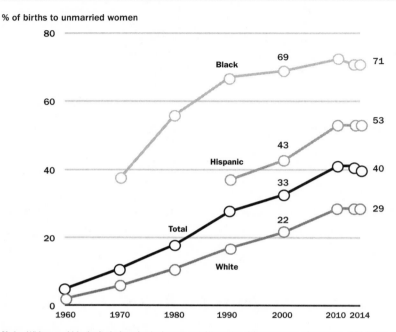

% of births to unmarried women

Note: Whites and blacks include only single-race non-Hispanics. Hispanics are of any race. 2014 data are preliminary. Data for Asians only not available.
Source: National Center for Health Statistics natality data. PEW RESEARCH CENTER.

We see in Figure 8.4, from Pew Research, that the out-of-wedlock birth rate appears to level off by 2014. But the apparent gap between the black rate and the white rate remains significant, and the growth slope for black mothers appears to have slowed relative to the growth slopes for other groups.

Marriage

The Institute for Family Studies reports that since 1970 there has been dramatic increase in the incidence of never-married Americans and dramatic drops in the percentage of American adults that are married, as shown in Figure 8.5.

Figure 8.5   Share of Never-Married Adults Reaches New High[13]

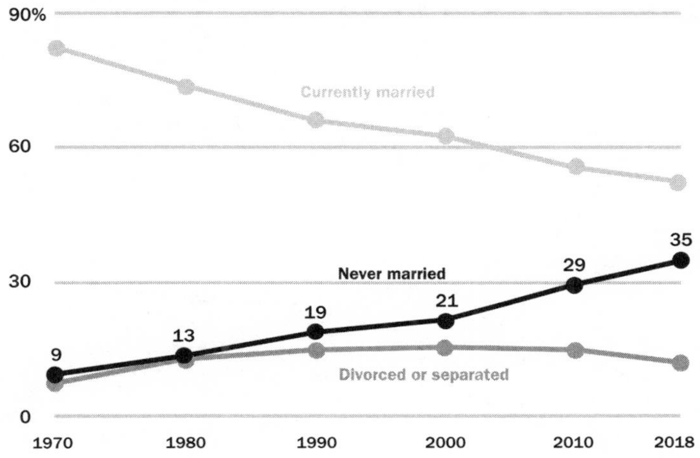

Note: Based on adults ages 25–50. A small share of widowed adults is not shown.
Source: U.S. Census and American Community Survey, IPUMS. INSTITUTE FOR FAMILY STUDIES.

In Figure 8.6, from Pew Research, we see that in 1960, the percentage of white Americans and American blacks that had been never married was almost identical. By 2012, a gap of 20 points had emerged. From 1960 to 2012, the percentage of never-married black American adults increased by 300 percent, while the percentage of never-married white adults increased by 100 percent. This is significant, for it demonstrates that the disparity in marriage rates between white Americans and American blacks is a relatively recent development.

Poverty, Family, and Race

We observe that, since the 1960s, a dramatic decline in traditional family structure in all American families has occurred. The percentage of married Americans has declined dramatically

Figure 8.6 Share of Never-Married Adults, Growing Race Gap[14]

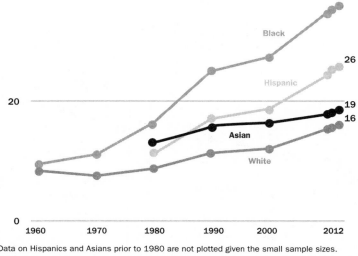

% of adults ages 25 and older who have never been married

Note: Data on Hispanics and Asians prior to 1980 are not plotted given the small sample sizes.
Source: Pew Research Center analysis of the 1960–2000 decennial census and 2010–2012 American Community Survey, Integrated Public Use Microdata Series (IPUMS). PEW RESEARCH CENTER.

and the percentage of babies born to women not married has increased dramatically. If we see the breakdown of traditional marriage and family structure in America as a pathology, the whole nation, regardless of race or ethnic background, suffers from this pathology and from the high rates of abortion and out-of-wedlock births that it tends to produce. However, this pathology has struck American blacks far more severely than other communities.

If the problem we are trying to better understand is the incidence of poverty, and if we conclude that high poverty rates relate to the breakdown of traditional family structure, then we must in turn consider what is causing family breakdown. We have two questions before us:

1. What is driving the breakdown of family in America?
2. Why has this pathology struck American blacks so much more severely than other groups?

Changing Values

Polling data show the clear change in values in America over the last twenty years, such that the importance of traditional values has dramatically deteriorated.

Consider the data in Tables 8.6 and 8.7, from Gallup:

Table 8.6   Changes in Perception of Moral Acceptability[15]

Percent saying morally acceptable, by year			
	2001	2015	2020
Gay/lesbian relations	40	63	66
Having baby outside of marriage	45*	61	66
Sex between unmarried man/woman	53	68	72
Divorce	59	71	77
Abortion	42	45	44

*First measured in 2002

Source: Megan Brenan, "Record-Low 54% in U.S. Say Death Penalty Morally Acceptable," Gallup, June 23, 2020, https://news.gallup.com/poll/312929/record-low-say-death-penalty-morally-acceptable.aspx; Frank Newport, "Americans Continue to Shift Left on Key Moral Issues," Gallup, May 26, 2015, https://news.gallup.com/poll/183413/americans-continue-shift-left-key-moral-issues.aspx.

Table 8.7   Moral Acceptability of Out-of-Wedlock Births—Changes Over Time[16]

Is it important for couples with children to legally marry?			
	2006	2013	2020
% saying very important	49	38	29
% saying not too/not important	23	35	40

Source: Jeffrey M. Jones, "Is Marriage Becoming Irrelevant?" Gallup, December 28, 2020, https://news.gallup.com/poll/316223/fewer-say-important-parents-married.aspx.

Table 8.8   Americans More Likely to Say Career Enjoyment Key to a Fulfilling Life than Marriage[17]

Percent saying essential/important/not important, for men and women		Essential	Important, but not essential	Not important
Marriage	For a man	16	54	29
	For a woman	17	54	28
Having children	For a man	16	58	25
	For a woman	22	57	21
Having a job/career they enjoy	For a man	57	39	3
	For a woman	46	48	5

Source: Amanda Barroso, "More than Half of Americans Say Marriage Is Important but not Essential to Leading a Fulfilling Life," Pew Research Center, February 14, 2020, https://www.pewresearch.org/fact-tank/2020/02/14/more-than-half-of-americans-say-marriage-is-important-but-not-essential-to-leading-a-fulfilling-life/.

Table 8.8 presents data from Pew Research based on polling done in 2019.

We can see just over the last twenty years a dramatic deterioration of the traditional values essential to maintaining marriage and traditional family structure. We suggest that these changes are likely related to deeper shifts in cultural philosophies and attitudes, most notably the rejection of Christian moral teaching and the prevalence of materialism.

For perspective and contrast, here are the words of Alexis de Tocqueville, describing the reality of the young American nation in 1835, from his classic work *Democracy in America*:

America is, however, still the place in the world where the Christian religion has most preserved genuine power over souls; and nothing shows better how useful and natural to man it is in our day, since the country in which it exercises the greatest empire is at the same time the most enlightened and free.

Therefore one cannot say that in the United States religion exerts an influence on laws or on the details of political opinions, but it directs mores, and it is in regulating the family that it works to regulate the state.

Of the world's countries, America is surely the one where the bond of marriage is most respected and where they have conceived the highest and most just idea of conjugal happiness.[18]

Why Have Things Changed?

How do we account for the dramatic change that has taken place since Tocqueville recorded his observations in 1835? It is, of course, far easier to describe what happened than to explain why. We can point to fundamental changes that have occurred over time with regard to the general understanding of our Constitution and the extent to which it limits the role of government in American society. We may also observe changes in Americans regarding attitudes toward religion.

We have gone from an understanding of the United States defined fundamentally as a free country, where individuals are granted freedom to exercise self-government and personal responsibility and our Constitution limits the ability of government to infringe on that freedom, to the belief that government itself should be a primary means for improving people's quality of life.

This is a far cry from how America's founders defined the role of government, as written in the Declaration of Independence:

We hold these Truths to be self-evident, that all men are created equal, that they are endowed by their Creator with certain unalienable rights, that among these are Life, Liberty, and the Pursuit of Happiness, —That to secure these Rights, Governments are instituted among Men, deriving their just powers from the Consent of the Governed, that whenever any Form of Government becomes destructive of these ends, it is the Right of the People to alter or abolish it, and to institute new Government, laying its Foundation on such Principles and organizing its powers in such form, as to them shall seem most likely to effect their Safety and Happiness.

In the founding vision of America, the truth of human nature precedes the institution of government. Citizens form government to protect their life, liberty, and agency (pursuit of happiness), and to secure equality under the law which reflects the truth that all people are equal before God. The source of the truths articulated in the Declaration of Independence is God, our Creator and wise Governor.

In a departure from the initial understanding that government's job is to protect our God-given freedom, especially the freedom to practice true religion, the government itself is now seen as the *source* of freedom. For some, indeed, government has become the new religion.

Consider the words of the late Claremont Institute scholar Harry V. Jaffa, in his classic essay "The American Founding as the Best Regime":

> The Preamble of the Constitution crowns its enumeration of the ends of the Constitution by declaring as its purpose "to secure the blessings of liberty to ourselves and our posterity"...Alone among the ends of the constitution, to secure liberty is called a securing of "blessings." What is a blessing is what is good in the eyes of God. It is a good whose possession—by the common understanding of mankind—belongs properly only to those who deserve it.[19]

Jaffa noted that the blessing of liberty comes to those who deserve it, and Tocqueville pointed out that the Christianity that prevailed in the lives of Americans in the early nineteenth century provided the means, as it was incorporated in individual behavior, for Americans to act worthily of their freedom.

Today, Americans' sense that government is not a tool for protecting their freedom, rather the vehicle for improving their lives, is reflected in federal expenditures. Figure 8.7, from American Enterprise Institute economist and blogger Mark Perry, illustrates this well.

Prior to 1960, some 15 percent of the federal budget consisted of transfer payments. Today transfer payments—the federal government taxing one set of citizens and transferring the revenue to another set of citizens—make up almost 70 percent of the federal budget. Government has become the source and substance of many Americans' lives. We may posit a connection between the data above

Figure 8.7   Composition of U.S. Federal Outlays, 1952–2020[20]

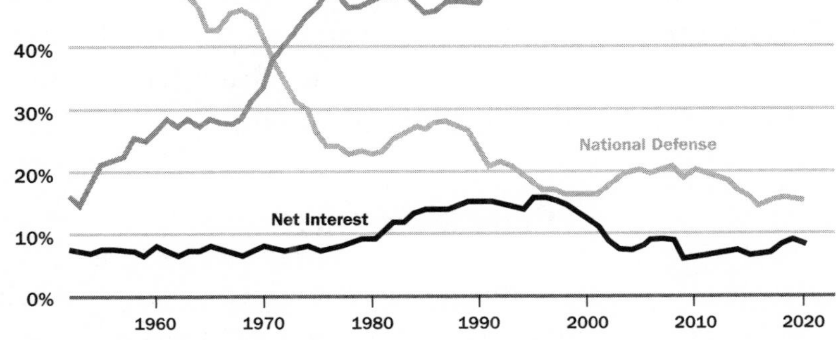

Source: White House Office of Management and Budget.

Figure 8.8 A Majority Still Say Religion Is Important in Their Lives[21]

How important would you say religion is in your own life—very important, fairly important or not very important?

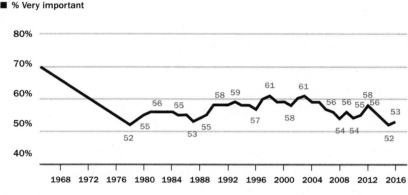

■ % Very important

Source: GALLUP.

and Figure 8.8, from Gallup, which captures changes in Americans' attitudes regarding the importance of religion in their lives.

Note that in the 1950s/1960s, almost three quarters of Americans said religion was "very important" in the own lives. By the end of the 1970s, this had dropped to about half. We might turn back to the words of Tocqueville: "Therefore one cannot say that in the United States religion exerts an influence on laws or on the details of political opinions, but it directs mores, and it is in regulating the family that it works to regulate the state." Conversely, we suggest that as Americans turn less to religion to regulate their lives, they turn more to government.

Enter *Roe v. Wade*

Exactly in the middle of this period of dramatic change, the *Roe v. Wade* decision of 1973 legalized abortion on demand.

Was *Roe v. Wade* the result of dramatic change in attitudes among Americans regarding the importance of religion and of the acceleration of government dependence? Or was it the cause? Causation likely runs in both directions. But it is safe to say that the decision made a dramatic difference in the behavior and attitudes among American regarding the importance of marriage and family and played a role in bringing about the deleterious results that have already been discussed.

The Constitution and "General Welfare"

We must also point out that the turn to more government has been enabled by Supreme Court decisions that significantly attenuated constitutional limits on the federal government's taxing and spending. A watershed moment occurred in 1937 in the Supreme Court's decision *Helvering v. Davis*, in which the constitutionality of the new Social Security Act, signed into law by President Roosevelt in 1936, was challenged. In *Helvering v. Davis*, the Court decided that it is within the purview of the Constitution for Congress to redistribute wealth in the form of "payments to individuals," as depicted in Figure 8.7. This was a reinterpretation of the General Welfare clause of the Constitution, Article I, Section 8:

> The Congress shall have the power to lay and collect taxes, duties, imposts and excises, to pay the debts and provide for the common defense and general welfare.

Prior to *Helvering*, "general welfare" was understood to be a "catch-all" phrase concerning the other explicit tax and spend authorities given to Congress. *Helvering*, in finding the Social Security Act constitutional, opened the door to understanding "general welfare" as a specific spending authority for Congress in itself. One might say this opened the door to today's massive welfare state.

How do we understand the change from the America described by Tocqueville, in which religion is the regulator of individual behavior and government exists to protect religion and individual freedom, to an America where government can enter and direct individual lives as long as one can rationalize that the measures taken are for the sake of the "general welfare"? The "chicken" and the "egg" are hard to identify. We can only say the change has happened, with profound implications for the American republic.

We might also point out that Social Security, which essentially played the midwife for the modern welfare state, is an unsustainable system due to the social problems associated with the welfare state. Because Social Security is financed by payroll taxes collected from those working, the viability of the system is predicated on stability of the nation's fertility rate—which largely determines the number of working Americans per retiree collecting benefits. In fact, because of breakdown of marriage and family, fertility rates in America have dropped. Per the Social Security Trustees 2020 report, changes in the number of working Americans per retirees collecting benefits over time is shown in Table 8.9.

Per this analysis, Social Security will have insufficient funds to meet obligations by 2034, just 13 years from now.

Table 8.9 Covered Workers and Beneficiaries, Calendar Years 1945–2040[22]

1945	41.9
1950	16.5
1960	5.1
1970	3.7
1980	3.2
2019	2.8
Projected	
2030	2.4
2040	2.2

Source: OASDI Trustees, "The 2020 Annual Report of the Board of Trustees of the Federal Old-Age and Survivors Insurance and Federal Disability Insurance Trust Funds," April 22, 2020, https://www.ssa.gov/oact/tr/2020/tr2020.pdf, 62, Table IV.B3.

Why Disproportionately among Blacks?

Why has the pathology that has afflicted the whole nation, leading to breakdown of family and the exacerbation of poverty, so disproportionately affected black America? In keeping with the spirit of analytical humility which we have tried to maintain throughout this discussion, we can only suggest, not definitively explain, why this is the case.

To summarize the picture we have developed thus far:

1. Poverty in America appears to correlate strongly with family structure. The less likely a household is headed by a married couple, the higher the incidence of poverty.
2. We observe dramatic deterioration in marriage and the traditional family in the United States beginning in the 1960s.
3. We propose that deterioration of marriage and the traditional family is a result of changes in attitudes both toward religion and toward government.
4. These changes in attitude were strengthened, accelerated, and enabled by Supreme Court decisions which weakened constitutional restrictions on federal government involvement in individual lives.

This crisis has disproportionately impacted the lives of American blacks. Family breakdown has been much more severe, abortion more widespread, and out-of-marriage births more common compared to national averages.

Why has the impact on American blacks been more severe? We suggest that it is relevant to consider that the civil rights movement in the mid-1960s coincided with a time when belief in big government was accelerating and belief in traditional values was deteriorating. Precisely when black reality in America was being "reinvented," it was increasingly accepted that the government should step in aggressively to "help" disadvantaged groups, including American blacks.

In a five-year window from 1963 to 1968, under the presidency of Lyndon Johnson, almost 200 pieces of legislation were enacted into law as part of what Johnson called "the Great Society." These included, as reported in the *Washington Post*:

> Medicare and Medicaid; food stamps; urban renewal; the first broad federal investment in elementary and high school education; Head Start and college aid; an end to what was essentially a whites-only immigration policy; landmark consumer safety and environmental regulations; funding that gave voice to community action groups; and an all-out War on Poverty.[23]

It was in the midst of all this that the civil rights movement came to fruition and the Civil Rights Act became law.

President Johnson spoke at Howard University in 1965, on the occasion of signing the Voting Rights Act, and shared his vision that freedom was an insufficient answer for American blacks to move forward in America:

> But freedom is not enough. You do not wipe away the scars of centuries by saying: Now you are free to go where you want, and do as you desire, and choose the leaders you please.
>
> You do not take a person who, for years, has been hobbled by chains and liberate him, bring him up to the starting line of a race and then say, "you are free to compete with all the others," and still justly believe that you have been completely fair. Thus it is not enough to open the gates of opportunity. All our citizens must have the ability to walk through those gates.[24]

We might note that the civil rights movement was animated by the imagery of the Bible. It was inspired by the story of the

Hebrew slaves in Egypt, and Moses telling Pharoah, "Let my people go." In this sense, the biblical story has a message similar to the message of President Johnson. Freedom is more than just breaking the chains of bondage. The message of Moses to Pharoah, however, was to let the people go so they could leave and worship their God. The aspiration to freedom was the aspiration to self-govern.

The message of President Johnson undermined the people's confidence in their capacity to self-govern. This message contributed to a culture among American blacks, post–civil rights movement, that reflected the conviction that they did not have the tools to live free. They needed the government to provide what was necessary for life.

A Census Bureau report in 2015 summarized participation of the general population in government mean-tested programs from 2009 to 2012. According to the report, an average of 21.3 percent of the American population participated in these programs per month. However, the highest rate of participation was among American blacks, 41.6 percent of whom participated in government assistance programs in a given month.[25]

Additionally, surveys show that American blacks believe, to a higher degree than other Americans, that a more active government is necessary. Consider the results of the 2019 Pew Research survey shown in Figure 8.9.

It is worth noting, however, that although black attitudes about government activism are very much in line with general opinion within the Democratic Party (with whom American blacks largely vote), on issues touching on religion and morality, black attitudes are not in line with most Democrats, as shown in Figures 8.10 and 8.11.

These figures gesture at the spiritual and moral strength that persists in communities of American blacks despite the social and economic difficulties some among them face. Politicians

Figure 8.9 Wide Racial, Age, and Partisan Differences on Role of Government[26]

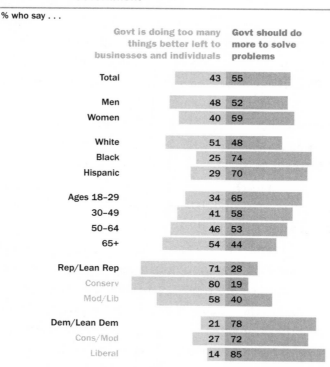

% who say . . .

	Govt is doing too many things better left to businesses and individuals	Govt should do more to solve problems
Total	43	55
Men	48	52
Women	40	59
White	51	48
Black	25	74
Hispanic	29	70
Ages 18–29	34	65
30–49	41	58
50–64	46	53
65+	54	44
Rep/Lean Rep	71	28
Conserv	80	19
Mod/Lib	58	40
Dem/Lean Dem	21	78
Cons/Mod	27	72
Liberal	14	85

Note: No answer responses not shown. Whites and blacks include only those who are not Hispanic; Hispanics are of any race.
Source: Survey of U.S. adults conducted Sept. 3–15, 2019. PEW RESEARCH CENTER.

and elites should trust these communities to govern themselves instead of imposing secular ideals on them and claiming that they cannot flourish without additional intervention from the federal government.

Conclusions

In thinking about the problem of poverty in America, we should direct more focus toward family structure and marriage. The

Figure 8.10 Wide Racial Difference among Democrats on Whether Belief in God Is Necessary to Be Moral[27]

Among Democrats and Democratic leaners,
% who say it is . . .

	Necessary to believe in God in order to be moral	Not necessary to believe in God in order to be moral
Total	26	73
White	11	89
Black	55	44
Hispanic	41	57

Note: Based on Democrats and Democratic-leaning independents. No answer responses not shown. Whites and blacks include only those who are not Hispanic; Hispanics are of any race.
Source: Survey of U.S. adults conducted Sept. 3–15, 2019. PEW RESEARCH CENTER.

Figure 8.11 Black Democrats Far Less Likely than White Democrats to Say Legalizing Same-Sex Marriage Is a Good Thing[28]

Among Democrats and Democratic leaners, % who say same-sex marriage now being legal in the U.S. is a _____ thing for our society

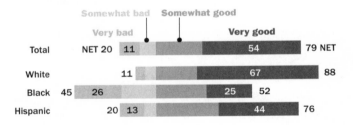

	Somewhat bad	Very bad	Somewhat good	Very good	
Total	NET 20	11		54	79 NET
White		11		67	88
Black	45	26		25	52
Hispanic		20	13	44	76

Note: Based on Democrats and Democratic-leaning independents. No answer responses not shown. Whites and blacks include only those who are not Hispanic. Hispanics are of any race.
Source: Survey of U.S. adults conducted Sept. 3–15, 2019. PEW RESEARCH CENTER.

deterioration of marriage and the traditional family has been particularly severe in black America and is likely one of the main culprits behind persistently high poverty rates.

We suggest that deterioration of family in black America relates to the widespread adoption of attitudes among American blacks, beginning in the 1960s and 1970s, that they should welcome government direction of their lives. Despite high church attendance in black America, the culture of government dependence has pervaded many low-income black communities.

It is an unfortunate historical fact that the civil rights movement coincided with the prevalence of a certain cultural arrogance which deemphasized religion and pretended that the federal government could solve all social ills. Also contributing to the problem were changes in the understanding of the U.S. Constitution that made possible a vast new welfare state, in which blacks would disproportionately participate. Legalization of abortion, too, wreaked havoc in black marriages and black families. Other relevant court decisions not addressed in this discussion, beginning in the 1950s and continuing to the present, marginalized religion in the public square in America. All these developments hastened the breakdown of the healthy American social and political order that Tocqueville praised, taking an especially large toll on American blacks.

Going forward, if we wish to see American blacks reach their potential, restore family, escape poverty, and build wealth, we recommend raising awareness among black civil and religious leadership about the destructiveness of a culture of government reliance. We also urge policy reforms in education, housing, retirement savings, health care, and elsewhere that will diminish the influence of government in the lives of American blacks and increase the scope of freedom and choice in all areas of private life.

ACKNOWLEDGMENTS

This volume is the work of many hands, hearts, and minds working in unison. Beyond the contributors acknowledged within, we are grateful for the following supporters, champions, and visionaries who brought this work to fruition:

We could not have initiated this project without the support and encouragement of Tom Klingenstein, who generously provided the initial funding and inspired the contributions of others.

CURE Vice President for Policy Robert Borens, besides participating as a contributor, sparked the deliberations that led us to the book's focus.

Star Parker blessed the project with her vision and labors, authorizing the dedication of CURE's Annual Policy Summit to the purpose.

A special thank-you to William B. Allen for his leading role in the creation of *The State of Black America*. He continues to be a constant source of support and inspiration.

Mikael Good's editorial eye constituted the "that without which" none of this would have been realized, or at least not so well realized.

CURE is much obliged to Austin Stone's advocacy in bringing our scholarship to print. His industry knowledge connected us to Encounter Books and their editors, who shepherded us through the process of publishing *The State of Black America* with a clear focus. We are indebted to them for their patient guidance and support.

It is, moreover, important to observe that the cadre of CURE supporters and funders have been instrumental in advancing these labors, particularly those who participated in the 2020 and 2021 Annual Policy Summits. Bolstered by the generous support of the Ken W. Davis Foundation and other donors, CURE has been able to produce a distinctive contribution to our nation's sustained discussion of pathways to bring relief into America's distressed zip codes and, at the same time, hope for America's future.

CONTRIBUTORS

William B. Allen is a resident scholar and the former chief operating officer of the Center for Urban Renewal and Education in Washington, D.C. He is emeritus professor of political philosophy in the Department of Political Science and emeritus dean of James Madison College at Michigan State University. In 2018–20 he was senior scholar in residence at the University of Colorado Boulder. He served previously on the United States National Council for the Humanities and as chairman and member of the United States Commission on Civil Rights. Recognized for excellence in liberal education on the 1997 Templeton Honor Roll (individually and institutionally), he also has been a Kellogg National Fellow, received the international Prix Montesquieu, and was the 2014 Salvatori Award winner. He has published extensively, including *George Washington: A Collection* (Liberty Fund, Inc.), *Rethinking Uncle Tom: The Political Philosophy of H. B. Stowe* (Lexington Books), and *George Washington: America's First Progressive* (Peter Lang, Inc.).

Robert D. Bland is an assistant professor of history and Africana studies at the University of Tennessee. His scholarship explores the legacy of the Reconstruction era in American memory. He earned his PhD at the University of Maryland in 2017. His forthcoming book, *Requiem for Reconstruction: The South Carolina Lowcountry and the Making of the Black South*, explores the previously unexamined struggle over the legacy of Reconstruction during the Gilded and Progressive eras in the black public sphere. A portion of his research has been published in the *Journal of the Gilded Age and Progressive Era*, where it was awarded an Honorable Mention for the journal's 2020 Best Article prize. His work has been supported by the Woodrow Wilson Foundation, the Social Science Research Council, and the National Endowment for the Humanities.

Robert Borens has worked with Star Parker and the Center for Urban Renewal and Education for over twenty years. He has over thirty years' experience in government affairs and public policy. Borens began his career in corporate planning at Getty Oil Company. He then became director of government affairs and built Getty's government affairs program in Washington, D.C. He later became a vice president at the Cato Institute and subsequently did consulting work with Empower America and the Hudson Institute. Robert currently lives in Jerusalem, Israel, where he is the director of the Friedberg Economics Institute.

Daphne Cooper is an associate professor of political science at North Carolina Agricultural and Technical State University in Greensboro, North Carolina. She was awarded a master of arts in public administration and a doctor of philosophy in political science from Clark Atlanta University in Atlanta, Georgia. Her research focus is on public policy, poverty, and African American politics.

Edward J. Erler is a senior fellow at the Claremont Institute and a professor of political science emeritus at California State University, San Bernardino. He is the author of *Property and the Pursuit of Happiness: Locke, the Declaration of Independence, Madison, and the Challenge of the Administrative State* (2019) and *The United States in Crisis: Citizenship, Immigration and the Nation State*, Revised Edition (forthcoming 2022); co-author of *The Found-*

ers on *Citizenship and Immigration: Principles and Challenges in America* (2007); co-editor of *The Rediscovery of America: Essays by Harry V. Jaffa on the New Birth of Politics* (2019) and *The American Polity: Essays on the Theory and Practice of Constitutional Government* (1991); and the author of numerous articles in law reviews and professional journals. He has testified before Congress on immigration and civil rights issues in addition to serving on the California Advisory Commission on Civil Rights.

Mikael Rose Good is a former policy analyst and editorial assistant at the Center for Urban Renewal and Education. She earned a bachelor's degree in political philosophy from Patrick Henry College in Purcellville, Virginia. She is an alumna of the Intercollegiate Studies Institute, the Hertog Foundation, the American Enterprise Institute's Summer Associates Program, and *The American Conservative*'s Constitutional Fellowship.

Precious D. Hall is an assistant professor of government at Saint Lawrence University in Canton, New York, where she began teaching in 2019. Prior to joining the faculty of Saint Lawrence, she was a tenured professor of political science at Truckee Meadows Community College in Reno, Nevada, from 2012 to 2019. She hails from Baltimore, Maryland, having completed her undergraduate studies at High Point University in North Carolina and graduate studies at Georgia State University in Atlanta, Georgia, in the fields of American government and politics, political behavior, and political theory. She considers herself a race scholar, broadly defined, and has previously published in the *Journal of Race and Policy* and *Ethnic Studies Review*.

Thomas Klingenstein is the chairman of the Claremont Institute and has spent most of his career in the investment business. He was a securities analyst on Wall Street, the chief executive officer of a major Colorado bank, and a money manager at Cohen, Klingenstein, LLC, an investment firm he and his partner started in 1990. Klingenstein has served on many corporate and nonprofit boards. He is also a playwright. Currently he lives in New York City.

Glenn C. Loury is the Merton P. Stoltz Professor of Economics at Brown University. He received his BA in mathematics from Northwestern University and his PhD in economics from MIT. As an economic theorist, he has published widely and lectured throughout the world on his research. He is also among America's leading critics writing on racial inequality. He has been elected as a distinguished fellow of the American Economics Association, as a member of the American Philosophical Society and of the U.S. Council on Foreign Relations, and as a fellow of the Econometric Society and of the American Academy of Arts and Sciences.

Star Parker is the founder and president of the Center for Urban Renewal and Education. She is a nationally syndicated columnist and hosts a weekly television news show, *CURE America with Star Parker*. To date, Parker spoken on more than 225 college campuses, including Harvard, Berkeley, Emory, Liberty, Franciscan, UCLA, and University of Virginia. She is a regular commentator on national television and radio networks, including the BBC, EWTN, and FOX News, and the author of four books: *Necessary Noise: How Donald Trump Inflames the Culture War and Why This Is Good News for America* (2019); *Uncle Sam's Plantation: How Big Government Enslaves America's Poor and What We Can Do about It* (2003/2012); *White Ghetto: How Middle-Class America Reflects Inner City Decay* (2006); and *Pimps, Whores and Welfare Brats: From Welfare Cheat to Conservative Messenger* (1997). In 2016, CPAC honored Parker as the "Ronald Reagan Foot Soldier of the Year." In 2017, she was the recipient of the Groundswell Impact award, and in 2018, Bott Radio Network presented her with its annual Queen Esther award. She also serves on the National Religious Broadcasters Board of Directors and the Board of Directors at the Leadership Institute.

Ian V. Rowe is a senior fellow at the American Enterprise Institute, where he focuses on education and upward mobility, family formation, and adoption. Rowe is also the cofounder and CEO of Vertex Partnership Academies, a new network of character-based International Baccalaureate high schools opening in the Bronx in September 2022; a member of the board of advisors for FAIR for All; the chairman of the board of Spence-Chapin, a nonprofit adoption services organization; and the cofounder of the National Summer School Initiative. He concurrently serves as a senior visiting fellow at the Woodson Center and a writer for the 1776 Unites Campaign. Until July 1, 2020, Mr. Rowe was CEO of Public Prep, a nonprofit network of public charter schools based in the South Bronx and the Lower East Side of Manhattan. Rowe has been widely published in the popular press, including the *New York Post*, the *Wall Street Journal*, and the *Washington Examiner*. Mr. Rowe has an MBA from Harvard Business School, a BS in computer science engineering from Cornell University, and a diploma in electrical engineering from Brooklyn Technical High School.

NOTES

FOREWORD

1 Abraham Lincoln, "Speech at Springfield, Illinois," June 26, 1857, in *The Collected Works of Abraham Lincoln*, 8 vols., ed. Roy P. Basler (New Brunswick, NJ: Rutgers University Press, 1953), 2:406.

CHAPTER ONE

1 When, in 2007, the senior author pleaded to substitute the term "inclusion" for the term "diversity," he little expected the history that followed, in which the two were caught up in a general sweep of thoughtless unconcern for the jangling tensions they enunciate when conjoined as a pair.

2 Robert D. Putnam, *The Upswing: How America Came Together a Century Ago and How We Can Do It Again* (New York: Simon & Schuster, 2020), 11.

3 Ibid., 10, Figure 1.1.

4 Ibid., 34, Figure 2.8.

5 Ibid., 203 (emphasis added).

6 Ibid., 36, Figure 2.9.

7 Ibid., 42, Figure 2.10.

8 Ibid., 68, Figure 2.19.

9 Ibid., 234, Figure 6.9.

10 Ibid., 10, Figure 1.1.

11 Ibid., 87, Figure 3.3.

12 Ibid., 190–91.

13 Ibid., 192–93.

14 Ibid., 88, Figure 3.4.

15 Ibid., 107, Figure 3.11.

16 Richard Alba, *The Great Demographic Illusion: Majority, Minority, and the Expanding American Mainstream* (Princeton, NJ: Princeton University Press, 2020), 37, Figure 3.1.

17 Ibid., 71, Figure 4.2.

18 Ibid., 78, Figure 4.5.

19 Ibid., 97, Figure 5.2.

20 Ibid., 100, Figure 5.3.

21 Ibid., 110, Figure 5.5.

22 See Ibram X. Kendi, "Founder's Statement," Boston University's Center for
    Antiracist Research, July 1, 2020, https://www.bu.edu/antiracism-center/
    the-center/founder-statement/. In recent years, Kendi became one of the
    most quoted voices on antiracism, boasting three *New York Times* bestsellers,
    a National Book Award, and a prominent platform with *The Atlantic* and
    other national publications. Kendi's books *Stamped from the Beginning* (2016)
    and *How to Be an Antiracist* (2019) are considered essential reading for all
    Americans wishing to "educate themselves" on antiracism. They are featured
    front-and-center in the proliferation of antiracism handbooks and resource
    lists that are now regularly released by institutions as various as universities,
    museums, libraries, and corporations to guide the moral and spiritual
    formation of their members. Kendi himself published a widely disseminated
    antiracist syllabus in *The Atlantic*, hoping to steer teachable Americans
    toward "a lifetime of anti-racist action." Besides his influential roles as public
    speaker and popular-level author, Kendi is the director and founder of the
    burgeoning new Center for Antiracist Research at Boston University, whose
    mission, in Kendi's words, is "to use the blocks of thoughtful and exhaustive
    scholarship to build an antiracist future for America, for humanity"
    ("Founder's Statement," Boston University Center for Antiracist Research,
    July 1, 2020, https://www.bu.edu/antiracism-center/the-center/founder-
    statement/). See also Kendi, "The Anti-Racist Reading List," *The Atlantic*,
    February 12, 2019, https://www.theatlantic.com/ideas/archive/2019/02/
    antiracist-syllabus-governor-ralph-northam/582580/.

23 Granted, Robin DiAngelo may be an equally notable public figure, and
    her book *White Fragility: Why It's So Hard for White People to Talk about
    Racism* (2018) arguably made an even bigger splash than Kendi's *How
    to Be an Antiracist*. But DiAngelo is also the object of considerably more
    suspicion than Kendi, usually on the basis of her alleged opportunism and
    the unseriousness of her thought. See, for example, such damning critiques
    as Daniel Bergner, "'White Fragility' Is Everywhere. But Does Antiracism
    Training Work?" *New York Times*, July 15, 2020, https://www.nytimes.
    com/2020/07/15/magazine/white-fragility-robin-diangelo.html?referringS
    ource=articleShare; Bhaskar Sunkara, "Stop Trying to Fight Racism with
    Corporate Diversity Consultants," *The Guardian*, July 8, 2020, https://www.
    theguardian.com/commentisfree/2020/jul/08/diversity-consultants-racism-
    seminars-corporate-america; David Barber, "Renouncing White Privilege: A
    Left Critique of Robin DiAngelo's 'White Fragility,'" *CounterPunch*, August
    3, 2020, https://www.counterpunch.org/2020/08/03/renouncing-white-
    privilege-a-critique-of-robin-diangelos-white-fragility/; Helen Lewis, "How
    Capitalism Drives Cancel Culture," *The Atlantic*, July 14, 2020, https://www.
    theatlantic.com/international/archive/2020/07/cancel-culture-and-problem-
    woke-capitalism/614086/; and Ryan Cooper, "The Limits of *White Fragility*'s
    Anti-Racism," *The Week*, June 24, 2020, https://theweek.com/articles/921623/
    limits-white-fragilitys-antiracism.

24 Ibram X. Kendi, *How to Be an Antiracist* (New York: One World, 2019), 9.

25 Ibid.

26 Coleman Hughes, "Has Anti-Racism Become a New Religion? with John McWhorter (Ep. 2)," *Conversations with Coleman*, YouTube video, January 15, 2020, https://www.youtube.com/watch?v=UPiNiTwf5bM.

27 Kendi, *How to Be an Antiracist*, 38.

28 Ibid., 8.

29 Ibid., 35.

30 Ibram X. Kendi, *Stamped from the Beginning: The Definitive History of Racist Ideas in America* (New York: Bold Type Books, 2016).

31 Kendi, *How to Be an Antiracist*, 38.

32 Ibid., 31.

33 Ibid., 20. "The most threatening racist movement is not the alt right's unlikely drive for a White ethnostate but the regular American's drive for a 'race-neutral' one. The construct of race neutrality actually feeds White nationalist victimhood by positing the notion that any policy protecting or advancing non-white Americans toward equity is 'reverse discrimination.'"

34 Ibid., 18.

35 Ibid.

36 Ibid., 19.

37 Ibid., 214 (emphasis added).

38 Ibid., 231.

39 Ibid., 208.

40 Hernando de Soto, *The Mystery of Capital: Why Capitalism Triumphs in the West and Fails Everywhere Else* (New York: Basic Books, 2000).

41 Ibram X. Kendi, "A Battle between the Two Souls of America," *The Atlantic*, November 11, 2020, https://www.theatlantic.com/ideas/archive/2020/11/americas-two-souls/617062/.

42 Ibid.

43 Ibid.

44 Kendi, *How to Be an Antiracist*, 234.

45 Ibid., 132.

46 Kendi, "A Battle between the Two Souls of America."

47 Kendi, *How to Be an Antiracist*, 142.

48 Ibid., 23.

49 Ibid.

50 Ibid., 235.

51 Ibid., 54.

52 Ibid., 180.

53 Ibid., 238.

54 Ibid., 205.

55 Ibram X. Kendi, "We Still Don't Know Who the Coronavirus's Victims Were," *The Atlantic*, May 2, 2021, https://www.theatlantic.com/ideas/

archive/2021/05/we-still-dont-know-who-the-coronaviruss-victims-were/618776/.

56   Ibram X. Kendi, "What to an American Is the Fourth of July?" *The Atlantic*, July 4, 2019, https://www.theatlantic.com/ideas/archive/2019/07/resistance-patriotism-fourth-july/593344/.

57   Ibid.

58   Ibid.

59   Hughes, "Has Anti-Racism Become a New Religion?"

60   Martin Luther King Jr., *Letter from a Birmingham Jail*, https://www.csuchico.edu/iege/_assets/documents/susi-letter-from-birmingham-jail.pdf, 4, 2. Of interest are Coleman Hughes's candid musings about whether a nonreligious narrative can ever be compelling in the way that MLK's was: "[MLK] stood on this religious perch from which he could view the divisiveness of the Black Power movement and the white racists as petty and terrestrial, relative to the unity that he could say is true of our world in virtue of his being a Christian. He had a metanarrative that kind of dissolved all of the divisive narratives below. And I find, as an atheist entering this conversation that has a very religious character, I lack a metanarrative. You lack a metanarrative . . . I think that's a liability for us . . . I can't help but think that having a doctrine of universal humanity, something that was tied to tradition and a specific text and a long history, is largely what enabled him to [succeed]" (Hughes, "Has Anti-Racism Become a New Religion?").

CHAPTER TWO

1   Congressional Globe, 39th Cong., 1st Sess., 2459 (May 9, 1866); Stevens had explicated the theme that the Fourteenth Amendment was a completion of the founding on several occasions, beginning at least on January 22, 1862: "Let the people know that this Government is fighting not only to enforce a sacred compact, but to carry out to final perfection the principles of the Declaration of Independence" (Congressional Globe, 37th Cong., 2nd Sess., 441); see also Congressional Globe, 39th Cong., 1st Sess., 536 (January 31, 1866).

2   Congressional Globe, 39th Cong., 1st Sess., 674 (February 6, 1866).

3   Alexander Hamilton, James Madison, and John Jay, *The Federalist Papers*, ed. Clinton Rossiter, notes and introduction by Charles R. Kesler (New York: Signet Classics, 2003), No. 39, 236.

4   Congressional Globe, 39th Cong., 1st Sess., 684 (Sumner); 74; 322; 536; 2459 (Stevens).

5   Harry V. Jaffa, *Crisis of the House Divided: An Interpretation of the Lincoln-Douglas Debates* (Garden City, NY: Doubleday & Company, 1959), 158. Jaffa does not mention that Lincoln had said in his First Inaugural that "the intention of the law-giver is the law." Jaffa, of course, was well aware of Lincoln's statement. See Lincoln, "First Inaugural," in *The Collected Works of Abraham Lincoln*, 8 vols., ed. Roy P. Basler (New Brunswick, NJ: Rutgers University Press, 1953), 4:263.

6 Abraham Lincoln, "Fourth Debate with Stephen A. Douglas at Charleston, Illinois," September 18, 1858, in *The Collected Works of Abraham Lincoln*, 3:145.

7 Abraham Lincoln, "Speech at Chicago, Illinois," July 10, 1858, in *The Collected Works of Abraham Lincoln*, 2:499.

8 Article IV, Section 2, was regularly referred to as the "fugitive slave clause." Once fugitive slave legislation was passed, it in effect "nationalized" slavery by making slavery legal in every part of the United States. It depended on the status of the "person," not the status of the territory. As such, it was the most malicious of the "necessary evils" incorporated into the Constitution. See Edward J. Erler, *Property and the Pursuit of Happiness* (Lanham, MD: Rowman & Littlefield, 2018), 146, n. 21.

9 Abraham Lincoln, "Speech at Chicago, Illinois," July 10, 1858, in *The Collected Works of Abraham Lincoln*, 2:492. This idea is repeated many times by Lincoln. See 2:461, 498, 501, 514, 520–21; 3:18, 78, 87, 92–93, 117, 180–81, 254–55, 276, 307, 312–13, 333, 404, 406–7, 439, 483, 488, 489, 498, 535, 537–38, 550, 551, 553; 4:17–18, 21–22. Professor Michael J. Klarman, in *The Framers' Coup: The Making of the United States Constitution* (New York: Oxford University Press, 2016), 298–99, reports that this sentiment was expressed during the Constitutional Convention, quoting Thomas Dawes in the Massachusetts ratifying convention as saying that "we may say that, although slavery is not smitten by an apoplexy, yet it has received a mortal wound, and will die of consumption." "Another Massachusetts Federalist," Klarman notes, "writing pseudonymously, agreed that the Philadelphia convention went as far as policy would warrant or practicality allow. The friends to liberty and humanity may look forward with satisfaction to the period, when slavery shall not exist in the United States."

 James Wilson made similar arguments in the Pennsylvania ratifying convention, which, because he was a signer of the Declaration, a member of the Constitutional Convention, and later a member of the Supreme Court, deserve quotation at length: "With respect to the clause restricting Congress from prohibiting the migration or importation of such persons as any of the States now existing shall think proper to admit, prior to the year 1808, the honorable gentleman says that this clause is not only dark, but intended to grant to Congress for that time, the power to admit the importation of slaves. No such thing was intended; but I will tell you what was done, and it gives me high pleasure that so much was done. Under the present confederation, the States may admit the importation of slaves as long as they please; but by this article, after the year 1808, the Congress will have power to prohibit such importation, notwithstanding the disposition of any State to the contrary. I consider this as laying the foundation for banishing slavery out of this country; and though the period is more distant than I could wish . . . It is with much satisfaction I view this power in the general government, whereby they may lay an interdiction on this reproachful trade" [John McMaster and Frederick Stone, eds., *Pennsylvania and the Federal Constitution 1787–1788* (Indianapolis, IN: Liberty Fund, 2011, orig. pub. 1881)], 312.

10 Abraham Lincoln, "Address at Cooper Union," February 27, 1860, in *The Collected Works of Abraham Lincoln*, 3:545; see "Fifth Debate," 3:231.

11 *Dred Scott v. Sandford*, 60 U.S. (19 How.) 393, 452, 451 (1857) (Taney, C.J.) (emphasis added). Indeed, it could be shown that the word "property" was deliberately excluded even from the final version of the Declaration of Independence because of its slavery implications.

12 See Edward J. Erler, "The Political Philosophy of the Constitution," in *To Form a More Perfect Union: The Critical Ideas of the Constitution*, ed. Herman Belz et al. (Charlottesville: University Press of Virginia, 1992), 143–52.

13 Harry V. Jaffa, *American Conservatism and the American Founding* (Durham, NC: Carolina Academic Press, 1984), 133 ("Without recourse to the Declaration, there is no way of distinguishing principled from unprincipled compromises"); Jaffa, *Crisis of the House Divided*, 330; and Jaffa, *A New Birth of Freedom: Abraham Lincoln and the Coming of the Civil War* (Lanham, MD: Rowman & Littlefield, 2000), 339–40. I had an extended debate with Attorney Mark Pulliam on *American Greatness* and *Real Clear Policy*. Pulliam comments extensively on the Constitution and legal issues generally and is a follower of the jurisprudence of the late Judge Robert Bork. Bork often wrote that the Constitution must be interpreted strictly according to its text, structure, and tradition, contending that it was illegitimate to go outside the four corners of the Constitution to consult other sources. He directed particular animus at the Declaration of Independence, which, he insisted, represented only the "abstract theories" and "value judgments" of the social class to which its authors belonged. I supplied abundant evidence to Pulliam that Madison and the framers explicitly grounded the Constitution on the principles of the Declaration (see the discussion of *Federalist* 39 above) and challenged him to produce a single example of a framer who didn't accept the Declaration as the principled authority for the Constitution. He was unable to do so and, in an argument unknown in the canons of legal reasoning, said that since I challenged him to give an example of a framer who disagreed, it was my obligation to supply one! Obviously I could not, since it was my contention that no such framer existed. In a final act of desperation, Pulliam said I should leave constitutional interpretation to lawyers and not meddle as an amateur. I then had the ill grace to point out that the authors of the Declaration included the most prominent lawyers of the day, principal among them Thomas Jefferson and John Adams, and that the person who is justly celebrated as the "Father of the Constitution" was not a lawyer.

14 Abraham Lincoln, "Speech at Springfield, Illinois," June 26, 1857, in *The Collected Works of Abraham Lincoln*, 2:405–6 (all emphasis original).

15 *Dred Scott v. Sandford*, at 410.

16 Ibid., at 576 (Curtis, J., dissenting).

17 Ibid., at 574–75 (Curtis, J., dissenting).

18 Abraham Lincoln, "Speech at Springfield, Illinois," June 26, 1857, in *The Collected Works of Abraham Lincoln*, 2:406.

19 Ibid. See Stephen A. Douglas, "Remarks of the Hon. Stephen A. Douglas, on Kansas, Utah, and the Dred Scott Decision," delivered at Springfield, Illinois, June 12, 1857 (Chicago: Daily Times Book and Job Office, 1857), 9–10.

20 *Dred Scott v. Sandford*, at 407.

21 Ibid.

22 Ibid.

23 Letter to Henri Gregoire, February 25, 1809, in *Jefferson: Writings* (New York: Library of America, 1984), 1202.

24 "Speech of Stephen A. Douglas," Chicago, July 9, 1858, in *The Lincoln-Douglas Debates of 1858*, ed. Robert W. Johannsen (New York: Oxford University Press, 1965), 24, 28; "Fifth Debate," October 7, 1858, The Lincoln-Douglas Debates, in *The Collected Works of Abraham Lincoln*, 3:225–56; 3:315; 2:553.

25 Harry V. Jaffa, *American Conservatism and the American Founding* (Claremont, CA: The Claremont Institute, 2002 [orig. pub. by Carolina Academic Press, 1984]), 135–36; Jaffa, *New Birth of Freedom*, 314–15; and Jaffa, *Crisis of the Strauss Divided: Essays on Leo Strauss and Straussianism, East and West* (Lanham, MD: Rowman & Littlefield, 2012), 10.

26 Congressional Globe, 37th Cong., 2nd sess., 3338 (July 15, 1862) (Sen. Jacob Howard, Michigan).

27 Ibid. (Sen. James Harlan, Iowa).

28 Herman Belz, *A New Birth of Freedom: The Republican Party and Freedmen's Rights, 1861 to 1866* (Westport, CT: Greenwood Press, 1976), 20–21.

29 Ibid., 13.

30 *The Collected Works of Abraham Lincoln*, 5:330–31.

31 Ibid., 4:250.

32 Belz, *A New Birth of Freedom*, 13.

33 *The Collected Works of Abraham Lincoln*, 5:144–45. Lincoln uses the awkward term "abolishment" in an effort to disassociate himself from "abolition" and "abolitionist." Democrats constantly tried to pin the highly unpopular "abolitionist" label on him.

34 "Appeal to Border State Representatives to Favor Compensated Emancipation," in *The Collected Works of Abraham Lincoln*, 5:317–19. The border state congressmen responded to Lincoln on July 15, 1862. They argued that the cost of the compensation required plus the money required for colonization was not justified; it would "add this vast amount to our public debt, at a moment when the Treasury was reeling under the enormous expenditures of the war." Lincoln had argued that the savings from ending the expenses of the war effort would more than pay for compensated emancipation and colonization. Almost predictably, the congressmen seemed more interested in quibbling about what they considered the low estimate put on the compensation price of the slaves. The heart of their rejection, however, was undoubtedly their passionate attachment to the idea that "the right to hold slaves is a right appertaining to all the States of this Union. They have the right to cherish or abolish the institution as their tastes or their interests may prompt, and no one is authorized to question the right, or limit its enjoyment. And no one has more clearly affirmed that right than you have." They were mistaken to think that Lincoln's proposal threatened

to interfere with any rights of the states since compensated emancipation in Lincoln's proposal was strictly voluntary; a minority report was also included in which the minority pledged "to meet your address in the spirit in which it was made, and as loyal Americans declare to you and to the world that there is no sacrifice that we are not ready to make, to save the government and institutions of our fathers." Both can be found at https://www.loc.gov/collections/abraham-lincoln-papers/?q=Border+State+Congressmen+to +Abraham+Lincoln+July+15,+1862+1863. See also Charles H. McCarthy, *Lincoln's Plan of Reconstruction* (New York: AMS Press, 1966, orig. pub. 1901), 171–77.

35 "Proclamation Revoking General Hunter's Order of Military Emancipation of May 9, 1862," in *The Collected Works of Abraham Lincoln*, 5:222–23.

36 "To Henry W. Halleck," December 2, 1861, in *The Collected Works of Abraham Lincoln*, 5:35, granting him power to suspend the writ of habeas corpus within the limits of his command and "to exercise martial law as you find it necessary in your discretion to secure the public safety and the authority of the United States." Halleck's General Order No. 3 had been issued on November 20, 1861.

37 Michael Burlingame, *Abraham Lincoln: A Life*, 2 vols. (Baltimore: Johns Hopkins University Press, 2008), 2:348.

38 Letter to Horace Greeley, August 22, 1862, in *The Collected Works of Abraham Lincoln*, 5:388–89 (all emphasis original).

39 Both quotations in Burlingame, *Abraham Lincoln: A Life*, 2:410, 411.

40 Harry V. Jaffa, "The Emancipation Proclamation," in *Equality and Liberty: Theory and Practice in American Politics* (New York: Oxford University Press, 1965), 146 (emphasis original).

41 *New York Tribune*, September 24, 1862, quoted in Burlingame, *Abraham Lincoln: A Life*, 2:412.

42 Ralph Waldo Emerson, "The President's Proclamation," *Atlantic Monthly*, November 1862, 640, quoted in Burlingame, *Abraham Lincoln: A Life*, 2:412.

43 James M. McPherson, *Battle Cry of Freedom: The Civil War Era* (New York: Oxford University Press, 1988), 560.

44 Burlingame, *Abraham Lincoln: A Life*, 2:419–20. See William B. Hesseltine, *Lincoln and the War Governors* (New York: Alfred A. Knopf, 1948), 311–18. In this age of "cancel culture," when hysteria has replaced reason in public discourse, progressive-Left Democrats denounce Abraham Lincoln as a "racist." They seem blissfully ignorant of the fact—because it doesn't fit their narrative—that the Democratic Party was the party of slavery before, during, and after the Civil War. Jim Crow was the invention of the Democratic Party, and anyone with genuine insight into our political situation today can see clearly that the Democratic Party is still the party of Jim Crow— equality is denounced as "racist," and its replacement, "equity," an explicitly race-based test of racial results, has now become sacrosanct (meaning it is "racist" to argue against it) among the narratives of the progressive Left. If

anything is to be canceled because of its past racism, it is the Democratic Party! The epithets hurled at Lincoln reveal an utter ignorance of regime principles—without which there was never any hope of ending slavery— and the statesmanship required to implement those principles. But reason is useless against the hysterical narratives that dominate the public realm today. Lincoln must have advanced white supremacy—wasn't he white? The Democratic Party was white—*it did, in fact, advance white supremacy*, but no need to hold it to account, because the narrative of the progressive Left is an arbitrary and willful invention that does not have to give an account based on reasoned discourse. The facts dredged up from the hoary depths will never be summoned before the bar of reason. But then again, the narrative demands that we accept as one of those facts that reason itself is simply another form of white supremacy, and any attempt to use reason to refute the progressive-Left narrative is *ipso facto* an act of white supremacy—the principal source of "domestic terrorism" according to President Biden and the current Justice Department.

45 B[enjamin] R. Curtis, *Executive Power* (Boston: Little, Brown and Company, 1862), 9–10.

46 Ibid., 10.

47 Ibid.

48 Ibid., 19–22.

49 In his Annual Message delivered to Congress on December 19, 1859, President Buchanan congratulated the Supreme Court for its decision in the *Dred Scott* case, calling it "the final settlement . . . of the question of slavery in the Territories, which had presented an aspect so truly formidable at the commencement of my Administration. The right has been established of every citizen to take his property of any kind, including slaves, into the common Territories belonging equally to all the States of the Confederacy, and to have it protected there under the Federal Constitution. Neither Congress nor a Territorial legislature nor any human power has any authority to annul or impair this vested right. The supreme judicial tribunal of the country, which is a coordinate branch of the Government, has sanctioned and affirmed these principles of constitutional law, so manifestly just in themselves and so well calculated to promote peace and harmony among the States. It is a striking proof of the sense of justice which is inherent in our people."

We have already discussed Lincoln's opinion that Chief Justice Taney's ruling for the majority in *Dred Scott* that Congress has "the power coupled with the duty" to enact a slave code for the territories was the proximate cause of the Civil War. In his fourth Annual Message to Congress (December 3, 1860), Buchanan acknowledged that the Constitution contemplates a perpetual Union and therefore does not recognize the right to secession. By the same token, however, Buchanan argues that the Constitution does not delegate power to Congress or any branch of the government to keep a state from departing the Union. While secession is unconstitutional, there is no power to enforce the Constitution! The Constitution thus renders the government powerless to defend itself and thereby deprives the sovereign people of a right to self-preservation. Individuals are born and die, but the sovereignty of the people is perpetual—it passes from generation to generation. As long as the people are sovereign, the Union must be perpetual. Buchanan's understanding of the Constitution and Union was, to say the least, imperfect.

50 Curtis, *Executive Power*, 18.

51 *The Collected Works of Abraham Lincoln*, 4:430–31.

52 See Daniel Farber, *Lincoln's Constitution* (Chicago: University of Chicago Press, 2003), 160–70.

53 "Annual Message to Congress," December 1, 1862, in *The Collected Works of Abraham Lincoln*, 5:530.

54 Burlingame, *Abraham Lincoln: A Life*, 2:473.

55 See ibid., 2:595.

56 Congressional Globe, 38th Cong., 2nd Sess., 572 (February 10, 1864) (Rep. Eliot).

57 Ibid., 961 (February 21, 1865) (Sen. Sumner).

58 Ibid., 962 (February 21, 1865) (Sen. Henderson).

59 Ibid., 773 (February 23, 1864) (Rep. Kelley).

60 Mark A. Graber, "The Second Freedmen's Bureau Bill's Constitution," *Texas Law Review* 94, no. 7 (June 2016): 1361, 1363.

61 Congressional Globe, 39th Cong., 1st Sess., appendix, 66–67 (February 1, 1866) (Rep. Garfield, Ohio).

62 See Erler, *Property and the Pursuit of Happiness*, 189–93.

63 Congressional Globe, 39th Cong, 1st Sess., 474 (January 29, 1866) (Sen. Trumbull, Illinois). Trumbull was also co-author of the Thirteenth Amendment.

64 President Andrew Johnson, March 27, 1866, in *A Compilation of the Messages and Papers of the Presidents*, 9 vols., ed. James D. Richardson (Washington, DC: Bureau of National Literature and Art, 1905), 6:407.

65 Congressional Globe, 42nd Cong., 1st Sess., appendix, 83 (March 31, 1871) (Rep. Bingham, Ohio). "I had the honor to frame . . . the first section [of the Fourteenth Amendment] as it now stands, letter for letter and syllable for syllable . . . save for the introductory clause defining citizens." This was in debate over the Third Force Act of 1871.

66 Congressional Globe, 39th Cong., 1st Sess., 2542 (May 10, 1866) (Rep. Bingham, Ohio).

67 See Erler, *Property and the Pursuit of Happiness*, 182–93.

68 O. J. Hollister, *Life of Schuyler Colfax*, 2nd ed. (New York: Funk and Wagnalls, 1886), 270–71.

69 Congressional Globe, 39th Cong., 1st Sess., 5 (December 4, 1865) (Rep. Colfax, Indiana).

70 "Speech of Hon. Schuyler Colfax," *Cincinnati Commercial*, August 9, 1866, 2 (emphasis original). See remarks of Representative Thaddeus Stevens, Congressional Globe, 39th Cong., 1st Sess., 2459 (May 9, 1866).

71 Congressional Globe, 39th Cong., 1st Sess., 2765–66 (May 23, 1866) (Sen. Howard, Michigan).

72 See Edward J. Erler, *The United States in Crisis: Citizenship, Immigration, and the Nation State*, rev. ed. (New York: Encounter Books, 2022).

CHAPTER THREE

1 56th Cong., 1st sess., *Congressional Record* vol. 33 (February 26, 1900): 2243, 2245.

2 "Negroes in Congress. Rise and Overthrow of Colored Politician," *Boston Herald*, January 5, 1902.

3 "In Gay Washington, Grand Army Week Crowned with Festivities," *Indianapolis Freeman*, November 1, 1902.

4 On the Grand Army of the Republic and its role in shaping Republican Party politics in the late nineteenth century, see Barbara A. Gannon, *The Won Cause: Black and White Comradeship in the Grand Army of the Republic* (Chapel Hill: University of North Carolina Press, 2011).

5 George Tindall, *South Carolina Negroes, 1877–1900* (Columbia, SC: University of South Carolina Press, 1952), 73.

6 "Stalwarts" encompassed the Gilded Age wing of the Republican Party that supported the spoils system, patronage politics, and a continued commitment to the civil rights and voting rights that defined the party during the Ulysses S. Grant Administration. On the Stalwart wing of the Republican Party during the Gilded Age, see Allan Peskin, "Who Were the Stalwarts? Who Were Their Rivals? Republican Factions in the Gilded Age," *Political Science Quarterly* 99, no. 4 (Winter 1984): 703–16.

7 *New National Era*, Washington, DC, May 9, 1872.

8 On the formation of the Republican Party in South Carolina, see Thomas Holt, *Black over White: Negro Political Leadership in South Carolina during Reconstruction* (Urbana: University of Illinois Press, 1977).

9 Mary J. Miller, ed., *The Suffrage: Speeches by Negroes in the Constitutional Convention: The Part Taken by Colored Orators in Their Fight for a Fair and Impartial Ballot* (n.p., 1895).

10 On Klan violence in the South, see Elaine Frantz Parsons, *Ku-Klux: The Birth of the Klan during Reconstruction* (Chapel Hill: University of North Carolina Press, 2015); and Kidada Williams, *They Left Great Marks on Me: African American Testimonies of Racial Violence from Emancipation to World War I* (New York: New York University Press, 2012).

11 On the end of Reconstruction, see Gregory P. Downs, *After Appomattox: Military Occupation and the Ends of War* (Cambridge, MA: Harvard University Press, 2015); and Heather Cox Richardson, *The Death of Reconstruction: Race, Labor, and Politics in the Post–Civil War North, 1865–1901* (Cambridge, MA: Harvard University Press, 2001).

12 On the politics of the post-Reconstruction South, see Edward L. Ayers, *The Promise of the New South: Life after Reconstruction* (New York: Oxford University Press, 1992); Jane Dailey, *Before Jim Crow: The Politics of Race in Postemancipation Virginia* (Chapel Hill: University of North Carolina Press, 2000); Gregory P. Downs, *Declarations of Dependence: The Long Reconstruction of Popular Politics in the South, 1861–1908* (Chapel Hill: University of North Carolina Press, 2011); and Nicole Myers Turner, *Soul Liberty: The Evolution of Black Religious Politics in Postemancipation Virginia* (Chapel Hill: University of North Carolina Press, 2020).

13 William J. Cooper Jr., *The Conservative Regime: South Carolina, 1877–1890* (Baltimore, MD: Johns Hopkins University Press, 1968), 130.

14 On the South Carolina Lowcountry and Sea Islands during Reconstruction, see Willie Lee Rose, *Rehearsal for Reconstruction: The Port Royal Experiment* (Indianapolis: Bobbs-Merrill, 1964); Thomas Holt, *Black over White: Negro Political Leadership in South Carolina during Reconstruction* (Urbana: University of Illinois Press, 1977); Eric Foner, *Nothing but Freedom: Emancipation and Its Legacy* (Baton Rouge: Louisiana State University Press, 1983), Chapter 3; and Julie Saville, *The Work of Reconstruction: From Slave to Wage Labor in South Carolina, 1860–1870* (New York: Cambridge University Press, 1996).

15 "A Negro Paradise," *Washington People's Advocate*, August 11, 1883; "Negro Suffrage: A Representative Colored Man Thinks It Was Prematurely Bestowed," *Chicago Daily Tribune*, August 18, 1886.

16 Rupert S. Holland, ed., *Letters and Diary of Laura M. Towne, Written from the Sea Islands of South Carolina, 1862–1884* (Boston: Riverside Press, 1912), 254.

17 *Charleston News and Courier*, February 2, 1890.

18 "Grant's Flying Trip through the South—How the People Act and What They Say," *Chicago Daily Inter Ocean*, January 15, 1880.

19 *New York Freeman*, November 27, 1886.

20 "Grit," *New York Globe*, April 12, 1884.

21 Edward A. Miller Jr., *Gullah Statesman: Robert Smalls from Slavery to Congress, 1839–1915* (Columbia: University of South Carolina Press, 1995), 168.

22 Robert Smalls, "Election Methods in the South," *North American Review* 151, no. 408 (November 1890): 593.

23 Ibid., 600.

24 On Washington, D.C., during Reconstruction, see Kate Masur, *An Example for All the Land: Emancipation and the Struggle over Equality in Washington, D.C.* (Chapel Hill: University of North Carolina Press, 2010).

25 On Washington, D.C., as a beacon for late-nineteenth-century black life, see Chris Myers Asch and George Derek Musgrove, *Chocolate City: A History of Race and Democracy in the Nation's Capital* (Chapel Hill: University of North Carolina Press, 2017); Masur, *An Example for All the Land*; and Eric S. Yellin, *Racism in the Nation's Service: Government Workers and the Color Line in Woodrow Wilson's America* (Chapel Hill: University of North Carolina Press, 2013).

26 Eric Foner, *Freedom's Lawmakers: A Directory of Black Officeholders during Reconstruction* (New York: Oxford University Press, 1993).

27 T. Thomas Fortune, *The Negro in Politics: Some Pertinent Reflections on the Past and Present Political Status of the Afro-American, Together with a Cursory Investigation into the Motives Which Actuate Partisan Organizations* (New York: Ogilvie and Rowntree, 1886).

28 W. Calvin Chase, "The Negro and Republicanism: Denying That the Colored Vote Is Swinging Away from the Party," *Washington Bee*, August 18, 1883.

29 Asch and Musgrove, *Chocolate City*, 180–83.

30 "The Disgrace," *Washington Bee*, April 21, 1888.

31 "Stand by for Carson!" *Washington Post*, December 14, 1895.

32 Tindall, *South Carolina Negroes*, 62.

33 On the struggle to define and redefine the Republican Party in the South, see Boris Heersink and Jeffery A. Jenkins, *Republican Party Politics and the American South, 1865–1968* (New York: Cambridge University Press, 2020).

34 Miller, *Gullah Statesman*, 185.

35 W. J. Whipper, *Fusionists and Fusionism: Robert Smalls' Arraignment by the New York World and Other Matters* (Beaufort, SC: Sea Island News Press, 1889), YA Pamphlet Collection, Rare Book and Special Collections Division, Library of Congress; T. E. Miller, "General Smalls and the President: He Denounces the Charges against Him," *Washington Bee*, April 27, 1889.

36 *Edgefield Advertiser*, June 30, 1892.

37 On the rise of Benjamin Tillman and his push for disfranchisement in South Carolina, see Stephen Kantrowitz, *Ben Tillman and the Reconstruction of White Supremacy* (Chapel Hill: University of North Carolina Press, 2000).

38 Miller, *The Suffrage*, n.p.

39 Sarah V. Smalls, *Speeches at the Constitutional Convention* (Charleston, SC: Enquirer Printing Company, 1896).

40 "Blaine Invincibles Elect Officers," *Washington Evening Star*, May 18, 1903; and Heersink and Jenkins, *Republican Party Politics and the American South*, 302–6.

CHAPTER FOUR

1 Samuel I. Rosenman and William D. Hassett, eds., *The Public Papers and Addresses of Franklin D. Roosevelt, Volume One: The Genesis of the New Deal, 1928–1932*, vol. 1 (New York: Random House, 1950), 742–55, https://teachingamericanhistory.org/library/document/commonwealth-club-address/.

2 Franklin Delano Roosevelt, "State of the Union Address," January 6, 1941, https://millercenter.org/the- presidency/presidential-speeches/january-6-1941-state-union-four-freedoms.

3 Franklin Delano Roosevelt, "State of the Union Address," January 11, 1944, https://millercenter.org/the- presidency/presidential-speeches/january-11-1944-fireside-chat-28-state-union.

4 Ibid.

5 Lyndon Baines Johnson, "Remarks at the Howard University Commencement," June 4, 1965, https://millercenter.org/the-presidency/presidential-speeches/june-4-1965-remarks-howard-university-commencement.

6 Martin Luther King Jr., *Where Do We Go from Here: Chaos or Community?* (Boston: Beacon, 2010).

7 Ibid., 116.

8 Ibid., 68.

9 Ibid., 128.

10 Ibid., 121.

11 United States National Advisory Commission on Civil Disorders, "Report of the National Advisory Commission on Civil Disorders" [Washington, DC]: [For sale by the Supt. Of Docs., U.S.G.P.O.], [1968] (DLC) 68061127 (OCLC) 1362515.

12 King, *Where Do We Go from Here*, 122.

13 Martin Luther King Jr., "I Have a Dream," August 28, 1963, https://www.archives.gov/files/press/exhibits/dream-speech.pdf.

14 King, *Where Do We Go from Here*, 131.

15 Ibid., 142. "The Negro is called upon to be as resourceful as those who have not known such oppression and exploitation. This is the Negro's dilemma. He who starts behind in a race must forever remain behind or run faster than the man in front. What a dilemma! *It is a call to do the impossible.* It is enough to cause the Negro to give up in despair" (emphasis added).

16 Ibid., 144–45.

17 Ibid., 134.

18 Ibid., 142.

19 Ibid.

20 Ibid., 154–55.

21 Ibid., 157.

22 Ibid., 62.

23 Ibid., 142, 158.

24 See W. B. Allen, "The *New York Times* Resurrects the Positive Good Slavery Argument," *Law & Liberty*, October 2, 2019, https://www.lawliberty.org/2019/10/02/the-new-york-times-resurrects-the-positive-good-slavery-argument/.

25 Lee Rainwater and William L. Yancey, *The Moynihan Report and the Politics of Controversy* (Cambridge, MA: MIT Press, 1967).

26 W. B. Allen, *George Washington: America's First Progressive* (New York: Peter Lang, 2008).

27 Ida B. Wells, Preface to *The Reason Why the Colored American Is Not in the World's Columbian Exposition: The Afro-American's Contribution to Columbian*

Literature, ed. Ida B. Wells (Urbana and Chicago: University of Illinois, 1893), https://digital.library.upenn.edu/women/wells/exposition/exposition.html.

28 Ibid.

29 Frederick Douglass, Introduction to *The Reason Why*.

30 Ibid.

31 Ibid.

32 Booker T. Washington, "Address Delivered at Hampton Institute," November 18, 1895, Teaching American History, https://teachingamericanhistory.org/library/document/address-delivered-at-hampton-institute/.

33 Booker T. Washington, "An Abraham Lincoln Memorial Address in Philadelphia," February 14, 1899, Teaching American History, https://teachingamericanhistory.org/library/document/an-abraham-lincoln-memorial-address-in-philadelphia/.

34 Booker T. Washington, "The Educational and Industrial Emancipation of the Negro," February 22, 1903, Teaching American History, https://teachingamericanhistory.org/library/document/the-educational-and-industrial-emancipation-of-the-negro/.

35 Ibid.

36 Ibid.

CHAPTER FIVE

1 "6 Dead, 63 Wounded in Memorial Day Weekend Shootings," *Chicago Sun-Times*, May 31, 2016, https://chicago.suntimes.com/2016/5/31/18337210/6-dead-63-wounded-in-memorial-day-weekend-shootings.

2 See Randall Kennedy, *Race, Crime, and the Law* (New York: Random House, 1997).

3 Jennifer Lee and Min Zhou, *The Asian American Achievement Paradox* (New York: Russell Sage Foundation, 2015).

4 See Stacy Tisdale, "Study: Black Immigrants Earn More than U.S.-Born Blacks," *Black Enterprise Magazine*, September 24, 2015, https://www.blackenterprise.com/black-immigrants-in-u-s-earning-30-more-than-u-s-born-blacks/.

5 "Fatal Force," *Washington Post*, updated April 20, 2021, https://www.washingtonpost.com/graphics/investigations/police-shootings-database/.

6 Richard Rosenfeld and James Alan Fox, "Anatomy of the Homicide Rise," *Homicide Studies* 23, no. 3 (2019): 202–24.

7 It is important to note that this is a frequently repeated misrepresentation of what Lincoln said and did, as fully explored by W. B. Allen in "To Preserve, Protect and Defend: The Emancipation Proclamation," in *The Political Thought of the Civil War*, ed. Alan Levine, Thomas W. Merrill, and James R. Stoner Jr. (Lawrence, KS: University Press of Kansas, 2018), 249–72. Allen concluded that "Lincoln conveyed by [an] evasion both his readiness to declare practically general emancipation and, at the same time, his readiness to accept the defected states back into the fold. It must be understood, however,

that Lincoln himself had a firm understanding of which of those prospects was the more likely. The fact that he had already committed to emancipation reveals his judgment of the likely outcome. Lincoln arrived at that result by meticulously weighing not merely the politics but the substance of the matter."

8 For a detailed analysis of the status of black Americans in the 1940s, see Gunnar Mydral, *An American Dilemma: The Negro Problem and Modern Democracy* (New York: Harper and Row, 1944).

9 See Robert Higgs, *Competition and Coercion: Blacks in the American Economy, 1865–1914* (New York: Cambridge University Press, 1977).

10 See ibid., as well as Herbert Gutman, *The Black Family in Slavery and Freedom, 1750–1925* (New York: Random House, 1976).

CHAPTER SIX

1 Jeff St. Clair, "To Make Birding Inclusive, Some Birds Will Need New Names without Colonial Roots," *All Things Considered*, NPR, June 7, 2021, https://www.npr.org/2021/06/07/1004076000/to-make-birding-inclusive-some-birds-will-need-new-names-without-colonial-roots.

2 Zack Harold, "New River Gorge Rock Climbers Grapple with Racist Route Names," *Allegheny Front*, February 5, 2021, https://www.alleghenyfront.org/new-river-gorge-rock-climbers-grapple-with-racist-route-names/.

3 Neil Bhutta, Andrew C. Chang, Lisa J. Dettling, and Joanne W. Hsu, "Disparities in Wealth by Race and Ethnicity in the 2019 Survey of Consumer Finances," FEDS Notes (Washington, DC: Board of Governors of the Federal Reserve System, 2020), https://doi.org/10.17016/2380-7172.2797.

4 Ibid., Figure 1.

5 Tressie McMillan Cottom, "No, College Isn't the Answer. Reparations Are," *Washington Post*, May 29, 2014, https://www.washingtonpost.com/posteverything/wp/2014/05/29/no-college-isnt-the-answer-reparations-are/.

6 Reader Center, "When I See Racial Disparities, I See Racism," *New York Times*, March 27, 2018, https://www.nytimes.com/interactive/2018/03/27/upshot/reader-questions-about-race-gender-and-mobility.html?

7 Sara McLanahan and Isabel Sawhill, "Marriage and Child Wellbeing Revisited: Introducing the Issue," *Future of Children* 25, no. 2 (Fall 2015): 4, https://futureofchildren.princeton.edu/sites/futureofchildren/files/media/marriage_and_child_wellbeing_revisited_25_2_full_journal.pdf.

8 This section is adapted from a study released by the present author along with Wendy Wang and W. Bradford Wilcox, entitled "Less Poverty, Less Prison, More College: What Two Parents Mean for Black and White Children," originally published in June 2021 by the Institute for Family Studies. See https://ifstudies.org/blog/less-poverty-less-prison-more-college-what-two-parents-mean-for-black-and-white-children. We are grateful to Samuel McIntyre, Joseph P. Price, Peyton W. Roth, Scott Winship, Jared Wright, and Nicholas Zill for their input and assistance. Brad Wilcox is a professor of sociology and director of the National Marriage Project at the

University of Virginia, a senior fellow of the Institute for Family Studies, and a nonresident scholar at the American Enterprise Institute. Wendy Wang is the director of research at the Institute for Family Studies.

9 Sara McLanahan and Gary Sandefur, *Growing Up with a Single Parent: What Hurts, What Helps* (Cambridge, MA: Harvard University Press, 1994), 1.

10 See Paul R. Amato, "The Impact of Family Formation Change on the Cognitive, Social, and Emotional Well-Being of the Next Generation," *Future of Children* 15, no. 2 (Fall 2005): 75–96, https://eric.ed.gov/?id=EJ795852; Isabel V. Sawhill, *Generation Unbound: Drifting into Sex and Parenthood without Marriage* (Washington, DC: Brookings Institution Press, 2014); and Melanie Wasserman, "The Disparate Effects of Family Structure," *Future of Children* 30, no. 1 (Spring 2020): 55–81, https://futureofchildren.princeton.edu/sites/futureofchildren/files/foc_vol_30_no_1_combined_v6.pdf.

11 Christina Cross, "The Myth of the Two-Parent Home," *New York Times*, December 9, 2019, https://www.nytimes.com/2019/12/09/opinion/two-parent-family.html. For a response, see W. Bradford Wilcox, "Three Facts about Family Structure and Race: Responding to the New York Times," Institute for Family Studies, December 12, 2019, https://ifstudies.org/blog/three-facts-about-family-structure-and-race-responding-to-the-new-york-times.

12 Christina Cross, "Why Living in a Two-Parent Home Isn't a Cure-All for Black Students," *Harvard Gazette*, June 3, 2021, https://news.harvard.edu/gazette/story/2021/06/why-living-in-a-two-parent-home-isnt-a-cure-all-for-black-students/. See also Christina Cross, "Racial/Ethnic Differences in the Association between Family Structure and Children's Education," November 2019, https://www.researchgate.net/publication/337111440_RacialEthnic_Differences_in_the_Association_Between_Family_Structure_and_Children's_Education; and Christina Cross, "Beyond the Binary: Intraracial Diversity in Family Organization and Black Adolescents' Educational Performance," https://doi.org/10.13140/RG.2.2.36370.58563.

13 See Angela Chen, "The Rise of the 3-Parent Family," *The Atlantic*, September 22, 2020, https://www.theatlantic.com/family/archive/2020/09/how-build-three-parent-family-david-jay/616421/; and S. Golombok et al., "Single Mothers by Choice: Parenting and Child Adjustment in Middle Childhood," *Journal of Family Psychology* 35, no. 2 (2021): 192–202, http://dx.doi.org/10.1037/fam0000797.

14 Courtesy of Nicholas Zill, the analysis is based on the March 2020 Current Population Survey (CPS). The vast majority of black children in two-biological-parent families are in families headed by married parents; only a small fraction are in cohabiting families. See Nicholas Zill and W. Bradford Wilcox, "1-in-2: A New Estimate of the Share of Children Being Raised by Married Parents," Institute for Family Studies, February 27, 2018, https://ifstudies.org/blog/1-in-2-a-new-estimate-of-the-share-of-children-being-raised-by-married-parents.

15 Authors' analysis of American Community Survey (ACS) 2015–2019 five-year estimates. Data were accessed at Steven Ruggles, Sarah Flood, Sophia Foster, Ronald Goeken, Jose Pacas, Megan Schouweiler, and Matthew Sobek, IPUMS

USA: Version 11.0 [dataset] (Minneapolis, MN: IPUMS, 2021), https://doi.org/10.18128/D010.V11.0.

16 This includes intact same-sex families and intact adoptive families. However, the vast majority of children in intact, married families in the ACS are in intact heterosexual families. See, for instance, Wendy Wang, "A Portrait of Contemporary Living Arrangements for U.S. Children," Institute for Family Studies, April 14, 2020, https://ifstudies.org/blog/a-portrait-of-contemporary-family-living-arrangements-for-us-children.

17 For poverty estimates, households were identified as likely "stepparent" families if the parents were married and either parent reported they had been married more than once. Families headed by a single widowed parent were excluded from the analyses. Data were accessed at Steven Ruggles, Sarah Flood, Sophia Foster, Ronald Goeken, Jose Pacas, Megan Schouweiler, and Matthew Sobek, IPUMS USA: Version 11.0 [dataset] (Minneapolis, MN: IPUMS, 2021), https://doi.org/10.18128/D010.V11.0.

18 The comparison group is children in single-parent families, stepfamilies, and other families not headed by an intact married couple.

19 The vast majority of these families are headed by married biological parents but also include a small number of cohabiting biological parents. See Zill and Wilcox, "1-in-2: A New Estimate of the Share of Children Being Raised by Married Parents."

20 The comparison group here is children from single-parent families, stepfamilies, and other families not headed by two biological parents.

21 See Kristin Anderson Moore, Susan M. Jekielek, and Carol Emig, "Marriage from a Child's Perspective: How Does Family Structure Affect Children, and What Can We Do about It?" Child Trends Research Brief, June 2002, http://www.childtrends.org/wp-content/uploads/2002/06/MarriageRB602.pdf.

22 See Zill and Wilcox, "1-in-2: A New Estimate of the Share of Children Being Raised by Married Parents."

23 This section is adapted from the present author's remarks before the United States Congress Joint Economic Committee on "Examining the Racial Wealth Gap in the United States," delivered on May 12, 2021.

24 New York State Education Department, "NYC Geog. Dist. #8—Bronx Graduation Rate Data: 4 Year Outcome as of August 2019," https://data.nysed.gov/gradrate.php?year=2019&instid=800000046547.

25 New York State Education Department, "Boys Prep Charter School of NY Grades 3–8 Mathematics Assessment Data," https://data.nysed.gov/assessment38.php?subject=Mathematics&year=2019&instid=800000071084.

26 The Nation's Report Card, "NAEP Report Card: 2019 NAEP Reading Assessment," National Assessment of Educational Progress, https://www.nationsreportcard.gov/highlights/reading/2019/.

27 See the National Assessment of Educational Progress Assessment Data, https://nces.ed.gov/nationsreportcard/data/.

28 Bhutta et al., "Disparities in Wealth by Race and Ethnicity."

29 Chuck Collins et al., "Ten Solutions to Bridge the Racial Wealth Divide," Institute for Policy Studies, April 2019, https://ips-dc.org/wp-content/ uploads/2019/04/Ten-Solutions-to-Bridge-the-Racial-Wealth-Divide-FINAL-. pdf, 4.

30 William Darity Jr. et al., "What We Get Wrong about Closing the Racial Wealth Gap," Samuel DuBois Cook Center on Social Equity, April 2018, https://socialequity.duke.edu/wp-content/uploads/2019/10/what-we-get- wrong.pdf, 4.

31 Nikole Hannah-Jones, "What Is Owed," *New York Times*, June 30, 2020, https://www.nytimes.com/interactive/2020/06/24/magazine/reparations- slavery.html.

32 Angela Rachidi, "American Exceptionalism? Five Ways Government Spending on Low-Income Children and Child Poverty Is Misunderstood," American Enterprise Institute, November 12, 2019, https://www.aei.org/wp-content/ uploads/2019/11/American-Exceptionalism-Five-Ways-Government- Spending-on-Low-Income-Children-and-Child-Poverty-Is-Misunderstood-1. pdf?x91208, 4, Figure 1.

33 Ibid.

34 See Wendy Wang and W. Bradford Wilcox, "The Millennial Success Sequence: Marriage, Kids, and the 'Success Sequence' among Young Adults," American Enterprise Institute and Institute for Family Studies, June 14, 2017, https:// www.aei.org/research-products/working-paper/millennials-and-the-success- sequence-how-do-education-work-and-marriage-affect-poverty-and- financial-success-among-millennials/.

35 See Raj Chetty et al., "Where Is the Land of Opportunity? The Geography of Intergenerational Mobility in the United States," *Quarterly Journal of Economics* 129, no. 4 (November 2014): 1553–623, https://doi.org/10.1093/qje/ qju022.

36 Joyce A. Martin et al., "Births: Final Data for 2019," National Center for Health Statistics, *National Vital Statistics Reports* 70, no. 2 (March 2021): 1–51, https://dx.doi.org/10.15620/cdc:100472.

37 See the CDC Wonder Database, https://wonder.cdc.gov/.

38 See AEI/Brookings Working Group on Poverty and Opportunity, "Opportunity, Responsibility, and Security: A Consensus Plan for Reducing Poverty and Restoring the American Dream" (Washington, DC: American Enterprise Institute and Brookings Institution, 2015), https://www.aei.org/ wp-content/uploads/2015/12/opportunity_responsibility_security_doar_ strain_120315_FINAL.pdf.

39 See William T. Grant Foundation, "Closing the Opportunity Gap Initiative: Finding Solutions for Our Kids," August 17, 2016, http://wtgrantfoundation. org/closing-opportunity-gap-initiative-finding-solutions-kids.

40 Netflix, "Building Economic Opportunity for Black Communities," June 30, 2020, https://about.netflix.com/en/news/building-economic-opportunity-for- black-communities.

41 *Grutter v. Bollinger*, 539 U.S. 306 (2003), https://www.law.cornell.edu/supct/html/02-241.ZS.html.

42 Students for Fair Admissions, "About," https://studentsforfairadmissions.org/.

43 Issa Kohler-Hausmann, "What's the Point of Parity? Harvard, Groupness, and the Equal Protection Clause," *Northwestern University Law Review Online* 115, no. 1 (2020): 1, https://northwesternlawreview.org/articles/whats-the-point-of-parity-harvard-groupness-and-the-equal-protection-clause/.

44 Petition for Writ of Certiorari, *Students for Fair Admissions, Inc. v. President & Fellows of Harvard College*, No. 20-1199, at *11 (1st Cir. February 25, 2021).

45 Howard Gold, "The Harsh Truth about Black Enrollment at America's Elite Colleges," *MarketWatch*, June 25, 2020, https://www.marketwatch.com/story/the-harsh-truth-about-black-enrollment-at-americas-elite-colleges-2020-06-25.

46 Jesse J. Tauriac and Joan H. Liem, "Exploring the Divergent Academic Outcomes of U.S.-Origin and Immigrant-Origin Black Undergraduates," *Journal of Diversity in Higher Education* 5, no. 4 (December 2012): 244–58, https://www.ncbi.nlm.nih.gov/pmc/articles/PMC3816006/.

47 Richard Kahlenberg, *The Remedy: Class, Race and Affirmative Action* (New York: Basic Books, 1997).

48 Raj Chetty et al., "Where Is the Land of Opportunity? The Geography of Intergenerational Mobility in the United States," Executive Summary, January 2014, https://opportunityinsights.org/wp-content/uploads/2018/03/Geography-Executive-Summary-and-Memo-January-2014-1.pdf.

49 Raj Chetty et al., "Race and Economic Opportunity in the United States: An Intergenerational Perspective," *Quarterly Journal of Economics* 135, no. 2 (May 2020): 711–83, https://doi.org/10.1093/qje/qjz042.

50 Emily Badger et al., "Extensive Data Shows Punishing Reach of Racism for Black Boys," *New York Times*, March 19, 2018, https://www.nytimes.com/interactive/2018/03/19/upshot/race-class-white-and-black-men.html.

51 Reader Center, "When I See Racial Disparities, I See Racism."

52 W. Bradford Wilcox, Wendy R. Wang, and Ronald B. Mincy, "Black Men Making It in America: The Engines of Economic Success for Black Men in America," Washington, DC: American Enterprise Institute and Institute for Family Studies, 2018, https://www.aei.org/research-products/report/black-men-making-it-in-america-the-engines-of-economic-success-for-black-men-in-america/.

53 American Enterprise Institute, "Economic Success for Black Men in America," YouTube video, June 26, 2018, https://www.youtube.com/watch?v=wI2IdM3cIMg.

54 Wilcox, Wang, and Mincy, "Black Men Making It in America," 3.

55 Child Trends, "Children in Poverty," 2016, https://www.childtrends.org/indicators/children-in-poverty; Ron Haskins, "The Family Is Here to Stay—Or Not," *Future of Children* 25, no. 2 (September 2015): 129–53, https://www.researchgate.net/publication/283659683_The_family_is_

here_to_stay-or_not; Paul R. Amato, "The Impact of Family Formation Change on the Cognitive, Social, and Emotional Well-Being of the Next Generation," *Future of Children* 15, no. 2 (2005): 75–96, https://www.jstor.org/stable/3556564?seq=1; Cynthia C. Harper and Sara S. McLanahan, "Father Absence and Youth Incarceration," *Journal of Research on Adolescence* 14, no. 3 (September 2004): 369–97, https://onlinelibrary.wiley.com/doi/abs/10.1111/j.1532-7795.2004.00079.x; Wendy D. Manning and Kathleen A. Lamb, "Adolescent Well-Being in Cohabiting, Married, and Single-Parent Families," *Journal of Marriage and Family* 65, no. 4 (November 2003): 876–93, https://www.jstor.org/stable/3599897?seq=1#metadata_info_tab_contents; Melissa S. Kearney and Phillip B. Levine, "The Economics of Non-Marital Childbearing and the 'Marriage Premium for Children,'" working paper, National Bureau for Economic Research (Cambridge, MA: 2017), https://www.nber.org/papers/w23230; and R. Kelly Raley, Michelle L. Frisco, and Elizabeth Wildsmith, "Maternal Cohabitation and Educational Success," *Sociology of Education* 78, no. 2 (April 2005): 144–64, https://journals.sagepub.com/doi/10.1177/003804070507800203.

56 Lois M. Collins, "What Research Says about Two-Parent Families Keeping out of Jail and in School," *Deseret News*, June 17, 2021, https://www.deseret.com/2021/6/17/22538277/what-research-says-about-two-parent-families-keeping-kids-out-of-jail-brookings-aei-family-studies.

57 David Leonhardt, "A One-Question Quiz on the Poverty Trap," *New York Times*, October 4, 2018, https://www.nytimes.com/2018/10/04/opinion/child-poverty-family-income-neighborhood.html.

58 Natalie Moore, "Obama Wraps State of Union Speech Tour in Chicago," *WBEZ Chicago*, February 15, 2013, https://www.wbez.org/stories/obama-wraps-state-of-union-speech-tour-in-chicago/4d1e323a-692a-4a87-b907-b9bee7bc65e3.

59 1776 Unites, "Who We Are," https://1776unites.com/.

CHAPTER SEVEN

1 Iris Marion Young, "Five Faces of Oppression," in *Justice and the Politics of Difference* (Princeton, NJ: Princeton University Press, 1990), 39–65, https://contensis.uwaterloo.ca/sites/courses-archive/1185/PHIL-324/media/documents/10a-young-1990-five-faces-of-oppression.pdf.

2 Claire Kowalick, "Inequities Remain Despite Historic Drop in Poverty Level in 2019," *Times Record News*, September 16, 2020, https://www.timesrecordnews.com/story/news/local/2020/09/16/inequalities-remain-despite-historic-drop-poverty-level-2019/5816101002/.

3 Federal Interagency Forum on Child and Family Statistics, "Food Insecurity: Percentage of Children Ages 0–17 in Food Insecure Households by Selected Characteristics and Severity of Food Insecurity, Selected Years 1995–2018," https://www.childstats.gov/americaschildren/tables/econ3.asp.

4 U.S. Federal Reserve, "Report on the Economic Well Being of U.S. Households in 2019–May 2020," last modified May 21, 2021, https://www.

federalreserve.gov/publications/2020-economic-well-being-of-us-households-in-2019-retirement.htm.

5 Kaiser Family Foundation, "Poverty Rate by Race/Ethnicity: 2019," estimates based on the 2008–2019 American Community Survey, 1-Year Estimates, www.kff.org/other/state-indicator/poverty-rate-by-raceethnicity.

6 National Urban League, "The State of Black America: Unmasked: 2020 Executive Summary," 2020, https://soba.iamempowered.com/2020-executive-summary, 3.

7 Angela Hanks, Danyelle Solomon, and Christian Weller, "Systematic Inequality: How America's Structural Racism Helped Create the Black-White Wealth Gap," Center for American Progress, February 21, 2018, https://www.americanprogress.org/issues/race/reports/2018/02/21/447051/systematic-inequality/.

8 Deepa Narayan, *Voices of the Poor: Can Anyone Hear Us?* (New York: Oxford University Press, published for the World Bank, 2000), 31.

9 Ann Chih Lin and David R. Harris, "Why Is American Poverty Still Colored in the Twenty-First Century?" in *The Colors of Poverty: Why Racial and Ethnic Disparities Persist*, ed. Ann Chih Lin and David Harris (New York: Russell Sage Foundation, 2008), 4.

10 David Hulme, Karen Moore, and Andrew Shepherd, "Chronic Poverty: Meanings and Analytical Frameworks," Chronic Poverty Research Centre Working Paper No. 2, November 1, 2001, https://papers.ssrn.com/sol3/papers.cfm?abstract_id=1754546, 12, 21.

11 Ibid., 21.

12 Kaiser Family Foundation, "Poverty Rate by Race/Ethnicity."

13 Lin and Harris, "Why Is American Poverty Still Colored," 1.

14 Daniel R. Meyer and Geoffrey L. Wallace, "Poverty Levels and Trends in Comparative Perspective," in *Changing Poverty, Changing Policies*, ed. Maria Cancian and Sheldon Danziger (New York: Russell Sage Foundation, 2009), 56.

15 Ibid., 56–57.

16 Ibid.

17 Mary Corcoran, "Mobility, Persistence, and the Consequences of Poverty for Children: Child and Adult Outcomes," in *Understanding Poverty*, ed. Sheldon Danziger and Robert Haveman (New York: Russell Sage Foundation, 2001), 128.

18 Lin and Harris, "Why Is American Poverty Still Colored," 4.

19 Devah Pager, "The Dynamics of Discrimination," in *The Colors of Poverty*, 23.

20 Poverty rates obtained from the U.S. Census Bureau. Rates were not collected as a separate category for African Americans until 1974.

21 Maurianne Adams and Ximena Zúñiga, "Core Concepts for Social Justice Education," in *Readings for Diversity and Social Justice*, 4th ed., ed. Maurianne Adams et al. (New York: Routledge, 2018), 42.

22 Ibid., 43.

23 Young, "Five Faces of Oppression," 39–65.

24 Ibid., 40.

25 Ibid.

26 NBC News, "MLK Talks 'New Phase' of Civil Rights Struggle, 11 Months before His Assassination," YouTube video, filmed 1967, updated April 4, 2018, https://www.youtube.com/watch?v=2xsbt3a7K-8.

27 Ibid.

28 Ibid.

29 Ibid.

30 Adriana Belmonte, "Black Farmers, Left Out of Trump's Bailout, Find Relief in Biden's Stimulus," *Yahoo! Finance*, March 22, 2021, https://finance.yahoo.com/news/black-farmers-trumps-bailout-biden-stimulus-134134301.html.

31 Ibid.

32 Young, "Five Faces of Oppression," 49.

33 NBC, "MLK Talks 'New Phase' of Civil Rights Struggle."

34 Ibid.

35 Young, "Five Faces of Oppression," 53.

36 Ibid.

37 Ibid.

38 Ibid.

39 Ibid., 56–57.

40 Ibid., 58.

41 Ibid., 59.

42 Ibid.

43 NBC, "MLK Talks 'New Phase' of Civil Rights Struggle."

44 Jo Anne Schneider, "And How Are We Supposed to Pay for Health Care? Views of the Poor and the Near Poor on Welfare Reform," *American Anthropologist* 101, no. 4 (December 1999): 766.

45 Young, "Five Faces of Oppression," 61.

46 Ibid., 62.

47 Charles Jones, "The Political Repression of the Black Panther Party 1966–1971: The Case of the Oakland Bay Area," *Journal of Black Studies* 18, no. 4 (June 1988): 415.

48 See ibid.

49 See Bryce Covert, "The Myth of the Welfare Queen," *New Republic*, July 2, 2019, https://newrepublic.com/article/154404/myth-welfare-queen.

50 Linda Faye Williams, *The Constraint of Race: Legacies of White Skin Privilege in America* (University Park, PA: Pennsylvania State University Press, 2003), 125.

51 Lyndon B. Johnson, "Annual Message to the Congress on the State of the Union" (January 12, 1966), The American Presidency Project, https://www.

presidency.ucsb.edu/documents/annual-message-the-congress-the-state-the-union-27.

52 Doris Kearns Goodwin, *Lyndon Johnson and the American Dream* (New York: Harper & Row, 1976), 53–54.

53 Kenneth O'Reilly, *Nixon's Piano: Presidents and Racial Politics from Washington to Clinton* (New York: Free Press, 1995).

54 Daniel F. Halloran, "Progress against Poverty: The Governmental Approach," *Public Administration Review* 28, no. 3 (May–June 1968): 209.

55 Ibid.

56 Williams, *The Constraint of Race*, 125.

57 Robert Mark Rank, *One Nation, Underprivileged: Why American Poverty Affects Us All* (New York: Oxford University Press, 2004), 53.

58 Ibid., 54.

59 Ibid., 53.

60 Ibid., 59–60.

61 Ibid., 62.

62 Ibid.

63 Ted K. Bradshaw, "Theories of Poverty and Anti-Poverty Programs in Community Development," RPRC Working Paper No. 06-05, February 2006, https://ccednet-rcdec.ca/sites/ccednet-rcdec.ca/files/bradshaw-theories_of_poverty_2006.pdf, 11.

64 Michael A. Stoll, "Race, Place, and Property Revisited," in *The Colors of Poverty: Why Racial and Ethnic Disparities Persist*, ed. Ann Chih Lin and David Harris (New York: Russell Sage Foundation, 2008), 203.

65 Ibid.

66 Bradshaw, "Theories of Poverty," 22.

67 Ibid., 12.

68 Stoll, "Race, Place, and Property Revisited," 204.

69 Ibid., 207.

70 Ibid., 212.

71 Ibid.

72 Wendy Shaw, *The Geography of United States Poverty* (New York: Garland Publishing, 1996), 29.

73 Bradshaw, "Theories of Poverty," 12.

74 Ibid., 13.

75 Ibid., 14.

76 Ibid.

77 Ibid.

78 Ibid., 22.

79 Ibid., 15.

80 Ibid., 22.

81 Oscar Lewis, "The Culture of Poverty," *Scientific American* 215, no. 4 (October 1966): 21, https://www.jstor.org/stable/24931078.

82 Edward Banfield, *The Unheavenly City Revisited* (Boston: Little, Brown and Company, 1994), 129.

83 Patricia Cohen, "Culture of Poverty Makes a Comeback," *New York Times*, October 17, 2010, https://www.nytimes.com/2010/10/18/us/18poverty.html.

84 Ibid.

85 Bradshaw, "Theories of Poverty," 9.

86 Oscar Lewis, *Anthropological Essays* (New York: Random House, 1970), 69.

87 Cohen, "Culture of Poverty Makes a Comeback."

88 Ibid.

89 Stephanie Riegg Cellini, Signe-Mary McKernan, and Caroline Ratcliffe, "The Dynamics of Poverty in the United States: A Review of Data, Methods, and Findings," *Journal of Policy Analysis and Management* 27, no. 3 (Summer 2008): 583, https://doi.org/10.1002/pam.20337.

90 Hanks, Solomon, and Weller, "Systemic Inequality."

91 Ibid.

92 Ibid.

93 Ibid.

94 Rank, *One Nation, Underprivileged*, 53.

95 Meyer and Wallace, "Poverty Levels and Trends in Comparative Perspective," 57.

96 Adams and Zúñiga, "Core Concepts for Social Justice Education," 48.

97 Merhsa Baradaran, "The Real Roots of 'Black Capitalism,'" *New York Times*, March 31, 2019, https://www.nytimes.com/2019/03/31/opinion/nixon-capitalism-blacks.html.

98 Andre Dua, Deepa Mahajan, Lucienne Oyer, and Sree Ramaswamy, "U.S. Small Business Recovery after the COVID-19 Crisis," McKinsey and Company, July 7, 2020, https://www.mckinsey.com/industries/public-and-social-sector/our-insights/us-small-business-recovery-after-the-covid-19-crisis.

99 Heather Long, Andrew Van Dam, Alyssa Fowers, and Leslie Shapiro, "The Covid-19 Recession Is the Most Unequal in Modern History," *Washington Post*, September 30, 2020, https://www.washingtonpost.com/graphics/2020/business/coronavirus-recession-equality/?itid=ap_andrewvan%20dam&itid=lk_inline_manual_2.

100 Andrew Van Dam and Heather Long, "Moms, Black Americans, and Educators Are in Trouble as Economic Recovery Slows," *Washington Post*, October 2, 2020, https://www.washingtonpost.com/business/2020/10/02/september-jobs-inequality/.

CHAPTER EIGHT

1 Jessica Semega et al., "Income and Poverty in the United States: 2019," U.S. Census Bureau, Current Population Reports, P60-270 (Washington, DC: U.S. Government Publishing Office, 2020), 15, https://www.census.gov/library/publications/2020/demo/p60-270.html.

2 John Creamer, "Inequalities Persist despite Decline in Poverty for All Major Race and Hispanic Origin Groups," U.S. Census Bureau, September 15, 2020, https://www.census.gov/library/stories/2020/09/poverty-rates-for-blacks-and-hispanics-reached-historic-lows-in-2019.html.

3 Ibid.

4 Ibid., 58, Table B-2.

5 Ibid., 61, 63, Table B-5.

6 Statista Research Department, "Poverty Rate of Black Married-Couple Families in the U.S. from 1990 to 2019," January 20, 2021, https://www.statista.com/statistics/205097/percentage-of-poor-black-married-couple-families-in-the-us/; "Poverty Rate for Families in the United States from 1990 to 2019," January 20, 2021, https://www.statista.com/statistics/204745/poverty-rate-for-families-in-the-us/.

7 National Center for Education Statistics, "Characteristics of Children's Families," last updated May 2021, https://nces.ed.gov/programs/coe/indicator/cce, Figure 6. Data are from the American Community Survey (ACS), 2019.

8 Katherine Kortsmit et al., "Abortion Surveillance—United States, 2018," Centers for Disease Control and Prevention, *MMWR Surveillance Summaries* 69, no. 7 (November 2020): 19, Table 5, https://www.cdc.gov/mmwr/volumes/69/ss/pdfs/ss6907a1-H.pdf.

9 Ibid., 20, Table 6.

10 Ibid., 6, 8.

11 Joyce A. Martin et al., "Births: Final Data for 2019," *National Vital Statistics Reports* 70, no. 2 (March 2021): https://www.cdc.gov/nchs/data/nvsr/nvsr70/nvsr70-02-508.pdf, 27, Table 9; 13, Table 1.

12 Pew Research Center, "Parenting in America: Outlook, Worries, Aspirations Are Strongly Linked to Financial Situation," December 17, 2015, https://www.pewresearch.org/social-trends/2015/12/17/parenting-in-america/.

13 Wendy Wang, "More Than One-Third of Prime-Age Americans Have Never Married," Institute for Family Studies, September 2020, https://ifstudies.org/ifs-admin/resources/final2-ifs-single-americansbrief2020.pdf, 1.

14 Wendy Wang and Kim Parker, "Record Share of Americans Have Never Married as Values, Economics and Gender Patterns Change," Pew Research Center, September 24, 2014, https://www.pewresearch.org/social-trends/2014/09/24/record-share-of-americans-have-never-married/.

15 Megan Brenan, "Record-Low 54% in U.S. Say Death Penalty Morally Acceptable," Gallup, June 23, 2020, https://news.gallup.com/poll/312929/record-low-say-death-penalty-morally-acceptable.aspx; Frank Newport, "Americans Continue to Shift Left on Key Moral Issues," Gallup, May 26,

2015, https://news.gallup.com/poll/183413/americans-continue-shift-left-key-moral-issues.aspx.

16 Jeffrey M. Jones, "Is Marriage Becoming Irrelevant?" Gallup, December 28, 2020, https://news.gallup.com/poll/316223/fewer-say-important-parents-married.aspx.

17 Amanda Barroso, "More than Half of Americans Say Marriage Is Important but Not Essential to Leading a Fulfilling Life," Pew Research Center, February 14, 2020, https://www.pewresearch.org/fact-tank/2020/02/14/more-than-half-of-americans-say-marriage-is-important-but-not-essential-to-leading-a-fulfilling-life/.

18 Alexis de Tocqueville, *Democracy in America*, ed. and trans. Harvey C. Mansfield and Delba Winthrop (Chicago: University of Chicago Press, 2000), 278–79.

19 Harry V. Jaffa, "The American Founding as the Best Regime," *Claremont Review of Books*, July 4, 2007, https://claremontreviewofbooks.com/digital/the-american-founding-as-the-best-regime/.

20 Mark J. Perry, "Saturday Afternoon Links, All Chart Edition," American Enterprise Institute, March 13, 2021, https://www.aei.org/carpe-diem/saturday-afternoon-links-all-chart-edition/.

21 Frank Newport, "Five Key Findings on Religion in the U.S.," Gallup, December 23, 2016, https://news.gallup.com/poll/200186/five-key-findings-religion.aspx.

22 OASDI Trustees, "The 2020 Annual Report of the Board of Trustees of the Federal Old-Age and Survivors Insurance and Federal Disability Insurance Trust Funds," April 22, 2020, https://www.ssa.gov/oact/tr/2020/tr2020.pdf, 62, Table IV.B3.

23 Karen Tumulty, "The Great Society at 50," *Washington Post*, May 7, 2014, https://www.washingtonpost.com/wp-srv/special/national/great-society-at-50/.

24 Lyndon B. Johnson, "Commencement Address at Howard University," June 4, 1965, https://www.presidency.ucsb.edu/documents/commencement-address-howard-university-fulfill-these-rights.

25 U.S. Census Bureau, "21.3 Percent of U.S. Population Participates in Government Assistance Programs Each Month," May 28, 2015, https://www.census.gov/newsroom/press-releases/2015/cb15-97.html.

26 Pew Research Center, "In a Politically Polarized Era, Sharp Divides in Both Partisan Coalitions," December 17, 2019, https://www.pewresearch.org/politics/2019/12/17/views-of-government-and-the-nation/.

27 Ibid.

28 Ibid.

INDEX

"earned success," 223; economic standing, 233; "equity," 201; family structure, 204–5; higher education, 205–6; hyper-local factors, 231; marginalized populations, 201; national conversation, 200, 232; next generation of students (advice for), 233; 1776 Unites, 236–37; Students for Fair Admissions, 227–28; success (institutional engines of), 234; "success sequence," 221, 224, 236; two-parent family, 206–16, 235, 236; Vertex Partnership Academies, 225; wealth building (intergenerational), 205; wealth disparity, 202, 203; wealth gap (family formation and), 216–24; "Woodson Principles," 237
urban renewal, 290
U.S. Constitution. *See* Constitution
U.S. party system, 4

Vertex Partnership Academies, 225
visions, competing (leaders of), 149–72; anti-capitalist sentiment, 170; biblical promise, 150; black disadvantages, basis for (King), 153; "capacity for hardships" (mythical), 152; character, invocation of (King), 156; Christian virtue, cultivation of (Washington), 171; "color shock," 154; Commonwealth Club address (FDR), 150–51; economic advance (opportunities of), 161; fruits of economic endeavor, 149; inevitability for blacks, 155; Johnson, Lyndon, 151, King, Martin Luther Jr. ("dilemma of the Negro Americans"), 152–58; King, Martin Luther Jr. (failure of), 158–65; mistaken hypothesis, 151; "multiculturalism," 159; paradox, 160, 164; QED (reaching), 168–72; Roosevelt, Franklin D., 150–51; Roosevelt, Theodore, 151; self-sufficiency (reliance on), 172; social migration, 163; suffering (growing and prospering while), 165–68; Wilson, Woodrow, 151
Voting Rights Act, 123, 224, 290

Wallace, Geoffrey, 243
Wang, Wendy, 204, 206, 233, 234
War on Poverty (Johnson), 252–54, 290; definition of, 252; failure of, 268; purpose of, 253; rushing through of programs, 254
Washington, Booker T., 5, 13, 15, 165, 168, 170
Washington, George, 14, 158, 164
Washington Bee, 141, 146
Washington Post, 182, 193, 203 290
Wasserman, Melanie, 206
wealth: disparity, 202, 203; distribution (1913–2014), 19; economic power and, 240–43; gap (family formation and), 216–24; inequality, 13, 20, 203, 217
Welfare Queen, 252
Wells-Barnett, Ida, 165–66
Where Do We Go from Here: Chaos or Community?, 152
Whipper, William J., 135, 144, 145, 147
white backlash (threat of), 185–86
"white silence," 184
"white supremacy": expression of, 125; false narrative of, 183–84; Left's claim about, 177; metaphor of, 183–84; propaganda aiming to counteract, 176; reason as, 124; "structural racism" and, 181
Whitmore, Garvin, 175
Wilcox, W. Bradford, 204, 206, 233, 234
Williams, Linda Faye, 252
Williams, Thomas Chatterton, 44, 186
Wilson, W. J., 259
Wilson, Woodrow, 151
Woodson, Robert, 194
"Woodson Principles," 237
World Bank (definition of poverty), 242

Years of Poverty, Years of Plenty, 264
Young, Iris Marion, 240, 246

Zhou, Min, 179